PRIVILEGING THE PAST

RECONSTRUCTING HISTORY IN NORTHWEST COAST ART

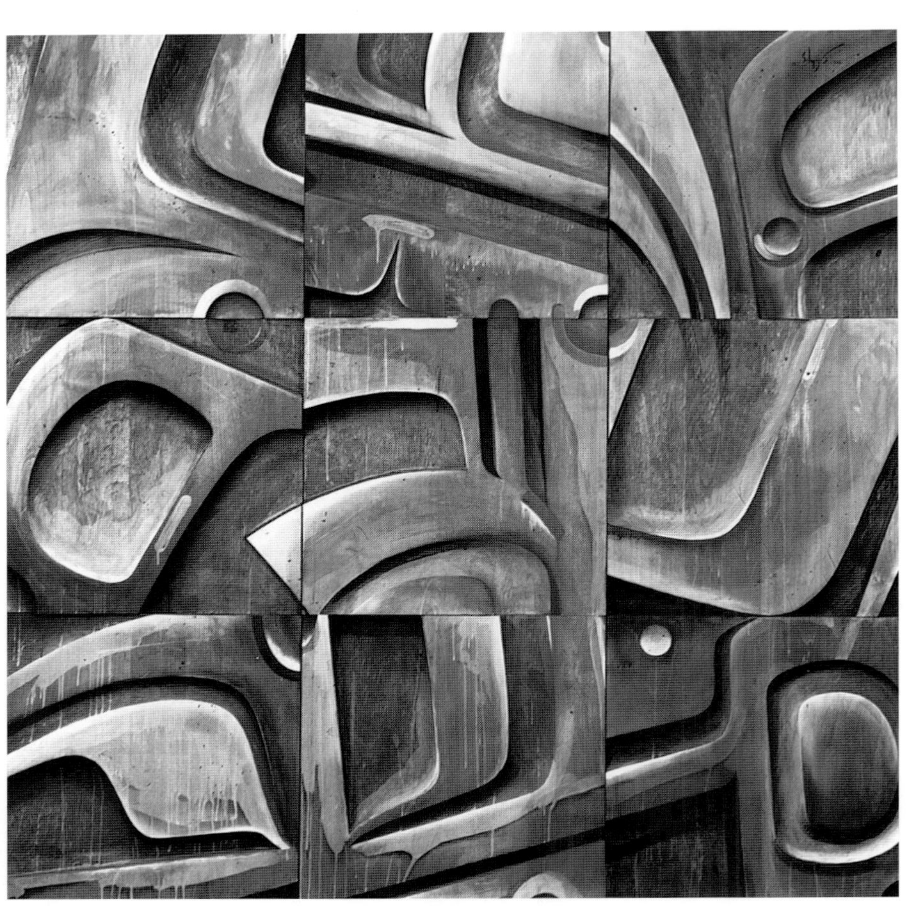

PRIVILEGING THE PAST

RECONSTRUCTING HISTORY IN NORTHWEST COAST ART

Judith Ostrowitz

FOREWORD BY
NELSON H. H. GRABURN

UNIVERSITY OF WASHINGTON PRESS
SEATTLE AND LONDON

UBC PRESS
VANCOUVER / TORONTO

Published with the assistance of the Getty Grant Program.

University of Washington Press
P.O. Box 50096, Seattle, WA 98145

UBC Press, 6344 Memorial Road,
University of British Columbia, Vancouver V6T 1Z2

Library of Congress Cataloging-in-Publication Data
Ostrowitz, Judith.
    Privileging the past : reconstructing history in northwest coast art /
Judith Ostrowitz ; foreword by Nelson H. H. Graburn.
        p.   cm.
    Includes bibliographical references and index.
    ISBN 0-295-97814-7 (alk. paper)
        1. Indian arts — Northwest Coast of North America.   I. Title.
E78.N78084   1999
700'.89'970795 — dc21   99 − 42684
                                                                                              CIP

Canadian Cataloguing in Publication Data
Ostrowitz, Judith, 1953 −
    Privileging the past
    Includes bibliographical references and index.
    ISBN 0-7748-0753-9

    1. Indian art — Northwest Coast of North America.   I. Title.
E78.N78087   1999   704.03'9970795   c99-910953-7

Cover and Interior Design by Stan Green

Contents

Foreword

AFTER TWENTY YEARS or so of relative stagnation, the "anthropology of art" or "comparative art history" is finally being stirred by the stimulating work of a younger generation of scholars. Though occasional publications focusing on arts and creativity in Africa, Australia, Japan, and New Zealand have made significant marks, most of the recent works, like this one, concern the indigenous but not untouched arts of North America.

Judith Ostrowitz sets out to examine for the field of Native American, specifically Northwest Coast, historical and contemporary arts the same problem that Johannes Fabian posed more generally in his now classic *Time and the Other* (1983). Fabian wanted to explore why agents of the Western world—explorers, travel writers, anthropologists, and the general public—consistently deny the coevalness, the simultaneous co-existence, of the "West and the Rest." That is to say, why do "we" insist on the "pastness" of the cultures of the "Other," typically viewing their culture as some kind of survival from past ages, for example, the "Stone Age," thought to be characteristic of "our" ancestors? While Fabian set up something of a straw man in criticizing his contemporary colleagues, this attribution of the "Other" to the dust heap of history did characterize the anthropologists of the last century and the first part of this one, and it certainly describes the common feelings of many western inhabitants of industrialized countries in their attitudes towards today's "ex-primitives" (MacCannell 1992).

This imperious attitude has two underlying modes, both of which are applicable to the narrower field of the "ex-primitive arts": That (1) these are peoples of the past who no longer exist, who are extinct, who have left their material remains and their formerly inhabited lands to us, or (2) these surviving peoples are the unchanged remnants of a past and glorious age, whose cultures still bear qualities that we, of urban industrialized societies, no longer embrace or cannot attain.

In artistic terms, these two propositions can be transformed into two statements: (1) There are no great contemporary nonwestern artists, for all the classic artists died out in the face of colonialism, commercialism, and hybridity or even of the fruit of the "tree of knowledge" in the form of the self-consciousness brought by western formal training in art and art history, an attitude that has appeared from Japan (Moeran 1998) to West Africa (Carroll 1967). Or (2) contemporary nonwestern artists, especially many Northwest Coast Indians, Ainu, and Australian Aborigines, are the last remaining bearers of the primal classic qualities in the arts, now lost to the western, self-conscious avant-garde art world, and that these arts are preferred by many Western critics and consumers over the acres of non-imagery or of politicized postmodernity that characterize most western serious artists and even many art-schooled-trained Native American artists of the Plains and the Southwest (Graburn 1993).

Ostrowitz focuses on the latter case. She contends that Native arts, especially those of the Northwest Coast, are perceived, judged against, and valued almost entirely for their historicism, that is, for their resemblance to the great styles, artists, and art objects of the past. Further, she contends that these contemporary Native arts, though much admired, can never be compared with or be as highly valued as the mainstream arts of the western world where value is equated with nonhistoricism, that is, originality, hybridity, and breaks from the past. Ostrowitz shows us that these contemporary Native artists are fully aware of the values of western modernity but are constrained from developing their arts in that direction (with the possible exception of Lawrence Paul Yuxweluptun) both by the continuity of the age-old Northwest Coast cultural imperative of reproducing art as a vital expression of rank and clan membership necessary for the recognition of inherited privileges and by the desire of non-Native authorities—gatekeepers, collectors, curators, advisors—to see, possess, and display replicas of the past, because of the second value orientation outlined in the prior paragraph.

Ostrowitz demonstrates this historical fact not by outlining once again the romantic story of the discovery and rediscovery of these classic arts but by following this history through the punctuated evolution of specific critical events (cf. Das 1995). On such occasions as the replication of Chief Shakes community house, the construction of the Northwest Coast housefronts at the Canadian Museum of Civilization, and the Kwakw<u>aka</u>'wakw dance performance at the American Museum of Natural History, the renegotiations among the Native peoples themselves and with white patrons exemplify these complex processes and bring to light these value orientations. Ostrowitz's reexamination of these crucial cases not only makes them come alive again but renders them more deeply meaningful than they were even to many of the participants.

Important conclusions emerge from Ostrowitz's Northwest Coast materials that are applicable to many other artistic "evolutions." First, replicas and restoration are always selective in matching certain features of the past in order to suit a particular historically situated group of authorities, positioned by their ethnicity and class. Until the twentieth century, Native restorations of material symbols of power and rank included necessary signs of compliance with the dominant non-Native world and its valued symbols and material displays. But more recently, both Native and non-Native authorities measure authenticity by the degree of "ethnic cleansing"—ridding the ethnic replica of any associations with the present and with the dominant non-Native culture. Second, the overwhelming focus on the mid-nineteenth century as "the classic period" and the model for reproduction by Native and non-Natives alike is not because of the ethnically purer Native culture of that time but because early *photography* first enshrined and preserved images that last over time, whereas material items and tribal ideas of style did not last unchanged over the same period. Third, contemporary Native artists and their patrons *do* make a distinction between the reproduction of art forms for rituals of rank and privilege and for ritual events of the dominant society. However, as institutions of the dominant society begin to value ritual as the *sine qua non* of authenticity and as Native peoples seek ever more acceptance by the mainstream as a mark of social reality, the two get conflated, with "real" rituals of privilege and political ascendancy being carried out not only in isolated villages but on the stage of the world's cultural institutions (cf. *Te Maori*, Mead 1984). In these departures from the strict historical model, adherence to the spirit rather than the form suffices for these ritual purposes.

Judith Ostrowitz has brought to our attention critical events in the history of these magnificent Canadian and American Native arts and their artists for a retelling that is at once exciting, moving, and very meaningful for our understanding of the persistence of such arts in our contemporary world.

Nelson H. H. Graburn
Berkeley, California
May 1999

References

Carroll, K. 1967. *Yoruba Religious Carving*. London: Geoffrey Chapman.

Das, Veena. 1995. *Critical Events: An Anthropological Perspective on Contemporary India*. New York: Oxford University Press.

Fabian, Johannes. 1983. *Time and the Other: How Anthropology Makes Its Object*. New York: Columbia University Press.

Graburn, Nelson H. H. 1993. "Ethnic Arts of the Fourth World: the View from Canada." Pp. 171–204 in Dorothea S. and Norman E. Whitten, eds., *Imagery and Creativity: Ethnoaesthetics and Art Worlds in the Americas*. Tucson: University of Arizona Press.

MacCannell, Dean. 1992. "Cannibalism Today." Pp. 17–73 in *Empty Meetings Grounds: the Tourist Papers*. London: Routledge.

Mead, Sidney Moko. 1984. *Te Maori: Maori Art from New Zealand Collections*. New York: Abrams.

Moeran, Brian. 1998. *Folk Art Potters of Japan: Beyond an Anthropology of Aesthetics* London: Curzon Press and Honolulu: University of Hawaii Press.

Preface

R IGHT AT THE BEGINNING, when I first began to study Northwest Coast native art, I was struck by certain practices that seemed incongruous when considered in relation to basic assumptions held by non-natives. I had come to these studies as an artist as well as an art historian. Whether perusing the galleries in SoHo or in the privacy of my own studio, I knew what a premium the non-native "art world" placed upon novelty and invention. I remember, as an undergraduate student at Pratt Institute in the 1970s, the sharp criticism of any "derivative" works that we saw in the galleries, and even the disdain in which one professor held "tubey" colors — paints that had been applied almost straight from the tube, unmediated by the artist's adjustments.

These sentiments certainly remain evident today. A recent interview with the well-known artist Chuck Close, published in *The New York Times*, included Close's reminiscence of fielding some tough questions from a group of children. They challenged him in a completely unabashed manner, asking, "Do you work from photographs or can you really draw?" Close, probably taken aback, finds this parable important enough so that he still explains today: "Looking at a photograph means you're not really looking, as if you're cheating. I found a way of working with photographs in which verisimilitude was just an automatic byproduct of the process" (Kimmelman 1997: C1, C23).

Apparently to proceed from existing images, to make something that cannot be presented as having sprung whole and complete from the artist's mind without reference to any model, is a position that must still be explained, even in this age of mechanical and cyber-reproduction. Imagine how astonished I was in the early 1990s to discover that many prominent native artists from the Northwest Coast have not only increased their participation in the production of historical restorations, but most often carve and paint what can loosely be called "copies." Just as perplexing, these pieces are often destined to be viewed by non-native collectors and museum-goers who have been accustomed to value above all else the new and the unique in the fine arts. Yet the artists and other people of Northwest Coast native descent whom I met in the course of my studies (which began when I worked as a curatorial assistant to Aldona Jonaitis for the exhibition of Kwakwaka'wakw potlatch art, *Chiefly Feasts: The Enduring Kwakiutl Potlatch* at The American Museum of Natural History), were quite savvy about this artwork. These artists were fiercely proud of their historical citations. Although some outsiders might categorize them as makers of curiosities based upon antiquities, they were actually influential people who took every opportunity to present their work and the important cultural transactions that accompanied its manufacture as meaningful and central to their up-to-the minute concerns.

I was fortunate in the course of my subsequent research to have been assisted, advised, and supported by a great many people. The most significant contribution to my project was made by the native artists of British Columbia and Southeast Alaska who created the compelling works of art discussed here as well as other native people who have participated in the interpretation of their meanings. Many freely answered my persistent questions, graciously offered their hospitality, and shared their insight into their cultural heritage. Among those whom I questioned and consulted are Ethel Alfred, Joe Becker, Marge Byrd, Mervyn Child, Edward P. Churchill, Margaret Cook, Agnes Cranmer, Bill Cranmer, Doug Cranmer, Robert Davidson, Adam Dick, Beau Dick, Jim Hart, Emma Hunt, Calvin Hunt, Richard Hunt, Stephen Hunt, Tom Hunt, Tony Hunt, Nathan Jackson, Susan Point, Israel Shotridge, Terry Starr, Dick Stokes, Glen Tallio, Art Thompson, Nellie Torgramsen, Gloria Cranmer Webster, Elsie Williams, Lyle Wilson, and Lawrence Paul Yuxweluptun.

Many scholars and other experts were kind enough to offer their advice and provide essential information: Steve Brown, Peter Corey, Karen Duffek, Diana Fane, Ian Gregory, Steve Henrikson, Bill Holm, Richard Inglis, Andrea LaForet, Leona Lattimer, Mary Jane Lenz, Judith Levinson, George MacDonald, Peter Macnair, Randall Macnair, Lee-Ann Martin, Mardonna Austin-McKillop, Bill McLennan, Gerald McMaster, Diana Nemiroff, Pat Greene Ockert, Drew Oswell, Isabel Proctor, Nora Rhinehart, Margaret Stott, Wayne Suttles, Robin Wright, and Gary Wyatt. Special thanks go to Aaron Glass for archival materials from Alert Bay, and to R. Tripp Evans for material on the Disney movie *Pocahontas*.

I am most deeply indebted to Aldona Jonaitis, whose advice and friendship made this work possible. As her curatorial assistant for *Chiefly Feasts*, I became acquainted with many of the people mentioned here and with those issues that grew to be central to this project. I have been inspired by Aldona's scholarship and was educated in her classroom. Her many close readings of early versions of the manuscript of this book, first written as a Ph.D. dissertation in the Department of Art History and Archaeology at Columbia University, have been of inestimable value. Aldona also helped to make me aware that each and every experience that we have with works of art, the people who make them, and the circumstances under which we come to know something about them is truly authentic.

I am pleased to have the opportunity to express my gratitude to Esther Pasztory. She too supervised my work at Columbia University, offering excellent advice and suggestions. Although I take complete responsibility for any shortcomings in the preparation of this work, I would like to acknowledge her guidance, which led to some of the best aspects of it. Earlier versions of the manuscript were also read by Diana Fane, Keith Moxey, Natalie Kampen, Janet Catherine Berlo, and Nelson Graburn. I have benefited enormously from their comments.

My field research was partially funded by a Graduate Student Fellowship from the Canadian Embassy (1992–93) and by two Lewine Summer Travel Grants from Columbia University (1991, 1992). An earlier and shorter version of the essay "Making Dance History: A Case Study in Kwakwa̱ka̱'wakw Performance Art at The American Museum of Natural History" appeared in *American Indian Art Magazine* in 1994. My thanks and esteem go to Naomi Pascal, Julidta Tarver, Lorna Price, and many others at the University of Washington Press for their part in making these thoughts concrete.

Finally, I would like to express my gratitude and affection for my family. My husband, Martin Levine, and my son, Sasha Ostrowitz-Levine, provided help, patience, and support. I would like to dedicate this book to the memory of my mother, Doris Ostrowitz.

PRIVILEGING THE PAST

RECONSTRUCTING HISTORY IN NORTHWEST COAST ART

Introduction

Everything made now is either a replica or a variant of something made a little time ago and so on back without break to the first morning of human time. This continuous connection in time must contain lesser divisions.

The narrative historian always has the privilege of deciding that continuity cuts better into certain lengths than into others. He is never required to defend his cut, because history cuts anywhere with equal ease, and a good story can begin anywhere the teller chooses.

—George Kubler, The Shape of Time (1962): 2.

THIS LINEAGE OF FORM proposed by Kubler suggests a great chain of events, instances of artistic manufacture that might be teased out and inspected productively at any point along a lengthy continuum. Although each segment in Kubler's series maintained traces of those that came before it, recent and inventive forms have habitually been privileged by most modern observers as more valuable and progressive, indicating a certain reticence to cut the procession of history just anywhere. On the other hand, the significant influence of history itself as a criterion of value has greatly affected the reception of other designated segments in this narrative. Native arts, for example, have been set apart, perceived and valued almost entirely through historicism. On the Northwest Coast of North America[1] in particular, where copies and creative translations of past form are not only legitimate but are also considered central to practitioners of traditional culture as well as to the interests of non-native patrons and scholars, the association of contemporary artworks with earlier prototypes is practiced assiduously. References to the origin of objects and the appropriate designation of stylistic conventions known from the analysis of native antiquities are therefore thought by the majority of outsiders to completely exhaust the meaning of these works.

Interestingly, these Northwest Coast "near replicas" and other works of art that refer to nineteenth-century prototypes are not created in complete isolation and apart from the contemporary western art milieu. Many, in fact, are generated through cross-cultural dialogue and made specifically to be viewed by audiences unfamiliar with their cultures of origin. Furthermore, in this last decade of the twentieth century, almost all native people have visited and interacted with those well beyond their home villages.[2] Artists in particular may play the part of cultural intermediaries for whom regular encounters with print and electronic media may be augmented with occasional international travel. Formal art education and training is also increasingly possible, though not yet commonplace.

Today none would deny most Northwest Coast artists' familiarity with a larger "art world," thus making it implausible to conceive of their carvings and prints as originating in a world set apart, without awareness of other traditions. Appropriately, their works must now be considered in relation to the tenets of modern and postmodern art historical discourse and to the various practices of non-native art production that they knowingly transgress. Yet acceptance by the mainstream is not forthcoming for these native artists, even in light of the postmodern agenda and the practices of collage and selective historical appropriations that have become associated with it. Intertextual references by native Northwest Coast artists apparently function quite differently in reference to local historical context and are not, for the most part, directed to the global audience conceptualized by their counterparts in New York. Therefore native formal transcriptions still imply a certain lack of progress, and even dissimulation, to an authoritative culture of outsiders who overvalue the new and the original, as may even be asserted through the eccentric combination of past form and other wide-ranging references now seen in some contemporary non-native works.

Other artists of native descent who live and work east of the Rocky Mountains and at points farther north and south also persist in referencing their heritage in works of art. It should be noted at the outset, however, that a good many do so with much greater formal and conceptual experimentation than their Northwest Coast contemporaries. This phenomenon was demonstrated with clarity, for instance, at the influential exhibition *Land, Spirit, Power: First Nations at The National Gallery of Canada*, held in Ottawa, Ontario, in 1992. An international audience was confronted there by a variety of approaches to the simultaneous representation of contemporary identity and native history. For example, Carl Beam (Ojibwa) exhibited frankly assertive photo collages, some with images of the bare-chested artist himself with hand on hip, and others of insects and historical figures. They were scarred by dripping strands of photo emulsion, a reminder of the artist's process and an adjunct to the edgy atmosphere of the works. Domingo Cisneros (Tepehuane) showed installation pieces composed of animal skins, bones, and snowshoes suspended in midair. Some of Jimmie Durham's (Cherokee) idiosyncratic assemblages were also in the show. Durham is the creator of the soul-searching *Self Portrait* of 1986 that combines a kind of paranoid face, text, and a hugh phallus on its flat figure; it gives play to cultural stereotypes just as it pulls these illusions apart. *Tlunhdatsi*, also Durham's piece, is composed of a section of police barricade surmounted by a terrifying open-jawed creature made of fur and bone. The show also included Faye Heavy-Shield's (Blood) abstract and somewhat minimalist sculptures, Alex Janvier's (Dene) stylized paintings of native people confined within swirls and cartouches, and James Lavadour's (Walla Walla) landscapes that are assembled, mosaic style, from a combination of painted canvases. The appearance of these works suggested that Indian art might now be considered "up-to-date."

Inserted in the same exhibition without explanation, however (though they seemed quite anomalous), were Robert Davidson's transformation mask *Eagle Transforming into Itself* and his *Gagit Mask*, masterfully carved and painted in traditional Northwest Coast style and clearly suitable for use in Haida ceremony. Dempsey Bob's masks carved in alder, so smoothly contoured that they looked as if they had been formed in a mold, also represented animals and supernatural beings. They too are to be understood historically, in reference to the Tahltan-Tlingit background of the artist. Dorothy Grant had also contributed two appliquéd wool and cashmere blankets based on Davidson's designs, which recalled Haida button blankets and the regalia customarily worn at potlatches. The works of these three artists of Northwest Coast descent were different. Though able to stand alone as tours de force in terms of skilled execution and aesthetic appeal, they were the only works in the show that relied upon tradition and past form to thoroughly explain their significance.[3]

Historical references and even "copies" developed by influential artists and encouraged by other authorities distinguish the appearance of most of the art of the Northwest Coast. This results in the unyielding definition of some of these works as mere reproduction, especially when native artists from other regions strive to make unique and forward-looking experiments. This definition has become inadequate, however. Various new criteria for authenticity, beyond the designation of ground-breaking "masterpieces" in the form of great coups by artist-elites, have now been proposed by postmodern scholars of both native and non-native art, encouraging a somewhat broader perspective. In addition, the appearance of these historically based pieces at various well-traveled and cross-cultural venues, from museums and galleries to films and theme parks, now makes the critical reevaluation of replicated art works and a greater understanding of their exact relationship to Northwest Coast history more urgent than ever before.

On many Northwest Coast reserves,[4] allusions to the past are still diligently maintained, particularly in ceremony, through the complexities of potlatch protocol, and remain based upon the exclusive prerogatives of clans and lineages to represent their "crests." These treasured representations of animals, heavenly bodies, important geographical features, supernatural beings, and ancestral heroes figure in oral histories that are sometimes related to the origin of the group. The practices of social units represented by such crests, in the form of painted and carved images, songs, dances, and oratory, vary from one Northwest Coast group to the next. The Kwakwaka'wakw, for instance, display their privileges to guests from other Kwakwaka'wakw tribes and today to visitors from all over the world. Tlingit hosts, however, must affirm their treasures, or *at.óow*, before members of their opposite moiety.[5] Contemporary Haida people still in the process of reconstructing ceremonial practice perform songs and dances and bring out artworks before a heterogeneous audience.

The display of these privileges at a potlatch is typically accompanied by payment or gift-giving by hosts to guests who signify, by their acceptance of these payments, the legitimate right of the host group to engage in such a demonstration. These ceremonies served in the past and continue now to reaffirm crucial affiliations and prerogatives in cultures preoccupied with rank and status. Today more general assertions of ethnic identity and the ability to link the activities of the present generation with the venerable practices of the past function alongside the desire to delineate distinct tribal subdivisions.

The high valuation of these historical crest prerogatives, embodied and displayed by relatively fugitive forms such as speechmaking, song, dance, and carved works, may be a source of some confusion for western observers. These ephemeral art forms may only be representative for as long as a generation or two, or as briefly as the duration of a single ceremonial appearance, unless they are preserved in museums or private collections. These practices often call for the replacement of artworks or "replication" for native use. Yet many recast objects are considered valuable treasures, and they are strikingly elaborated. Bill Holm, for instance, has narrated one segment in the life story of the accoutrements of a particularly valuable *hamat'sa* dance. This dance privilege, considered the most prestigious ceremonial display of the Kwakwaka'wakw, was the property of Willie Seaweed, the well-known 'Nak̓waxda'x̱w Kwakwaka'wakw artist-chief. Seaweed's dance, which he originally acquired as a boy, was later elaborated by his right to use two unusual masks, one called a Raising-Top *hamat'sa* mask and the other a Both-Sides-Face *hamat'sa* mask. Both of these forms were acquired in ceremony, passed on to him on the occasion of his marriage to a woman of Oowekeeno ancestry, sometime around 1910 (Holm 1983: 28–29, 88–93; Macnair et al. 1984: 75–77).

The Raising-Top represents a creature known as the Crooked-Beak-of-Heaven, who is said to attend the Cannibal-at-the-North-End-of-the-World, or Baxwbakwalanuxwsiwe' in Kwak̓wala, the initiating spirit that is supposed to possess the *hamat'sa* dancer. This unusual bird mask is structured so that its forehead area could be raised by means of a rod, like an articulated puppet, to reveal an inner surface of shining copper, a material associated in Northwest Coast cultures with wealth and high status. The Both-Sides-Face *hamat'sa* mask is also extraordinary and valued. It is carved to combine multiple cannibal bird faces, that of Raven and Crooked-Beak, which are positioned back-to-back with a small hooked-beak mask attached under the chin of the large Crooked-Beak.[6]

In 1910 Seaweed commissioned the young Mungo Martin, another famous Kwakwaka'wakw carver, to carve his Both-Sides-Face mask, and Seaweed himself made the Raising-Top. Holm remarks on the prestigious display enacted by these two masks, but then immediately informs his readers that only four years later, in 1914, they were sold to Charles Newcombe for the collection of the British Columbia Provincial Museum in Victoria. Holm then reflects:

> Selling masks, which represented noble prerogatives, to outsiders might seem to be a strange act for a conservative chief steeped in the traditions of his people. Yet it seems never to have been really troublesome for the Kwakwaka'wakw. A fine mask was and is prized, especially if it is an heirloom, but it is the right to display it, derived from ancient tradition, that is jealously guarded. (1983: 29)

This "strange act" was followed by another one, but once again strange only in reference to the viewpoint of outsiders. Around ten years after the two masks had been carved, Seaweed made what he called "copies" of them for his own use. Holm has documented their relationship to the older set, at least in reference to the creatures they represent, delineating the changes that are a part of this second-known formal expression of the privilege (ibid.: 90–92).

The term 'copies' here is at issue, however, as it suggests the spurious nature of facsimile for the modern western viewer and heralds, in the minds of some, the decline of the tradition. Ironically, it is in the context of the steady interaction with non-native audiences since the nineteenth century that the existing practice of "replication" by native people on the Northwest Coast was so broadly encouraged. Artworks that clearly cite past form have been considered representative of traditional culture, particularly as devices for the education and enjoyment of outsiders, from at least since the mid 1800s, when the carving of "motif pipes" in argillite became popular souvenirs of the Queen Charlotte Islands (Wright 1982, 1985, 1983). The increasingly vigorous market for native art since that time continues to select for recognizable works that may be associated with older models or ones that closely follow established stylistic conventions.[7] Such works are positioned by some outsiders to characterize a high point in the history of these native groups and consequently have come to be considered as "classic."

Although contemporary Northwest Coast native art has changed to include materials and aesthetic references to twentieth-century sensibilities, such as the development of serigraph printing and further experimentation with abstraction, its reference to historically based form persists. Contemporary artists themselves, along with the influential non-native institutions that function as their patrons, still insist upon this association with the past. To varying degrees, most are pre-occupied with issues of ethnic identity and family history, even though they may experiment with bronze casting or block out their carvings with chain saws. Their works often appear as the creative translation of nineteenth-century form, but in no instance known to me do they produce completely westernized images that do not refer at all to their native identities.[8] To some extent, this phenomenon has been determined by the market for valuable contemporary works of native Northwest Coast art, as I will elaborate upon in Chapter Four of this volume.

This strategy for making art, although it persists energetically in the 1990s, is clearly inconsistent with the non-native view that characterizes the history of modern art as a history of the avant-garde. Although recognized artist-personalities have emerged on the Northwest Coast in the twentieth century, the tradition is not first and foremost a striving toward novel expression as outlined by Belting (1987: 3 and passim) in relation to western art history or about "Modernism as the pursuit of better futures . . ." as suggested by David Harvey (1999: 53–54). That procession was thought to be accomplished through the artist as autonomous agent of idiosyncratic expression. The break with the past that was supposed to underlie the modernist project cannot be reconciled with the inherited subject matter and conventionalized stylistic devices still used on the Northwest Coast.[9] Yet new works of Northwest Coast native art that refer to the past proliferate, and their makers strongly assert the vitality and relevance of their practices. These artists have developed their own alternate strategies for recognition and the increasing authority to participate fully in contemporary life. This study documents some of the processes by which they have accomplished these goals.

From Benjamin to Baudrillard

The strange acts remarked upon here—the sale of inherited treasures, the insular preoccupation with matters of local importance, and in particular the repeated translation of antique form as near replica—are positioned within cross-cultural dialogue in direct relation to issues of authority and the right to produce meaning for artistic display. Any fundamental or unified meaning for native art practice may never have existed, but it is now further complicated when contextualized by non-natives who commission works of art and by theoreticians who interpret them, frequently for museum representation or for the lucrative native art market. Therefore it is essential to identify the native and non-native authorities who mandate certain standards for historical accuracy in Northwest Coast art reproduction as well as those who authorize each departure from tradition.

These are hybrid works, created as collaborative acts, and they are not considered, even by their most enthusiastic western admirers, as central to "art world" concerns. This marginalization has developed in tandem with the invention of a romanticized Indian past, still valued at a remove from the achievements of the contemporary world.[10] Instead, non-native institutions and influential individuals have highlighted and sanctioned repeated references to this past by underwriting those expressions that validate native identity as historically based. This widespread phenomenon is illustrated here, for example, in Chapter One, "Expedience and Classicism at the Chief Shakes Community House," which describes a series of architectural restoration projects on the Northwest Coast designed to produce results that may be considered as "traditional" as possible.

The Shakes house, an example of Tlingit architecture, stands today in Wrangell, Alaska, and has a very long and well-documented history of reproduction. No tribal houses actually built in the nineteenth century or earlier remain on the Northwest Coast, although house pits and fragments in situ are known. The photographic record, however, has been thoroughly mined in recovering the tradition. Documents made by photographers, like the accounts of anthropologists recorded at the turn of the twentieth century, have therefore come to be considered authoritative, resulting in a designated high point or "origin" for authentic architectural representation. Designating this time period as a reference point for works of art and architecture that follow is made even more implausible in light of the persistence of native cultures in the area, according to archaeological evidence, for a period of at least 12,000 years duration (Carlson 1976: 13).

The recorded history of the Shakes house, for example, began in the 1830s, when Chief Shakes IV relocated his entire clan and significant examples of its prestigious crest art to the Wrangell site from an older village located some 20 miles away. Although this move was clearly associated with the exigencies of a world rapidly modified by white-native interaction, Shakes's program for artistic embellishment of the house referenced practices for high status display of considerable historical depth. Chief Shakes IV not only transported important carved works from the "Old Town" location to Wrangell, but he or his immediate descendants also commissioned the near replication of certain carved and painted works for the new site. Kow-ish-te, his nephew, became Chief Shakes V, and George Shakes, or Shakes VI, who bore this title from 1878 until his death in 1916, amassed additional valuable items of both native and non-native manufacture for the comfort and high repute of the inhabitants of the clan house, which by now had windows, doors, and a cast-iron stove. Many other household possessions were displayed alongside masks and crest hats for the information of these many outsiders with cameras, who were dedicated to the recording of traditional Tlingit culture.

In the 1930s, the Civilian Conservation Corps, a New Deal program designed to remedy unemployment during this period of economic crisis, reconstructed the entire Shakes building, then dilapidated and overgrown with moss and bushes. Features of the original structure were meticulously replicated in this phase of the project, even when considered impractical, by the team of both white and native workers. Finally, the criteria specific to a 1984 restoration of the house affected the reproduction of four interior houseposts, considered "masterpieces" by museum specialists around the world. They were faithfully replicated, bringing forward a rendition of the particular "hand" of an old Tlingit master artist. Although each of these generations restored and redefined the house according to particular audience-specific standards of authenticity, they all emphasized history, the old Tlingit tribal house.

Ironically, the demands of the present—the desire to "push the envelope" that preoccupies contemporary non-native architects, artists, and performers—function along with this insistence upon "origin" for Indian art, considered to be in its heyday before white contact. At best, native art has been associated with a more authentic or "Edenic" state, as source or precedent perpetuated through historicism. Similar "first acts" in the dramatic unfolding of human history have long been esteemed. It is well known, for instance, that Plato delineated an essential role for "Form" as primal, succeeded by the execution of crafted or artistically interpreted representations, mere imitations associated with the procession of form and human mediation. This originality was even associated with divine intervention, as Socrates explains to his interlocutor in *The Republic*:

> Now the god made only one ideal or essential Bed, whether by choice or because he was under some necessity not to make more than one; at any rate two or more were not created, nor could they possibly come into being.
>
> Why not?
>
> Because, if he made even so many as two, then once more a single ideal Bed would make its appearance, whose character those two would share; and that one, not the two, would be the essential Bed. Knowing this, the god, wishing to be the real maker of a real Bed, not a particular manufacturer of one particular bed, created one which is essentially unique. (Book X: 597c–d)

The most "real" or authentic form is already associated here with the original act of creation, with the sanctity of divine authorship, and with unique qualities that cannot be duplicated without consequent loss. Similar relationships between historical depth and authenticity are assumed by many modern scholars.

For Eric Hobsbawm and Terence Ranger, editors of *The Invention of Tradition* (1983: 2–3), for example, the crafting of "custom," characterized as repeated acts not rooted in antiquity, may be distinguished from the legitimacy of tradition itself. The provenance of tradition, also preserved in repeated acts, but ones said to originate in "time immemorial," has been used to sanction claims of legitimacy by ceremonial practitioners in particular. Their authority may seem to derive from the historical past, but the basis of the studies in Hobsbawm's and Ranger's influential work is the debunking of the supposed antiquity of their acts and thus their true authenticity. The *Invention of Tradition* literature roots out examples of ceremony, performance, and other customary behavior that may actually be associated not with ancient but rather more recent inventions constructed for use in various cultures.

The composition of a 1991 dance presentation, for example, is described in Chapter Three, "Making Dance History: Kwakwa̲ka'wakw Performance Art at the American Museum of Natural History." A specific group of native performers from Vancouver Island, British Columbia, composed a dance presentation for the opening celebration of the exhibition *Chiefly Feasts: The Enduring Kwakiutl Potlatch* at the American Museum of Natural History (AMNH) in New York, according to selected references to the past. This case study follows the history of similar performances constructed as entertainment for tourists and other "outsider audiences" by this same group and its immediate forebears (grandparents, aunts, uncles, cousins) since the middle of the twentieth century. The events staged by these individuals were used as effective displays in the 1950s and 1960s, a key period in the reconstruction of public image for native residents of British Columbia seeking a voice in Canadian politics. These public performances, by virtue of the roster of participants as well as the format of presentation, may be understood as recent historical precedent for the dances, songs, and speeches that opened the New York exhibition in 1991.

The *Chiefly Feasts* "re-enactment," based in part upon the traditional Kwakwa̲ka'wakw potlatch, is analyzed here in reference to the standards of these "insiders" (the native people who constructed the display). Some of their conventions for legitimate performance were transferred to New York and played out before an audience unfamiliar with them. Accuracy in speechmaking, customary gift-giving or payment, and the selection of repertoire according to traditional native concerns were considered important and were reenacted in the performance, although the practices of the performers' precontact forebears were not and could not be duplicated. These elements were adapted instead for contemporary circumstances and embedded within a complex and lengthy theatrical presentation. The consequent form of the New York event established the authority of this generation of Kwakwa̱ka'wakw participants to arbitrate appropriate adjustments in the representation of their own past at a prestigious non-native institution.

It is interesting to consider the significance of this dance display in reference to the work of Walter Benjamin, now cited by many contemporary scholars who are attempting updated determinations of authenticity. Benjamin considered the original venue and first art practice to be of central importance. He insisted upon the primacy of the original as "the technique of reproduction detaches the reproduced object from the domain of tradition" (1968: 221). This, he thought, would result in the loss of the valued "presence of the original" which he considered prerequisite to the concept of authenticity (ibid.: 217–51). Benjamin's essays do not simply degrade the historical processes of simulation. His writings actually laud the mimetic faculty, "the very highest capability to produce similarities," as central to human nature and suggest that such acts account for the procession of change in history (1979: 65–69). Allusions to the nature of first events, however, untainted by the objectives of those who arbitrate change, may explain Benjamin's preoccupation with this origin, rather than the authority of mere chronology.[11]

Benjamin had also delineated an exceptional and legitimate status for replicas made by Renaissance art students in the manner of the master, a phenomenon well understood and acceptable in the West, similar in fact to the educational process for traditional carvers on the Northwest Coast. These copies vary significantly, however, from the reproductions most familiar to contemporary audiences, those made in the twentieth century, that Benjamin called "mechanical reproductions." These are created through technical processes and are associated with the loss of the valued first status of the work that is embedded in the circumstances of its original manufacture and function. Benjamin's assumption that works reproduced in this manner are decontextualized and therefore removed from the flow of tradition has a special resonance for the perception of meaning in replicated works of twentieth-century Northwest Coast native art, whether they are mass-produced or even when they are made by hand. Totem poles and carved masks have become familiar to most outsiders through tourist experience, museums, and print media. The recontextualization of these images, often as replica or restored form, outside of the original context of their use may indeed distance them from their prototypes. Their life histories as signifiers of social reality are not over, however. They may now be understood, like the *Chiefly Feasts* dances, against a backdrop of meanings delineated by the present generation.

Benjamin also conceded a certain "exhibition value" for works of art that had been removed from their time and place of origin (1968: 224). He assumed a basis for this phenomenon, however, only in aesthetic value or the beauty of the object. But even visual appeal is subject to fluid criteria developed by influential arbiters of form, whose identities vary from generation to generation. Some new replicated works of Northwest Coast art, for instance, have been commissioned specifically for display to both native and non-native connoisseurs. Many older pieces as well are significantly recontextualized for public viewing in photographs, museums, and at tourist venues. These works, many of which are discussed in the chapters that follow, have been assigned complex meanings in the course of such projects, not all of them related to aesthetic concerns. Contemporary authorities have conserved certain conventions of antique form at these venues and opted for the modification of other features, demonstrating that "place of origin" may not be limited to the native village of the nineteenth century.

Another contemporary theorist whose works have sparked considerable interest among art historians, Jean Baudrillard, has also posited a certain disconnection between signified and sign, a loss in meaning associated with processes of abstraction and decontextualization. This loss is particularly apparent in the duplication of the sign, according to Baudrillard, and results in the destruction of meaning, "the death of the original and the end of representation" (1983: 136). Like Benjamin, Baudrillard has aligned the case for meaning with a state of originality, within the context of earliest use or original representative function. Indeed, few of the objects in museums, reproduced images in the media, or public performances known to us remain in the original context of their use, and none stand unmodified by the perspective of those who participate in their construction. Baudrillard mourns these transformations, citing the case of the exhumed remains of the Egyptian Pharaoh Rameses, the product of museumification:

> For mummies do not decay because of worms: they die from being transplanted from a prolonged symbolic order, which is master over death and putrescence, on to an order of history, science and museums—our own, which is no longer master over anything, since it only knows how to condemn its predecessors to death and putrescence and their subsequent resuscitation by science. An irreparable violence towards all secrets, the violence of a civilization without secrets. (1983: 21)

Even contemporary museums, I will argue, have their secrets, and the death of one symbolic order may be succeeded by the birth of another viable order. For example, the development of a complete, replicated native village described in Chapter Two, "The Map and the Territory in the Grand Hall at the Canadian Museum of Civilization [CMC]," was accompanied by many significant displays of authority framed by contemporary arbiters of propriety and form. Unlike the series of Shakes restorations, the architectural replicas in the CMC Grand Hall did not evolve over time but were made all at once by contemporary native artists, together with non-native museum staff. This assemblage, comprising new houses, both old and new totem poles, and references to natural features of the Northwest Coast landscape, constitutes a huge environment that must be entered and negotiated on foot. The streetscape, echoing with bird calls and the sound of waves seemingly crashing somewhere on its polished stone floors, is powerful and convincing in its unity and in the elaborate artistry with which it is constructed. Its representative function however, has indeed been transformed. It consists of recreated houses and other objects from a variety of old villages, traditions, and family histories, all combined here in an unprecedented way, contrary to traditional protocol.

The influential representation in the Grand Hall may not refer accurately to nineteenth-century native life; its construction, however, does not by any means represent the "extermination of meaning" viewed with both fascination and horror by Baudrillard. The components of the hall are conventionalized representations that form a particular if subjective map of nineteenth-century life on the Northwest Coast, unrelated to their "first status." An ideal of historical accuracy applied during the development process certifies the legitimacy of this collaged display for the museum-going public as a genuine glimpse into the native past. Therefore issues of propriety in museum representation are explored in the Grand Hall chapter as well as the authoritative role of the staff and selected native consultants. A replication project on this scale, particularly one that employed native workers and functioned as a training program for young people, may even come to influence new forms of native Northwest Coast art and architecture. It may ultimately bring home to native territory some of the ideals and criteria established for the construction of this lavish and influential map.

Umberto Eco, like Baudrillard, is a traveler drawn to this type of replicated landscape. He too peruses *hyperreality*, making pilgrimages from historical reconstruction to wax museum in the United States, critiquing the American obsession with representations that may be more real than their referents. "The sign aims to be the thing," proposes Eco "to abolish the distinction of reference, the mechanism of replacement" (1968: 7). These are the simulacra, "the generation by models of a real without origin or reality" that have also preoccupied Baudrillard (1983: 2).

Both Eco and Baudrillard have responded as if impoverished by replicated forms of expression, associating imitation with degradation, devoid of nuance and reference. Eco is driven to show how "completely fake" these constructed realities are, even though they may be more vivid and more attractive than the originals from which they derive. He is chilled by the exactness of horrifying detail in wax museums but complains of incongruous combinations of subject matter that transgress the reality of experience and his sense of propriety. Eco's critique calls for symbolic allusion rather than crude fact, an intellectual orientation that he is familiar with from his own "old world." At the same time he treats inconsistency and distance from those "facts" as being vacuous and without purpose.

Edward Bruner has critiqued both Baudrillard and Eco, calling for more illuminating evaluations of simulacra that may transcend the sharp lines previously drawn between original and copy, authentic and inauthentic. Rather than dismiss historical reproductions as mere fabrication, without origin or referential value, Bruner takes what he has called "a constructivist position that sees all culture as continually invented and reinvented" (1994: 397). For instance, in his analysis of Lincoln's New Salem, a historic site in central Illinois, he observes an educational function not strictly limited to historical illustration. He extrapolates instead a timely system of values embedded in this simulated town, which may be associated with the overvaluation of progress, the celebration of the "rags to riches" myth of opportunity in America, and the conscious "playing with time frames" enjoyed by tourists and other visitors to the site (ibid.).

The New Salem reconstruction need not be obviated as the focus of historical scholarship because it does not duplicate the exact conditions of that village in the 1830s. For instance, Bruner notes the weathered patina of the exteriors of the reconstructed buildings there, but remarks that they could not have looked that old in the 1830s, as New Salem was abandoned within ten years of its original construction. The patina of age is more closely associated with the historical sensibilities of contemporary people. This "inauthentic" aging process is valuable to observe, however, despite its historical inaccuracy. It may be read instead as a mirror to the 1990s, constructed to meet the requirements of contemporary staff and visitors and as such a significant historical document.

Contrary to Eco and Baudrillard, Bruner's "constructivist" approach positions the invention of experience as central to the creation of meaning. In a volume edited by both Bruner and Victor Turner, *The Anthropology of Experience* (1986), each new event or hybrid experience not rooted in a unified way with the antique is described as a text full of meanings. In the epilogue written for this book, Clifford Geertz proposes:

> Experiences, like tales, fêtes, potteries, rites, dramas, images, memoirs, ethnographies, and allegorical machineries, are made; and it is such made things that make them. The "anthropology of experience," like the anthropology of anything else, is a study of the uses of artifice and the endlessness of it. (1986: 380)

The role of invention in social reality and the perpetuation of selected cultural phenomena has been taken up by Chris Jenks as well. He has interpreted the concept of "cultural reproduction" as a strategy for social inculcation. Referring to cultural theorist Pierre Bourdieu and his analyses of educational systems as devices for the perpetuation of cultural dominance and class structure (Bourdieu 1997; Bourdieu and Passeron 1977), Jenks makes a case for imitation as regeneration. Enculturation, and preferred styles of presentation, reflect self-sustaining cultural process. This may be accomplished through the perpetuation of form and presentation as well as the adjustment of symbolic orders (Jenks 1993: 1–16). Repetitions of form and style, then, are not fully understood as mere evidence of historical accuracy, but are complex and influential acts, including those Bourdieu describes as "symbolic violence" (ibid.: 11).

The arguments of the scholars cited here rely upon their orientation to a presumed equation between legitimate representation and historical fact, between origin and authenticity. As a correlate, selective representation constructed according to the requirements of new and influential parties has been associated with falsification. Michael Taussig has suggested that the valuation of mimesis, "the faculty to copy, imitate, make models, explore difference, yield into and become Other," elicits admiration at times in the West, but may also elicit accusations of duplicity (1993: xiiiff). An ambiguous force, the mimetic faculty may capture power in a magical fashion, "yet that same power is a power to falsify, mask, pose" (ibid.: 42–43). To copy is also to invent. The western love/hate relationship with the ability to replicate has wavered between admiration and devaluation. The sanctions of supposed perpetuity and the hypnotic skills required for the practices of reproduction carry the impact of historical citation, not a mere recycling of form. Repetition may even model the future, whether encouraged by influential outsiders or designed by indigenous activists for their own use. Native Northwest Coast cultures do show reverence for their forebears by way of formal repetition, but their greatest authority, like that of their non-native sponsors, may be to respond to the present as expressed through selective reference.

Looking Backward at the Latest Thing

Some significant elements of past form are therefore customarily reproduced in the manufacture of masks and other items of regalia, both for potlatch practice on the reserves and for public exhibition. Ironically however, accurate renditions of old pieces, sometimes down to the last centimeter, are more often made for western admirers of the art form. The traditional appearance of a mask or totem pole, then, may not specify the identity of its audience. In Chapter Four, "False Cognates: Looking Backward at the Latest Thing in Contemporary Northwest

Coast Art," several generations of an old Kwakwaka'wakw painted screen, created in response to the requirements of different commissioners, are described. The prototype for this work was a nineteenth-century dance prop that has been recycled, so far, as a museum replication project, a serigraph print for sale, and as a wall-mounted art work intended for gallery viewing; it was ultimately purchased by a major corporation.

A set of carved and painted masks produced by an impressive roster of contemporary Northwest Coast artists for potlatch use, but known to a much broader audience, is also discussed in this chapter. The masks, commissioned by a non-native museum on Vancouver Island in cooperation with a native chief, are based upon historical precedent, known through an oral history. Another related set, carved in the nineteenth century strictly for native use, has recently been discovered as part of the collection of the American Museum of Natural History in New York. The comparison of these two mask sets as well as the various versions of the painted screen poses an unprecedented opportunity to explore new and changing criteria for relationships between crest prerogative, history, and the replication of form itself in Northwest Coast practice.

All of these works are contextualized for this study according to local history. This process is intended to update the cross-cultural dialogue that follows both from their presence and that of other historically based pieces in such diverse settings. The categorization of these arts by outside audiences as "timeless" at best, or on the other hand, as mere copies, unworthy of study, is addressed in this discussion. These definitions result from the apprehension of adaptations of past form as static within an international art environment that is driven by its keen admiration for invention. Translations of nineteenth-century works are typically regarded by outsiders as vestigial, forming what Baudrillard has called a "non-referential desert," even when they are invented as the new creations of particular parties. The present marginalization of these works and their makers is therefore presented here in contrast to the ennobling of the avant-garde in the West.

The contemporary native artists who produce these "copies" persist in their assertions of authority over the art form, even in these new arenas, which suggests a certain element of resistance in their practices. Some aspects of "identity politics" may be influential in the continuing conservative appearance of their work. Because generalizations and historical inaccuracies are also permitted in Northwest Coast art in the public domain and are acceded to, on some occasions, by these same artists, they too are analyzed at length here. Certain key decisions to homogenize native identity, for instance, may be seen as strategic in these settings. These modifications, as well as the selective conservation of antique formal practice, function as forceful assertions of ownership of the native past.

Current reproductions of Northwest Coast native art also result from the authority of powerful non-native institutions and the influence of the marketplace. These entities continue in many ways to define the conventions of style, attempt to designate group identity, and to confer value. From the government-funded totem pole restoration projects in Southeast Alaska of the 1930s through museum-sponsored dance reenactments of the 1990s, selected standards of authenticity and markers of Indian identity have been applied. Practices of inclusion, and the consequent exclusion, of certain native participants may also be observed in all of these projects. Furthermore these collaborative acts do not imply an equitable distribution of authority among all of the participants. Yet these practices have been instrumental in the creation of public image for native groups of both the United States and Canada, as constructed and certified for outsiders.

The resulting art works may even be considered "inventions by committee." In every case, the requirements of artists and patrons have run parallel, permitting just enough agreement to arrive at these forms. This may look like complicity, but the motives of these cooperating parties may be quite different. For their own reasons, native participants in these projects, and even individual artists who produce pieces for the commercial galleries, have seized important opportunities to interact with influential outsiders. They may advance their own needs and in some cases the goals of their communities. Non-native authorities, on their part, have found it helpful to align their replication projects with the imprimatur of authenticity offered by Indian consultation. The objectives of each of these participants may seem at first glance to coincide in their persistent references to history. Upon close examination however, these groups maintain their own subjective regard for the past.

For this reason, this is a historically based work that delineates the circumstances specific to discrete projects and focuses on case studies. The replicas, restorations, and reenactments discussed here may be regarded as unique documents of cross-cultural process. The individuals and groups who claimed the opportunity to work together on these projects made meaningful displays, influencing the perceptions of an international audience of observers. The effects of their decisions may even bring home some new criteria for traditional practice. The following sections of this work outline some of these group processes and introduce certain key personalities active in these local histories. This process is intended to recover some of the significance of recast or replicated forms according to the perceptions and objectives of those who had a hand in shaping them.

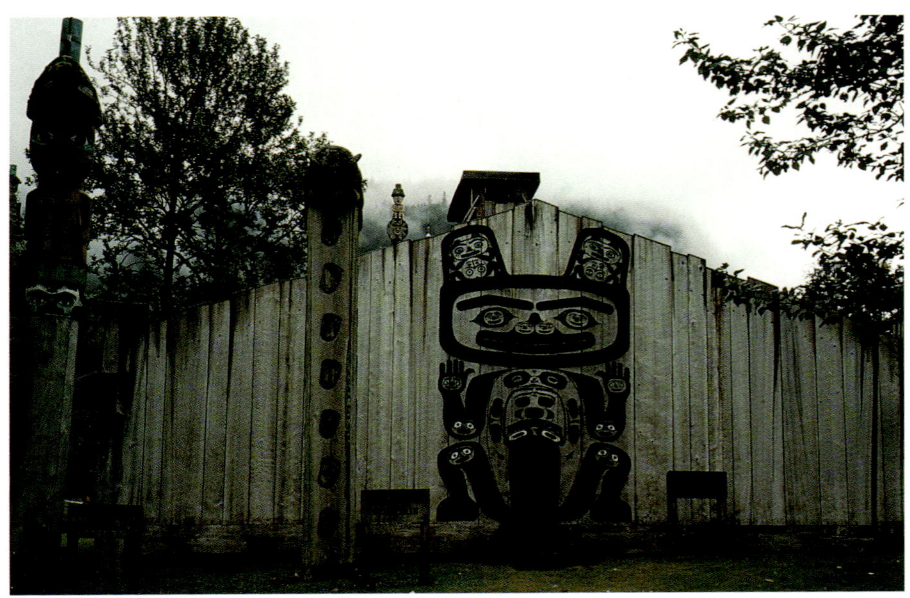

Plate 1 Chief Shakes Community House, Wrangell, Alaska, 1992. Photo: Judith Ostrowitz.

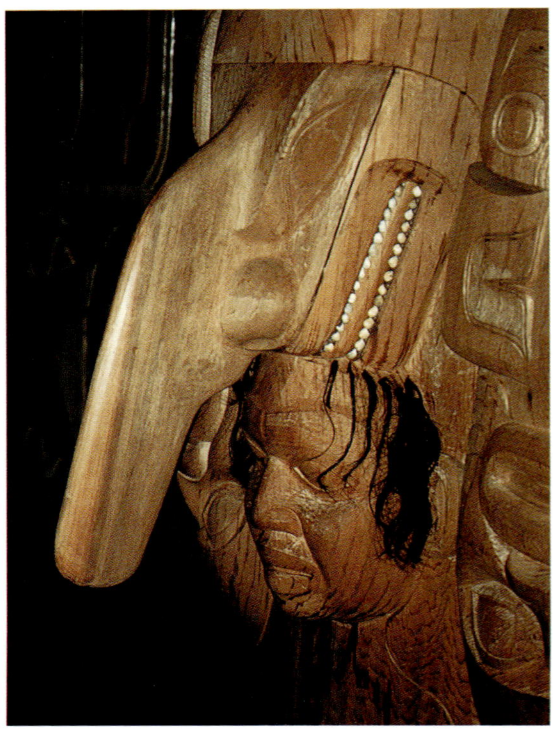

Plate 2 Detail of contemporary housepost carved by Steve Brown and assistants, now in the interior of the Chief Shakes Community House. Photo: Judith Ostrowitz, 1997.

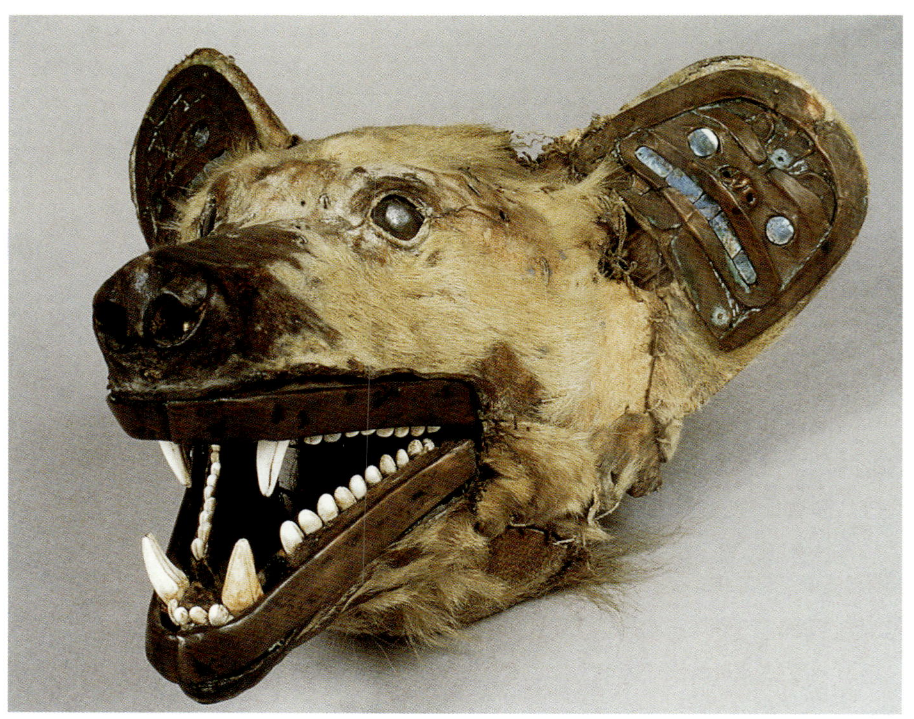

Plate 3 Chief Shakes' Grizzly Bear Mask, Stikine Tlingit, Nanya. ay i Clan, Wrangell, Alaska; courtesy of Burke Museum of Natural History and Culture, cat. no. 2.5E604.

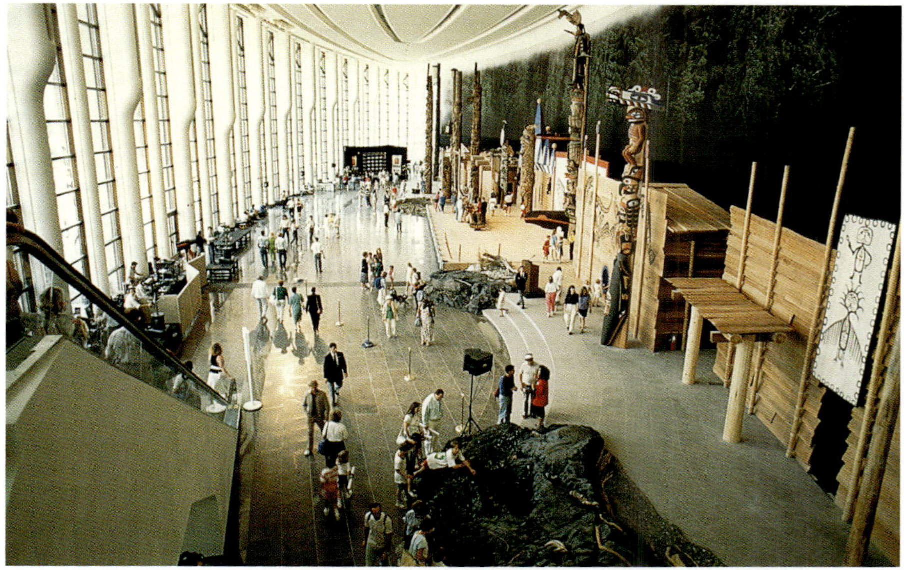

Plate 4 The Grand Hall, CMC, Hull, Quebec, 1989. S89-1896. Photo: S. Darby, June 29, 1989; courtesy Canadian Museum of Civilization.

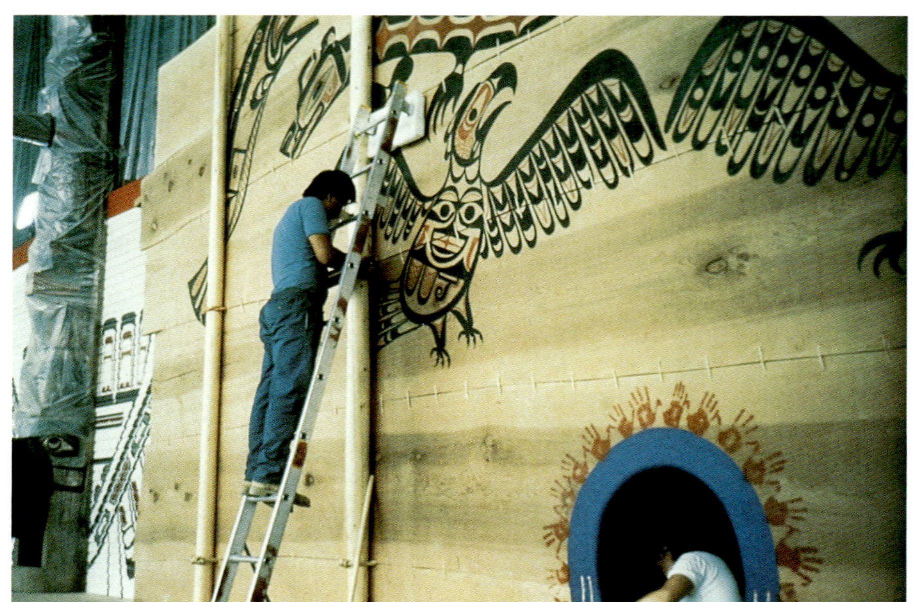

Plate 5 *The facade construction of the Nuu-chah-nulth House in the Grand Hall, in progress. Photo courtesy of Canadian Museum of Civilization, 1989.*

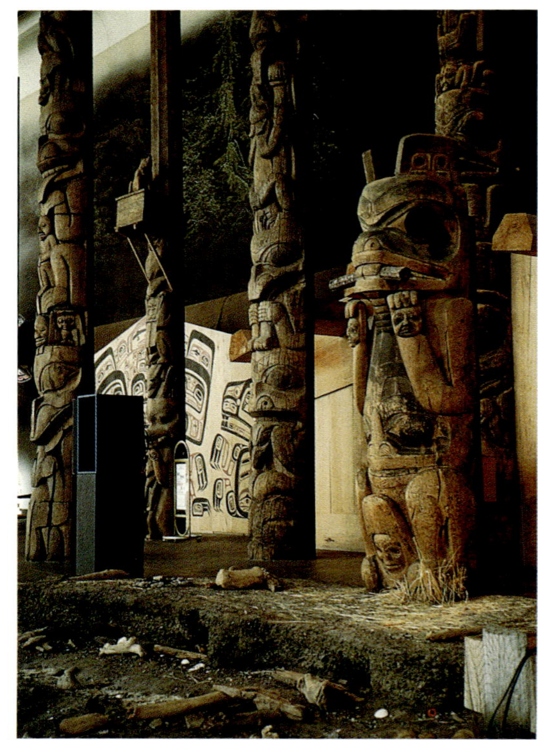

Plate 6 *Haida and Tsimshian totem poles in close prox-imity in the Grand Hall, overlooking the fabricated beach. Photo: Judith Ostrowitz.*

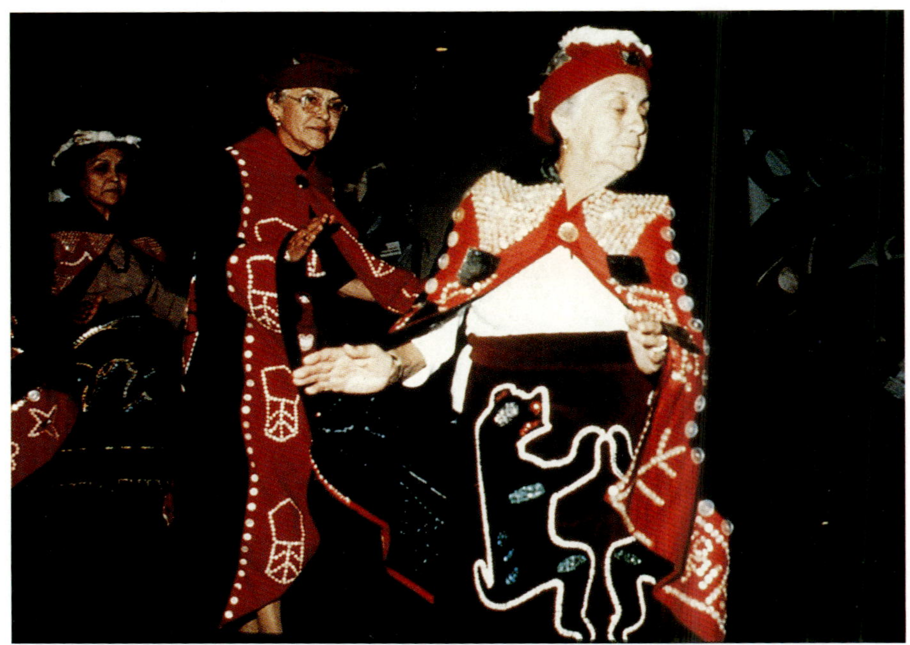

Plate 7 Ethel Alfred leads a line of dancers at the Chiefly Feasts *opening ceremonies, 1991. Gloria Cranmer Webster is on her immediate left. Uncatalogued photograph, AMNH, courtesy Department of Library Sciences.*

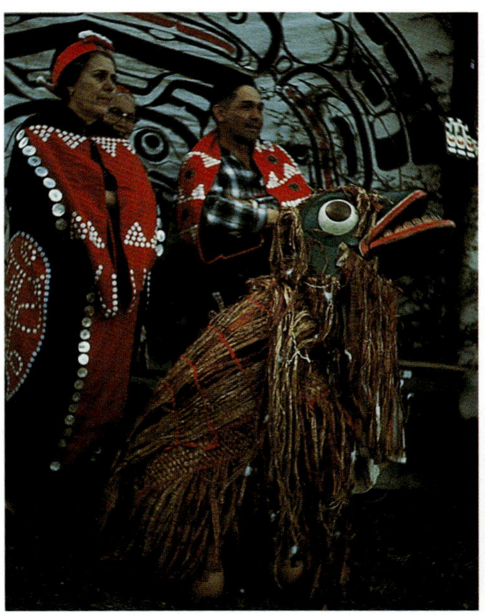

Plate 8 Outdoor dance presentation for June Sports Day, Alert Bay, c. 1962. Ethel Alfred, left, and James Sewid, right, with a Frog dancer. Photo: courtesy Drew Oswell.

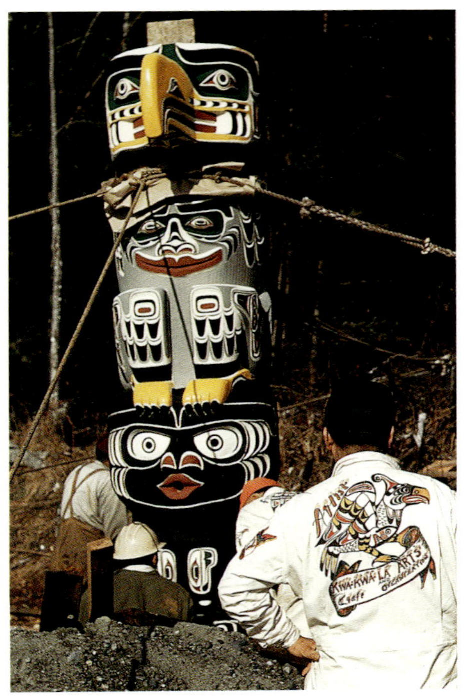

Plate 9 Alert Bay Big House under construction, c. 1965. Henry Speck (in white overalls with "Kwakwala Arts and Crafts" logo) stands before one of the massive house posts he carved and painted. Photo: courtesy Drew Oswell.

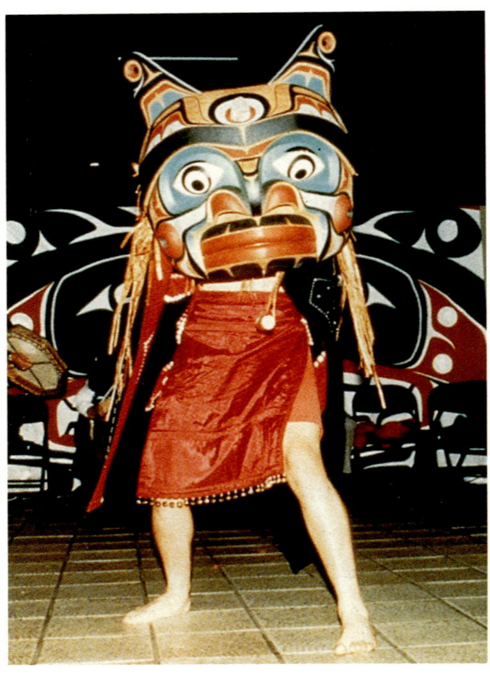

Plate 10 'Na̱mgis Sea Monster mask by Tony Hunt, Jr., c. 1990. Wood, cedar bark, copper, quartz crystal, cord. H: 69 cm. W: 60 cm. Danced by Kevin Cranmer at the *Chiefly Feasts* opening ceremonies, 1991. This mask is now in the collection of the Royal British Columbia Museum, Victoria, B.C. Uncatalogued photograph, AMNH; courtesy Tony Hunt, Jr., and Department of Library Services.

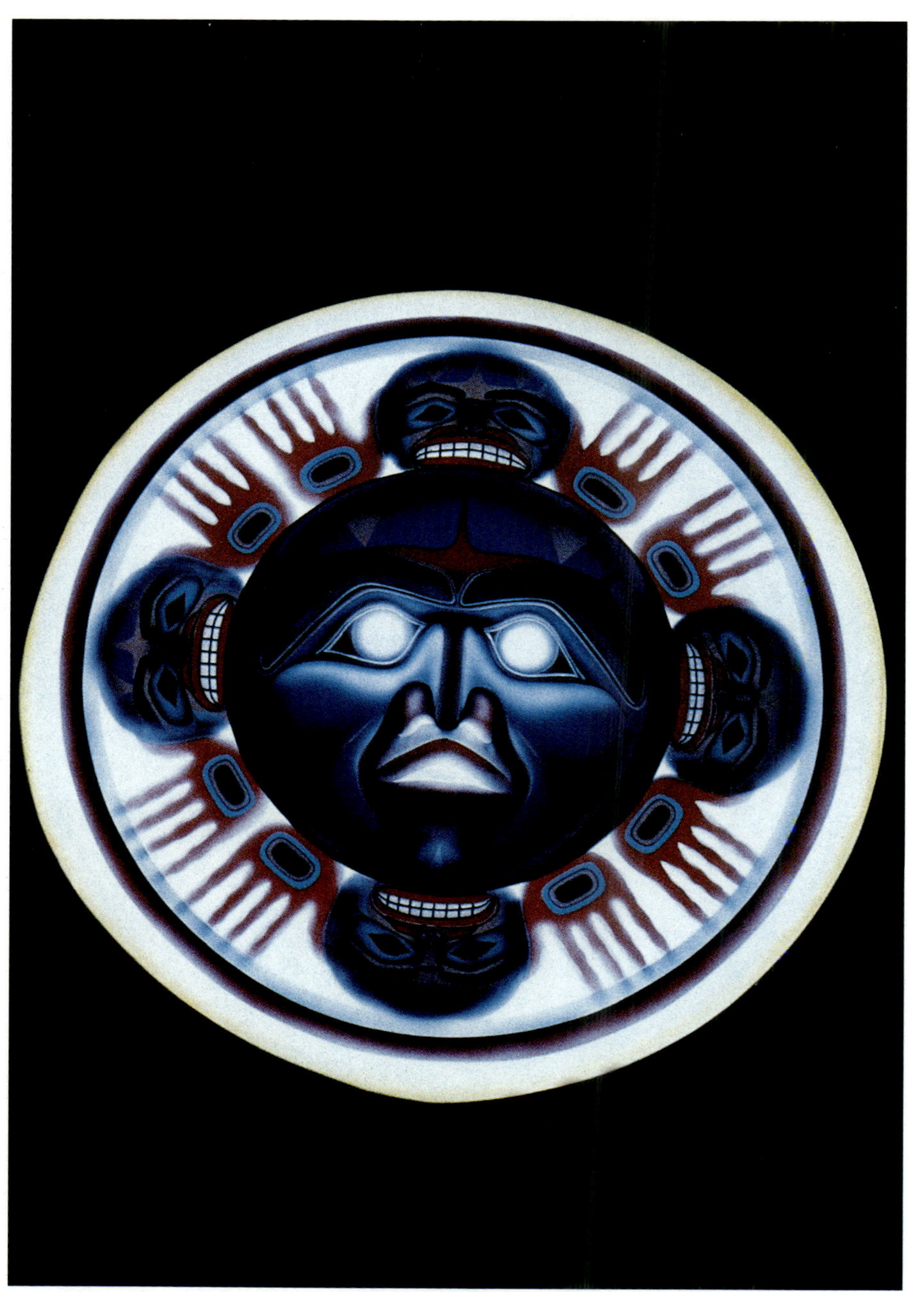

Plate 11 Sun mask with Heralder by Glen Tallio, 1992. Acrylic on wood, tubing. Photo: courtesy Glen Tallio and Inuit Gallery, Vancouver, B.C.

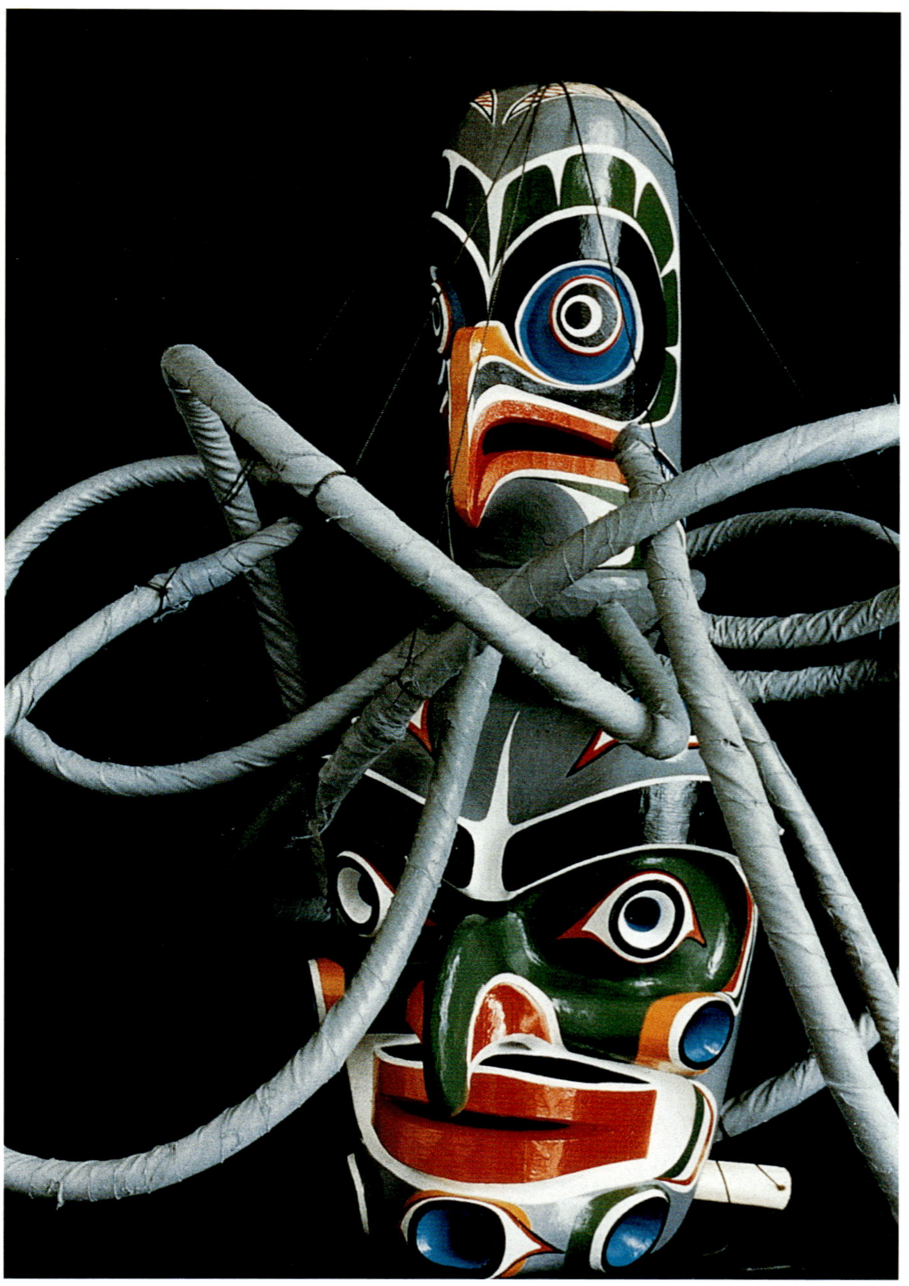

Plate 12 Kumungwe' mask with Octopus by Wayne Alfred, 1987. Acrylic on wood, tubing.
Photo: courtesy Wayne Alfred and Inuit Gallery, Vancouver, B.C.

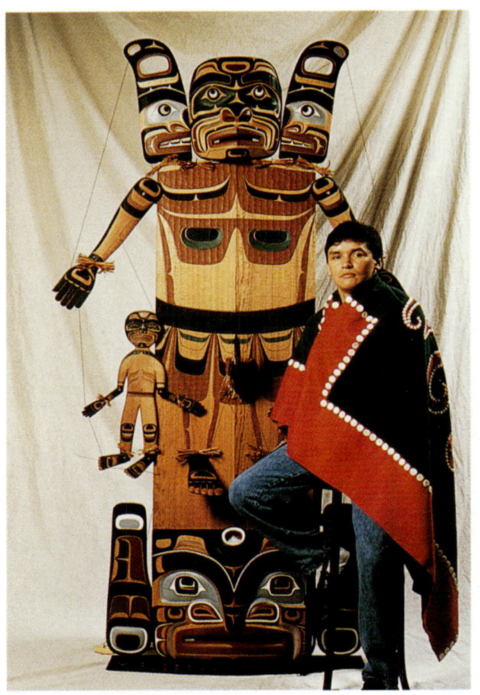

Plate 13 Tuxw'id *screen by Tom Hunt, 1990. Acrylic on wood. H: 96 in. W: 40 in. D: 3 in. Photo: courtesy Tom Hunt and The Legacy Ltd. Gallery, Seattle WA.*

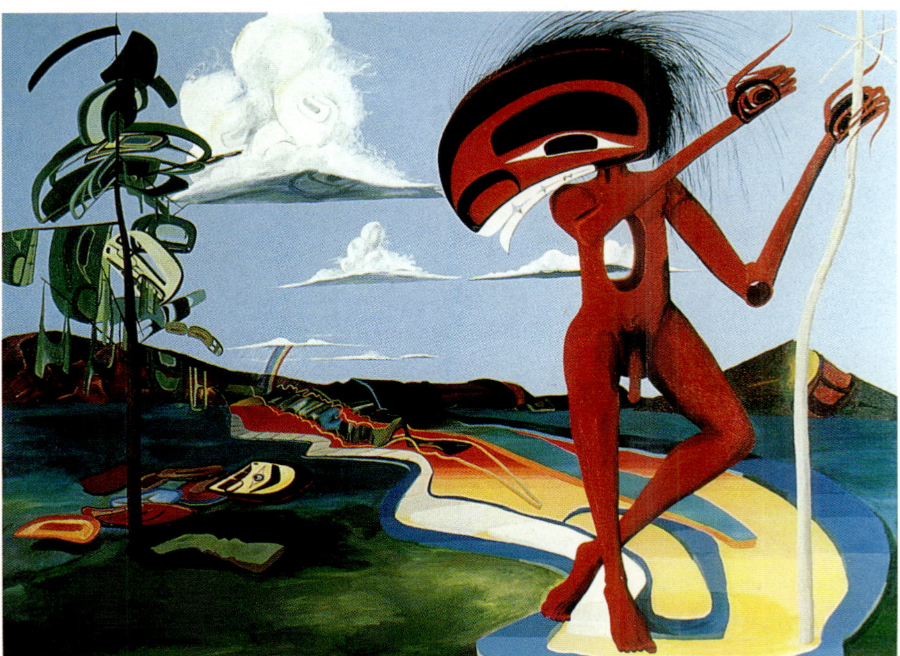

Plate 14 The Environmentalist *by Lawrence Paul Yuxweluptun, 1985. Acrylic on canvas. H: 66 in. W: 84 in. Photo: Peter Nebel; courtesy Lawrence Paul Yuxweluptun and Völker-kundemuseum der Universität Zürich.*

Expedience and Classicism at the Chief Shakes Community House

ETERMINING IDEAL FORM is a preoccupation consistent with the contemplation of the past, not with the production of unprecedented works. Only in historical perspective can the characteristics of a so-called classic phase be selected, their status mediated by cultural process and circumscribed by later authorities. Hans Belting, in *The End of the History of Art?* (1987), discussed a conjectured "universal classic" as posited by Vasari for Renaissance artists, for instance, necessarily associated with strict standards of shared value and a discernable progress toward ideal beauty. These were thought to be modeled upon the inexorable cycles of nature and further validated by the authority of precedent in antiquity. Although masterworks of native North American art are not frequently compared with the literary and artistic achievements of ancient Greeks and Romans, classicizing strategies have also been pursued in the evaluation of their forms and the appropriate circumstances of their manufacture. Such analyses have typically been constructed in relation to an unrelenting focus on the traditional and on the Native American past as an ahistorical ideal. Furthermore, the hypothesis of such a high point—a moment of equilibrium or even stasis within these non-western traditions—depends upon the delineation of common styles as well as the proposal of a completely unified canon derived from the meticulous analysis of a vast number of antiquities.

Certain standards of the traditional have, in fact, been established by scholars of native art and are frequently invoked as criteria for connoisseurship, affecting contemporary definitions of authentic native art and identity. The best-known example is Bill Holm's *Northwest Coast Indian Art: An Analysis of Form* (1965), a work originally undertaken to describe the stylistic characteristics of the northern graphic tradition. Holm's findings soon became a technical guide for many young Indian carvers who were passionately dedicated during the 1960s and beyond to rediscovering the artistic practices of their forebears. Holm's study also established, inadvertently, formal criteria still used by some individuals to evaluate these new works of Northwest Coast art, based upon the assumed authority of the past. Other scholars have disqualified post-contact works, those manufactured for sale to non-Indians, such as argillite and other tourist arts, from the roster of these so-called classic works.[1] Ironically, however, many highly visible works of Northwest Coast art, especially those created as representative examples of the Indian past for the general public, have been developed in just such cross-cultural milieux. These influential projects are frequently collaborative, created by both native and non-native arbiters of proper form and content according to selected standards and considerations.

The Chief Shakes Community House of Wrangell, Alaska, for instance, may be considered just such a "classic" example of Tlingit architecture (Plate 1). Shrouded under its usual canopy of mist, it has survived more than 160 years of life in its current location and has therefore been known by many generations of both native and non-native observers as representative of the building style of this Northwest Coast native group. The appearance of the house has been somewhat protean, however, forged in turn by various restoration projects that have concurrently transformed its public image. The present building is actually a "replica." Modeled upon a nineteenth-century community house that existed on the site, the contemporary structure was built in the late 1930s and has never been inhabited, nor has it been used extensively as a place for potlatching. Nonetheless, it continues to be admired by its various observers, not only for its stylistic accuracy, but because it has long been associated with the prominence of the Shakes family of the Nanya.ayí clan of the Stikine Tlingit and it functions still as an important symbol of contemporary native identity in Southeast Alaska.

Each restoration of the house has been motivated by audience-specific concerns so that its integrity as a prototype has been established as much by interpretation as by the durability of its post and beam construction. The circumstances that led to the representation of certain high points in its history or examples of what may be termed its "classic" form were specified as appropriate for public display, according to criteria developed by various consultants, supervisors and artists. These individuals have been considered authorities on the formal representation of native art and culture, according to the precepts of their respective generations.

Identifying Tlingit Architecture

George Thornton Emmons left copious notes on the identifying elements of authentic Tlingit architecture, establishing for the historical record certain norms of style as understood during his period of observation, which spanned the late nineteenth and early twentieth centuries. His notes include descriptions of general house types and specific examples as well, recording in particular the features of the Whale House at Klukwan. With minor provisos concerning the arrangement of wall planks and details of interior ornamentation, Emmons claimed that the description of the Whale House could be applied in general to any of the larger old community houses (Emmons/de Laguna 1991: 64):

> The larger and more important houses were partly subterranean, with one or two steplike platforms descending to a central square enclosure, from four to six feet below the surface of the ground. Such houses were ornamented with carved posts and screens, heraldic in character and illustrating important events in the life of the clan, while the small houses stood directly on the ground [lacking the excavated floor], and were crude and plain. . . . The old type of house was rectangular in plan, with a depth greater than the frontage. . . . The house front was often painted with animal figures [crests], or was ornamented with carved figures on either side of the entrance. . . . The doorway was oval and low, and was reached by several steps. . . . Windows that are seen on modern Tlingit houses [1900?] had no place in the past; the doorway and the smokehole in the roof were the only openings. (Ibid.: 60; Emmons 1916)

Analogous descriptions of Tlingit style houses have been recorded since Malaspina's expedition to Yakutat in 1791. Cordero and Suria, both members of the expedition, sketched old house frames, one of which was found on Ankau Point. Squared constructions of posts and beams with remnants of what de Laguna believes was probably plank siding were noted as the outstanding features of the structure.[2] Louis Shotridge (1913) is consistent in noting the salient features of Chilkat houses, and Vastokas (1966) continued the practice of listing posts, beams, wall planks, excavated floors, and smoke hole as intrinsic to the structure of the Tlingit house. Other contemporary authors and living individuals conversant with traditional or "authentic" Tlingit art and architecture also enumerate these details of construction as essential in community house form. In Nabokov and Easton's *Native American Architecture* (1989), for instance, construction techniques in which boards are fitted and overlap, requiring no nails or spikes to secure them are described. They too note the presence of a split-shingle smoke hole and the division of sleeping quarters in traditional houses by both stepped levels and screens as characteristic of Tlingit building style (277).

According to these definitions, the Chief Shakes Community House qualifies as just such an "old type, important house." Each reconstructed version of the building included in its composition most of the essential elements mentioned. The prestigious excavation is present in each version, as are the stepped levels, elaboration with heraldic or crest imagery,[3] appropriate dimensions, and in some phases, the necessary means of ingress and egress. These "building blocks of authentic form" as designated by scholars and other authorities, as well as the historical continuity associated with the house, have been maintained in part as a result of its repeated reproduction as a series of close copies. Ironically, however, creative adjustments in the interpretation of its forms over time have been just as useful in the maintenance of its important status as reckoned by key individuals.

Privilege and Artistic Reproduction on the Northwest Coast

Series of artistic recreations are actually well known within native Northwest Coast communities. Near copies or creative translations of ancestral works are routinely produced in relation to an enduring tradition in which the right to display specific imagery (previously referred to as heraldic by Emmons), in the form of carved works, items of regalia, and architectural elements, is ceremonially transferred from one generation to the next. Replacements are commissioned for old and worn-out heirlooms, providing a physical support for enduring but intangible prerogatives. The legitimate display of these inherited crests is exclusive and of central importance in ceremonialism.[4]

The facade of the contemporary Chief Shakes house, as an example, is carved in shallow relief and painted with the conventionalized image of a Brown Bear (or Grizzly) with faces superimposed on its upturned palms and the various joints of its body. This image was first applied to the housefront in 1939 in the course of a restoration project that I will discuss in greater detail. The painting is based upon the composition of an earlier work, an interior painted screen from the Chief Shakes house, now in the collection of the Denver Art Museum and once owned by the collector and enthusiast of the Surrealist movement, Wolfgang Paalen (Figure 1.1; see Paalen 1943: 16, Plate III). It differs only slightly from the contemporary facade image in the combination of painted and unpainted design elements, most notably in the stomach areas of the two bears. The Denver screen was photographed in situ in the late 1800s, but is itself a reproduction of an even older work.

A fragment of a wooden screen, actually just a plank, which was probably created for the Shakes family in the early eighteenth century, is preserved today in the collection of the Burke Museum of Natural History and Culture.[5] The image incised on this extremely deteriorated piece of wood appears to be quite similar to those on the other two extant Brown Bear screens, although only one hand and

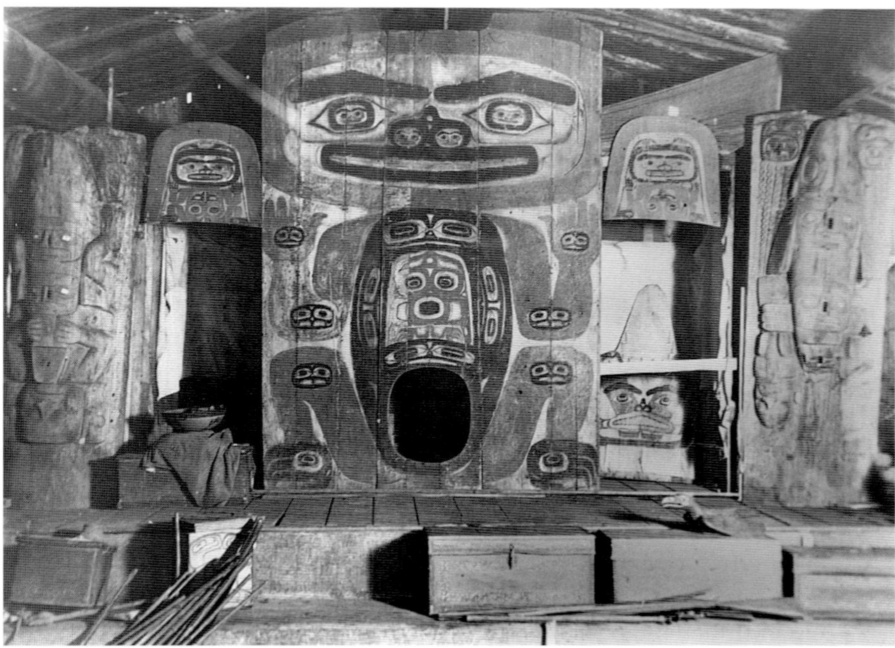

1.1 Brown Bear screen, interior of Chief Shakes House, c. 1890–1900. Photo: courtesy Wrangell Museum; P91.11.98, neg. 10.

a small section of the bear's face may still be discerned on its surface. No paint that is visible to the eye, however, remains on the Burke Museum's screen fragment.

Although it may be tempting to think so, we have no reason to believe that this older, suitably antique plank represents an original or first Brown Bear screen. It is simply the earliest surviving example in the series that we know of, each generation of which refers to the clan and its ursine tutelary. This particular creature is said to have accompanied Shakes' ancestors as they climbed up a mountain to escape the waters of a primordial flood, and its image is interpreted in various forms on much of the prestigious regalia of the Nanya.ayí.[6] The skin, teeth, and claws of this legendary bear are said to have been made into a mask (Plate 3) and full costume that became important items of regalia and theatrical props for the clan as well (Holm 1987: 192–95).[7]

The wooden fragment may still, however, be understood as a "classic," not because of its relative antiquity, nor for its adherence to universally accepted standards for proper form, but rather as an authoritative display of this crest within its own time period. The succeeding versions of this artwork were probably just as influential, and each was likely to have been validated in public ceremony when it was new. In this sense, each Brown Bear screen has been representative in its day. Each generation found it useful to display both Nanya.ayí identity and the prestigious affiliation of clan members in a particular manner. Minor modifications in the execution of the Brown Bear screen as well as the more significant change in its location, from the interior to the exterior facade of the house, have been affected by various compelling historical circumstances.

Over the last 160 years, the function of the entire house has fluctuated considerably. It has served as a greater or lesser public symbol of clan identity, according to the requirements of the Nanya.ayí and other interested parties. To illuminate the shifting status of the house and the consequent modifications in the appearance of the building as well as its contents, at least four delineated time periods should be considered. The early configuration of the house, beginning in the 1830s, for instance, and its associated totem poles as they were first established in Wrangell under the direction of Chief Shakes IV and his immediate successor Shakes V, are known. The house and the public display of its contents are also well recorded for posterity in the time period that I have named "The Photographic Period," coinciding with the reign of Chief Shakes VI, from the last quarter of the nineteenth through the early twentieth centuries. Later, in the late 1930s, a major restoration project conducted by the Alaska Civilian Conservation Corps resulted in the 1939 version of the house, and additional totem poles were also restored and moved to Shakes Island. Finally, the artistic replication of the famous interior house posts in the 1980s represents yet another shift in the appearance and role of the house as it is understood in the public domain.

The Recorded History of the Chief Shakes Community House: Establishing Nanya.ayí Dominion on the Stikine (c. 1830–1878)

The written history of the house began in the 1830s, during the lifetime of Chief Shakes IV, a powerful Stikine Tlingit chief, the fourth of seven consecutive house leaders known to have held this title.[8] His domain included access to the considerable resources of the Stikine River, valuable in the nineteenth century to both Indian groups and white traders, in particular for the fur trade. The Russians had built a fort, Redoubt St. Dionysius, in the harbor area of Wrangell in about 1833. Although we cannot be certain of his motives, Shakes was very likely aware of the advantages to be had by relocating his household in proximity to the fort, perhaps for protection (Keithahn 1981: 6), but just as likely to defend his interests and to establish trade relations with the Russian settlement.

In Tolmie's journal of an expedition to establish an outpost of the Hudson's Bay Company, which until 1840 was unsuccessful in its struggle to gain a hold on the fur trade on the Stikine, we get some sense of Shakes IV's true authority in the region and his determination to maintain his longstanding jurisdiction:

> We were visited for the second time by Seix of the Stikine. After a long conference he still refuses to permit our going up river to establish a post. Yet he is perfectly willing to let us settle at the entrance of the river. . . . He is a tall well-informed [sic] Indian, rather corpulent, but his size adds to his dignity and deportment. . . . He is forward and presuming. (Barbeau 1958: 38)[9]

By the early 1830s the formidable Shakes, also known as the first Nanya.ayí to have seen a white man (ibid.: 5), moved his entire clan to the small island in Wrangell Harbor. There he built a large communal house, very likely modeled upon one left behind in Khasitláan or "Old Wrangell," the former site of the clan house, about 20 miles further south.[10] Emmons identifies the house at Wrangell as the Dogfish House (the dogfish is a type of shark; Emmons/de Laguna 1991: 443, Table 14), and it may be possible to associate it with Swanton's record for the Nanya.ayí Shark House group at Old Wrangell (1908: 402). De Laguna has commented that it was not uncommon for a house name to be validated again if a building was reconstructed at a new site and extant carvings, related to the crests of the clan, were transported to a new house when possible (Emmons/de Laguna 1991: 67). These practices imply considerable historical depth in the public identity of particular Tlingit dwellings, even when newly reconstructed. Therefore the architectural conventions and crest images applied at the new home of Shakes's clan at Wrangell may be considered well-precedented, referring to the established prominence of the chief or house leader and the entire house group.

Shakes and his descendants, as concerned to demonstrate dominion among their Tlingit contemporaries as among the whites and other native groups who were rapidly descending upon their traditional territory, did bring various major carved images to the new site and commissioned the production of certain new ones. These artworks advertised Shakes's longstanding crest prerogatives and the famous history of the clan, both prerequisites to his claim. For example, two mortuary totem poles were placed before the house; they can be associated with older poles from the Khasitláan site. One of them, now referred to as the Gonakadet pole (Barbeau 1950, Vol. 1, 295–98), also the name of a lake monster, is carved with a seated figure wearing the double-headed Killerwhale crest hat of the Nanya.ayí.[11] This totem pole was photographed in situ by Eadweard Muybridge in 1868.[12] As Steve Brown, a scholar and artist who has worked extensively in the area has observed, it was already quite deteriorated by that date. Much of its painted surface had weathered away by 1868, and the base of the pole is shown to be propped up by a number of boards in this photograph. Its considerable age suggests that the pole may have been carved originally for the Khasitláan site and then moved for reinstallation before the new house. Alternately, it may have been carved anew in the early 1830s when the Nanya.ayí first relocated to Shakes Island (Brown 1994: 77–78).

The Gonakadet pole continued to be regarded as a significant image by succeeding generations of Shakes's clan. The figure with crest hat, composed in essentially the same manner, was again recarved around 1885, even seven years after the death of Shakes V (ibid.). In an 1886 photograph by Partridge[13] some minor alterations are visible in the artistic handling of the figure's features on the new pole and in the elaboration of the crest hat itself, notably in the reduction of the number of hat rings from four to three (ibid.). The new totem pole, however, functioned in much the same manner as did the older version, displaying the same crest privilege in the same location.

The other pole positioned before the Shakes house represents the Brown Bear of Nanya.ayí legend that gave its life for the clan; it appears on the various versions of the painted screen discussed earlier. A similar pole, surmounted by a horizontal bear, was sketched by John Muir at the Old Wrangell site in 1879 and photographed there as late as 1902, before its ultimate decomposition from old age.[14] The Old Wrangell version lacked the carved footprints on the cylindrical body of the pole that mark the legendary bear's progress up the mountain. Its basic composition, as well as its subject matter, however, probably link it with the pole before the new Shakes house.

Again following photographic evidence, the Brown Bear pole appears to have been freshly carved for display when the Shakes house was new to Wrangell (ibid.). The renewal of this totem pole in the early nineteenth century, though not in a manner quite identical to its Khasitláan predecessor, may be understood as a type of native "replication" project. Artistic references to the old site and to the prestigious history of the clan, as known by reputation to the other groups in the region, were designed to support and maintain the position of the clan in the new town, increasingly populated with a variety of outsiders.

The Photographic Period (1878–1916)

By 1878, the year of Kow-ish-te's, or Shakes V's death, the population at Wrangell was in the process of becoming even more heterogeneous. Members of other Tlingit clans were anxious to work in the town for the small wages offered them as day laborers and packers for the gold miners who passed through Wrangell to travel up the Stikine River. Others were attracted by the variety of supplies available from white merchants setting up shop in town (Young 1927: 80–81). Visiting

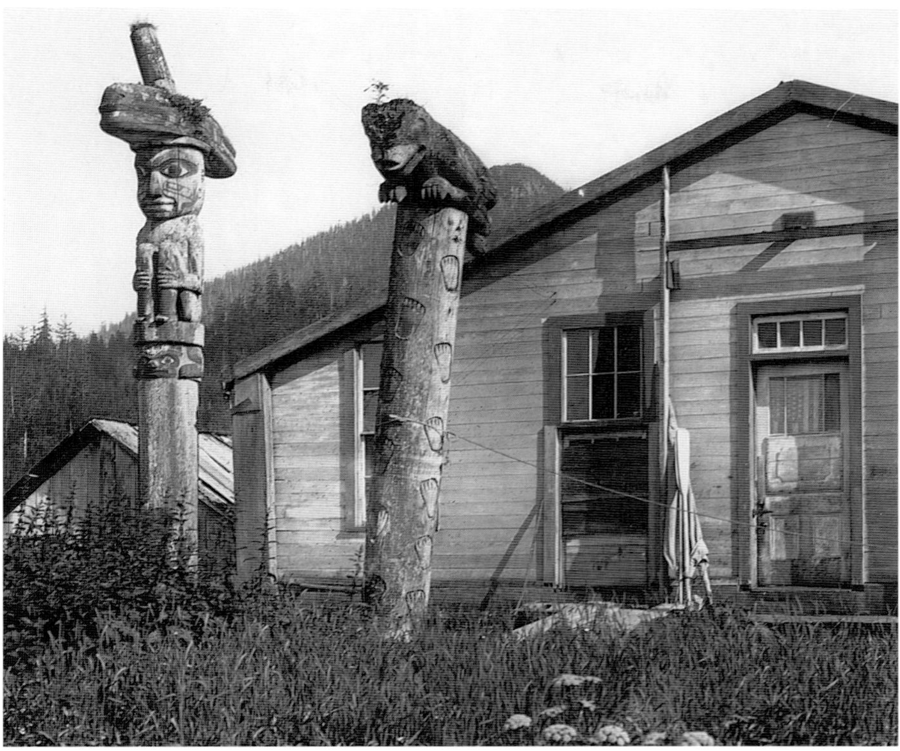

1.2 View of Chief Shakes house, Wrangell, Alaska, 1909. Photo: Harlan Smith. AMNH, 46122; courtesy Department of Library Services.

groups of both Tlingits and Haidas made their camps in what was called the "foreign village" section of Wrangell (Keithahn 1981: 7).

Interestingly, the photographic record for Wrangell, which had technically begun during Shakes V's lifetime, was expanded during this period of foreign influx. The well-known photograph of Kow-ish-te lying in state and surrounded by a large number of the clan's treasures may be said to mark the very beginning of this period, initiated during the last quarter of the nineteenth century and continuing through the first decade of the twentieth.[15] A number of photographers visited this exotic crossroads to document native life at the time, including Muybridge, Partridge, and Harlan Smith, thus fixing this stage of the town's appearance in the historical record. This wealth of documentation creates the impression of an "authoritative moment," worthy of notice and somehow more conclusive regarding authentic form and function in the arts than other moments when photos are lacking, or when extreme physical decline is evident.

This photographic period coincides roughly with the years also designated by scholars as "The Museum Period of Anthropology" and has been associated with

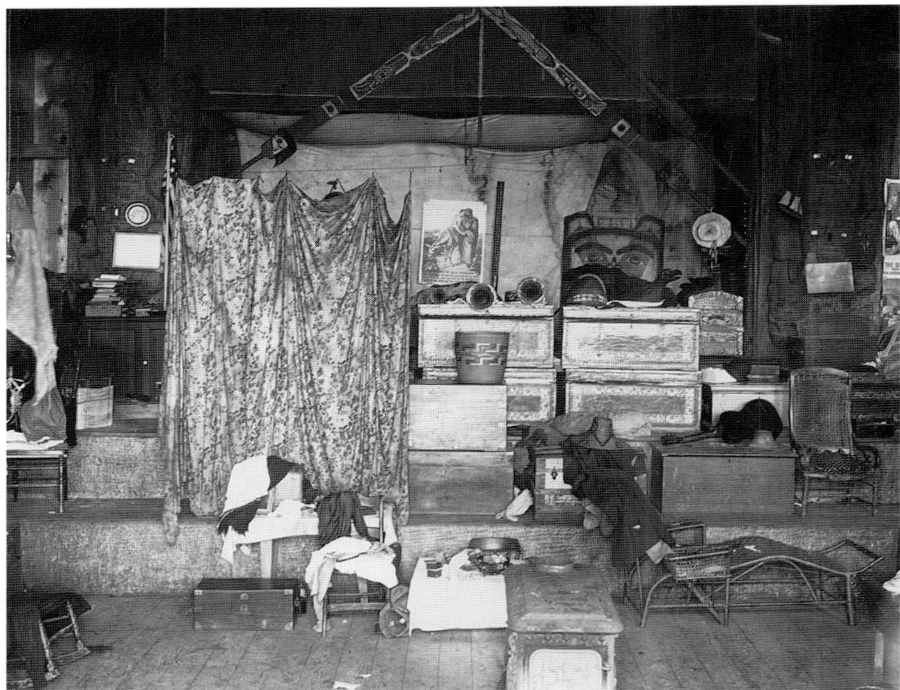

1.3 Interior of Chief Shakes house, Wrangell, Alaska, 1909. Photo: Harlan Smith. AMNH, 46123; courtesy Department of Library Services.

the fervent desire of museum professionals to thoroughly document native cultures while they were still intact.[16] Ironically, these photos of Wrangell, and the Shakes house in particular, illustrate a world already substantially altered. Although important artistic elements of the Chief Shakes Community House at the turn of the century, under the influence of George Shakes (Shakes VI), referred directly to the ancient stories of the Shakes clan, some renovations in emulation of white architectural conventions had also been incorporated into the facade (Figure 1.2). Harlan Smith's photographs, among others, show the wooden clapboard siding, double-hung windows, and a hinged door below a glass-paned transom visible on the exterior public face of the house. A bit of the American flag curtains part of the glass window in the upper section of the front door.[17] Similarly, photographs of the interior provide evidence of traditional Tlingit design but remind us that this "high point" in the history of the house included many hybrid forms as well.

In 1909, for instance, the house of Shakes VI was structured around a roughly square central enclosure excavated below ground level, and covered by a wood

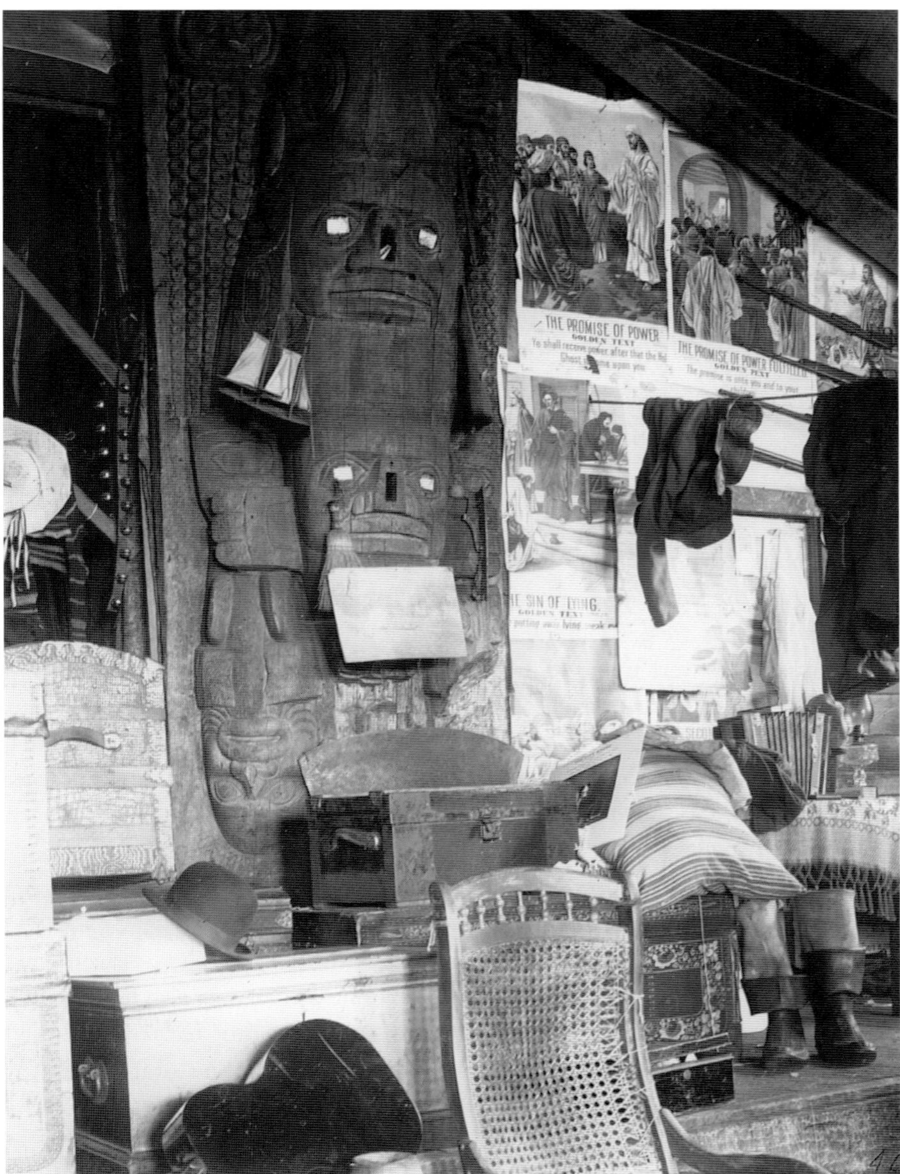

1.4 One of four Shark posts and various other prestige items, displayed inside the Chief Shakes house, 1909. Photo: Harlan Smith. AMNH, 46124; courtesy Department of Library Services.

floor with a cast-iron stove at its center, the location of a fire pit in older houses (Figures 1.3 and 1.4).[18] Consistent with descriptions of traditional style houses noted earlier, the steplike platforms that define this enclosure would have served as living, sleeping, and storage areas with a prestigious section, sometimes defined by screens or curtains, reserved for the use of the house leader at the rear.

As noted by Emmons and others, four heavy interior posts supported the roof beams of traditional houses, and were in some cases carved in high relief. One of the elaborately carved house posts seen in Figure 1.4 is an outstanding example of this art form; in fact, it is one of the four "Shark posts" sketched by Emmons for his notes.[19] The posts were transported to the house from the old site but well after the relocation of the clan, probably during the second half of the nineteenth century.[20] The Shark posts were not load-bearing in their new context at Wrangell, but were placed within the nineteenth-century house solely for display purposes. The house, photographed many times, was chock-full of such prestigious carvings and other objects that were included to announce the celebrated status of Shakes and his family, both in the idiom of the Tlingit and in manners of expression that were appropriated from other cultures.

Martha Black has characterized similar photographs that show the interiors of clan houses from various Northwest Coast groups as "contents displays," emphasizing the intentional arrangement of objects as set out by their owners. Funerary displays are particularly significant in this regard. Collections arranged by clan members were made primarily for the public display of clan history and a chief's high status to the various "witnesses" who entered the house to pay their respects. When recorded by the camera, these assemblages afforded an additional opportunity to document and publicize the clan's reputation in an even larger sphere (Black 1992). Such ensembles photographed at Wrangell may have been intended to broadcast aspects of Shakes's identity to a wider audience, functioning as a type of "official portrait," preserved for the future and transmitted to the "outside world."[21]

Figure 1.3 records, for example, that in 1909 decorated paddles were suspended diagonally across the back of the Shakes house, an area also hung with a painted curtain. An elaborately woven basket, a spruce-root hat, and a carved crest hat in the form of a Raven sit on Chinese camphorwood storage chests, as does a bowler hat and a guitar. Items of clothing, furniture, and boots from the white man's world have probably also been posed for the camera, indications of the wealth and modern ways of the inhabitants of the house. Printed posters, visible near the house post, were most likely provided by missionaries. Nailed to the walls, they appear to illustrate biblical scenes. Their texts advertise "The Promise of Power Fulfilled" for the reader and his children and also admonish against the sin of lying. Another photograph from the same period displays large framed objects, one of which is probably a painting or photograph and the other a mirror, shown "lined up" or contrived for the photographic record by this chief or other influential house group members. Appropriated from the cushioned living rooms of the white middle class, these objects were placed directly in front of the famous Nanya.ayí Brown Bear mask (see Plate 3), which in turn is positioned before the Brown Bear painted screen.[22] These signs of relative wealth and printed images that advertise Christian affiliation, shown alongside the powerful Shark posts and the traditional regalia of chieftainship, tell us a great deal about the man whose public image was expressed through this assemblage of elements.

The reign of this house leader, George Shakes, had begun some time after 1878, eleven years after the United States purchase of Alaska and the building of Fort Wrangell. E. L. Keithahn has suggested that the office of chief had been profoundly compromised since the days of Shakes V. The enforcement of the Emancipation Proclamation in the United States, for instance, placed native leaders, even those of the Shakes line, in the awkward position of being great men without slaves, formerly the customary evidence of their wealth and power. In addition, non-native immigrants to the region failed to recognize Shakes's traditional dominion as compared with lesser chiefs of the period (Keithahn 1981: 6–7). Although the influence and high status of chiefs from the Shakes line had previously been affirmed by potlatching, this practice was now discouraged by missionaries. For these reasons, the position of the Nanya.ayí chief became somewhat fragile under American jurisdiction, and Shakes's status required additional validation, now to be acquired, for the first time, at the pleasure of non-native authorities.

George Shakes's prominence was, for a time, acknowledged by American officials of the period. He was appointed Indian Policeman in Wrangell through 1898, charged with the commission to seize "hooch," or illegal liquor, and to make sure that the Indian children attended school. Among his valued "papers," now in the collection of the Alaska State Historical Library and Archives, is a letter of reference signed by the missionaries S. Hall Young, Sheldon Jackson, A. L. Lindsley, and M. Kendall, establishing his position and relative influence:

> The Undersigned, having been favorably impressed by personal interviews with Shaikes, the Stickeen Chief, and by information from other sources, respecting his disposition and intentions, comply with his request for a "Paper."
>
> We are inclined to believe that his disposition is pacific, and his intentions praiseworthy. He professes to be a good citizen, and promises to use his influence in favor of law and order.
>
> So far as he meets these engagements, he deserves the support of "the whites." And we cordially commend him to all good men.[23]

S. Hall Young in particular was influential in Shakes's "good citizenship," urging him to give up traditional practices in favor of Christianity and other "modern American ways." Young was particularly adamant about eradicating the practice of shamanic healing and the torturing of witches at Wrangell. To this end he created a "council" there, headed by George Shakes, that was supposed to put an end to the disruptive witch hunts that flared up among native residents from time to time. At Young's behest, Shakes even signed a document renouncing the practices of "medicine men" (1927: 134, 143–149 and passim). The missionary must have been something of a "success," as life had changed at Wrangell. When he prepared to leave town in 1888, he reflected with satisfaction upon his accomplishments and on the accompanying changes in the physical appearance of the town:

> The "old fashions" had been almost completely eliminated at Fort Wrangell; the medicine-men, witchcraft, persecution, potlatches, the old reprisal system, and especially heathenism, had been put down so completely that it had been several years since any of the Stickeens had dared to "dream" that anybody was a witch. The church membership had grown until it included practically all the adults in the place. The old community houses were fast disappearing, and neat cottages were replacing them. The transformation of the town was slow but quite remarkable. Government day schools, with good teachers, mostly nominated by our Christian missions, had taken the place of the mission day schools. (Ibid.: 311)

George Shakes had managed to piece together a new kind of chieftainship suitable for the climate of the times that Young describes. As the artworks and personal belongings assembled in his house indicate, the sixth bearer of the Shakes title was heir to an impressive lineage, but a man of the era as well. Conversion to Christianity and an interest in the trappings of gentlemen in the white world, those who held papers to recommend them, were aspects of his complex identity. Certain cross-cultural embellishments to Shakes's house might be disqualified by Emmons or other authorities from the roster of authentic forms that identify it as an example of classic Tlingit architecture. However, Shakes's "collection of treasures" comprised an ensemble that continued to define the house as a grand edifice. Still a place for ancient house posts, the turn-of-the-century version of the Chief Shakes Community House was made even more complete with the addition of modern doors, windows, and fancy picture frames.

Following George Shakes's death in 1916, the house continued to be occupied by family members, at least through the first quarter of the twentieth century. Then the structure itself and a portion of the island was purchased by Axel Rasmussen, superintendent of Wrangell Public Schools, from Mary Shakes, wife of the late chief. Rasmussen used the house as a carving studio and a place to display his private collection of native art, much of which is now owned by the Portland Art Museum (Rakestraw n.d.: 28). Later the building was abandoned and became quite ramshackle. Marius Barbeau remarked upon its dejected appearance during this period: "Just before the war, in 1939, the house looked as if marooned and forsaken in the midst of a cannery town, and the people considered it a crestfallen memorial of the past, its totem poles coated with green moss and flowering salal bushes" (1958: 142).

The CCC Indian Division and the Renewal of the Shakes House (c. 1938–1940)

The widespread economic crisis at the outset of the Roosevelt administration in the United States called for emergency measures and the creation of various New Deal programs, including the Civilian Conservation Corps. This project was originally designed both to provide jobs for the unemployed and to conserve what was already perceived in the 1930s as the depleted natural resources of the American landscape. The first efforts of the corps were directed to forestry, the prevention of soil erosion, flood control, and other projects. In Southeast Alaska, the CCC was administered by the U.S. Forest Service, and from 1937 to 1941 projects were developed in almost all native villages for the construction of roads, trails, bridges, breakwaters, and public buildings. Under the influence of Secretary of the Interior Harold Ickes and John Collier, Commissioner of Indian Affairs at the time, the economic and cultural value of Indian arts and crafts also received new attention as a part of the project. Collier and Ickes believed that a revival of Indian arts would provide economic opportunities for native people and lead ultimately to their greater capacity for self-administration (see Jonaitis 1989). As a result, some cultural resources were valued alongside the considerable natural resources of Southeast Alaska and they too were earmarked for conservation.

Major totem pole restoration and architectural replication projects were conducted by the CCC at some Alaskan sites. These became known as the Totem Parks of Saxman, Mud Bight, Sitka, Wrangell, Kasaan, Klawock, and Hydaburg. Under the supervision of Forester Frank B. Heintzleman, Director of the Alaska CCC, 250 native people were employed between 1938 and 1942 for the restoration of forty-eight old totem poles, the carving of fifty-four copies of poles that were considered beyond repair, and nineteen new poles, based upon "memory" or oral history. Traditional-style community houses were also constructed at Totem

Bight and Kasaan and eventually Shakes Island at Wrangell was selected for renewal. The Chief Shakes Community House was again to play a central role in the representation of Tlingit life and history, this time as the centerpiece of a Totem Park.[24]

Local residents, particularly non-native members of the Wrangell Women's Civic Club and Library Association, were the first to express interest in saving some of the decaying totem poles that remained in the area and in restoring the old house, which was thought to be the last remaining Tlingit tribal house in Alaska (Rakestraw n.d.: 28). After elaborate negotiations, both the island and the house were acquired by the Wrangell City Council, which transferred ownership to the Bureau of Indian Affairs.[25]

Forest Service architect Linn Forrest was put in charge of the project, and a team of local native artisans, working under white foreman Jimmy Dolan, set to work creating their version of an "authentic" Tlingit tribal house.[26] Tom Ukas, artist and cultural advisor on the project, is still spoken of in Wrangell today; he is considered the last great traditional carver from this town. Ukas was knowledgeable about traditional construction techniques and considered an authority on local history as well.[27] *The Wrangell Sentinel* (Oct. 27, 1931: 1) also named Joe Thomas, William Tamaree, George Collins and Phillip Kelly as CCC carvers on the Shakes Island project. Forrest DeWitt Sr. (1993: telephone interview) and Charley Jones—who later claimed the Shakes title—were also part of the restoration team. These men built the new Shakes house directly on the site of the nineteenth-century version, using as much of the existing excavation as possible. Formal continuity was also preserved through detailed measurement of the old structure.[28] Several totem poles from the Wrangell area were replicated for this project as well and moved to Shakes Island.[29]

In many ways, the version of the Chief Shakes Community House completed in 1940 recalls the period before the hybrid assemblage of Tlingit and white prestige objects that appear in the 1909 photographs. It is actually a distillation of the thoughts of the men who participated in the CCC project, representing their notions of the traditional or "classic" Tlingit house, which in this case privileges a compilation of unadulterated forms and devices conjectured as appropriate to a more distant past. Although the lumber used for the house was mill-cut in Wrangell, for instance, workers further processed the rough sawn wood, handadzing every piece to effect what was thought of as an "authentic look."[30] No clapboard siding or windows, seen in George Shakes's time, were allowed to mar this effect. Instead the Brown Bear image, known from the old interior screen, was adapted and painted on the facade of the house.[31]

The use of traditional joinery, the skilled construction of mortise and tenon connections that require only pegs to secure them, and the tongue-and-groove

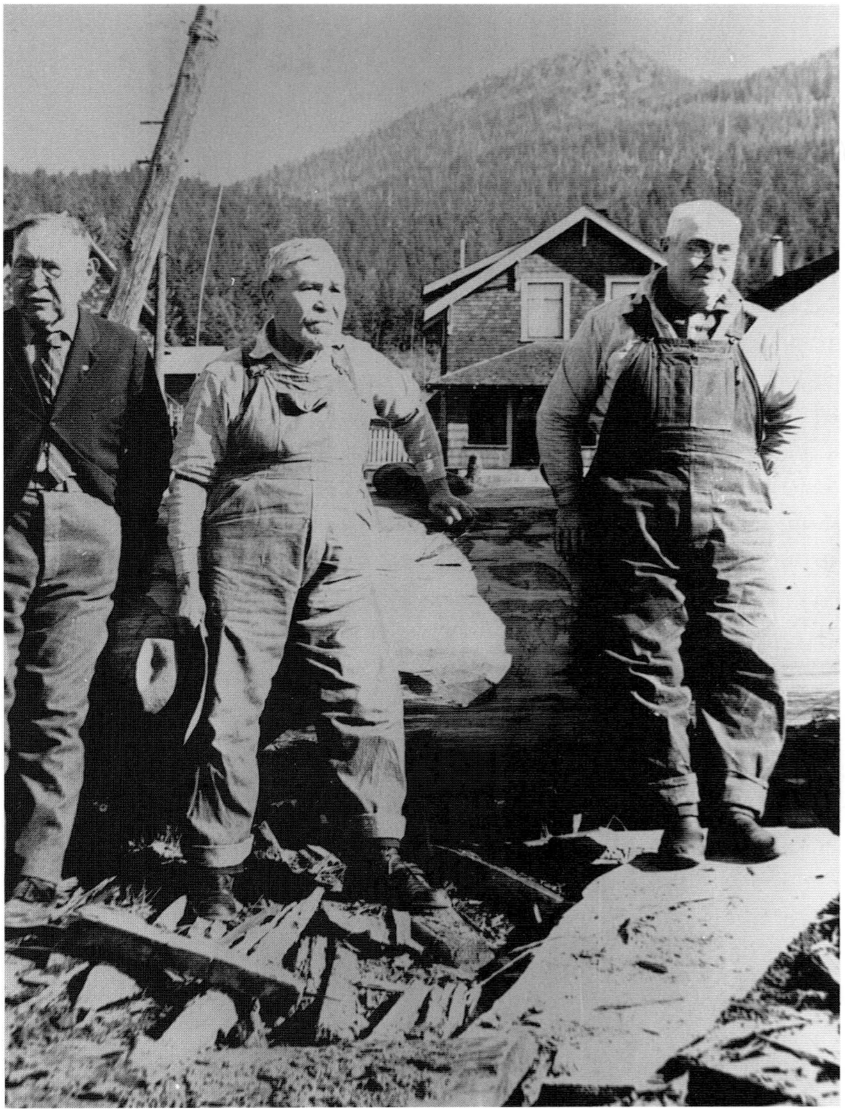

1.5 Some carvers and advisors who participated in the Civilian Conservation Corps' restoration of the Chief Shakes house, c. 1939. L. to r.: Charlie Jones (Chief Shakes VII), Joe Thomas, Joe Collins. Photo: courtesy Wrangell Museum, P80.12.305.

arrangement of planks were all important signs of this type of authenticity, valued and purposefully incorporated into the design by both the native and non-native workers on the project. These features were inextricably linked with a period understood by this team to be "aboriginal." When Linn Forrest, the Forest Service architect, was interviewed in 1983, for instance, he indicated the lengths to which a philosophy of historical accuracy had directed the reproduction of these time-honored construction techniques:

> Everything we did here on the reconstruction was faithful to the details as best we could determine. They [referring to the nineteenth century builders] did things we wouldn't do. For instance, when they put on the plank siding, they channeled out beams at the end and at the base to make a notch so they could get the siding boards in. Unfortunately, that detail was just made to receive water, and it rots. Still, we went ahead and did the same thing. (Wrangell Museum archives)

This imperative to replicate the structure with complete historical accuracy superseded Forrest's own judgement to the extent that it permitted the reproduction of unsound building practice.[32]

Forrest also attempted a historically accurate reading for the selection of paint colors for the Totem Parks projects. He had the native carvers gather traditional colors from graphite, clam shells, lichen, yellow stones, and copper pebbles. They ground these substances in mortars and then blended them with a saliva and oil mixture derived from chewing salmon eggs wrapped in cedar bark. In contrast to the extreme approach taken to the plank siding installation, which was replicated despite the fact that it collected water, some modification for practical purposes was allowed in this paint-making procedure. The colors that resulted from the old native practice were closely matched with commercial pigments and mixed as paints, a process necessary for the production of the larger quantities required for the Totem Parks. Forrest reminisced in a 1976 interview (June 16) at his home on Lena Cove: "Well, we had too big a project for that [making all the paint the native way], we would still be spitting for sure" (also see Forrest, Aug. 1, 1971: interview, and Rakestraw n.d.: 25).

On June 3 and June 4, 1940, a grand-scale potlatch was held in Wrangell to dedicate the completed CCC version of the Shakes house and to install Charley Jones as Chief Shakes VII (fig. 1.6).[33] The U.S. Forest Service, local office of the U.S. Bureau of Indian Affairs, and the Wrangell Chamber of Commerce organized this huge event, which brought approximately 1500 visitors to town, more than doubling Wrangell's usual population, according to *The Wrangell Sentinel* (June 7, 1940: 1). In accordance with traditional considerations (Rakestraw n.d.: 30), Charley Jones decided to adopt the entire Wrangell Chamber of Commerce into the Nanya.ayí clan in 1939 so that their financial support of this potlatch would be considered appropriate.

The provisionally established "Potlatch Central Committee" was in charge of a flurry of activity, encouraging female attendees to wear an official "Potlatch

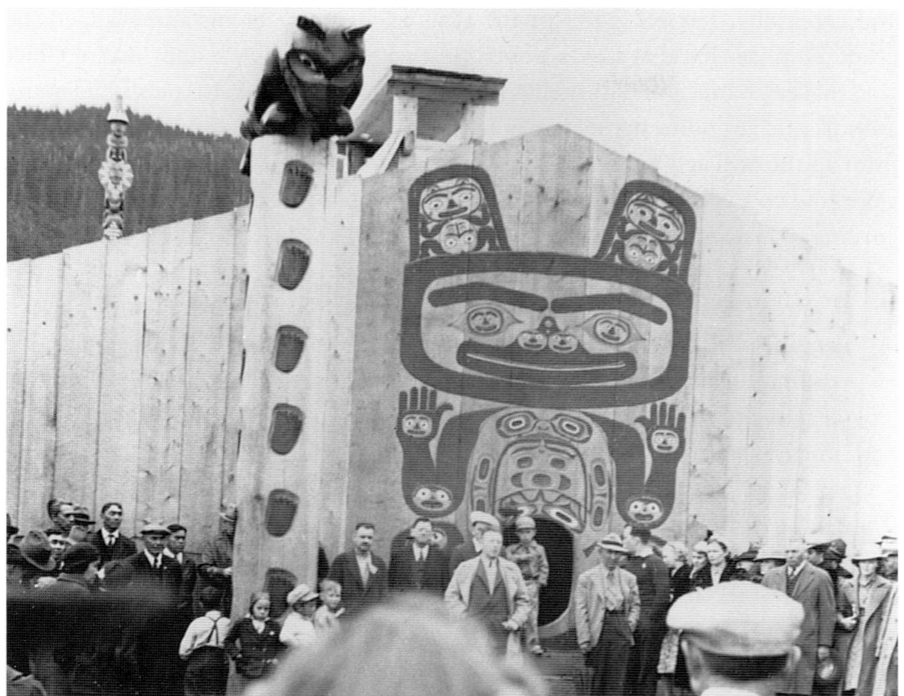

1.6 Gathering for the potlatch to dedicate the CCC's restoration of the Chief Shakes house, 1940. Photo: W. H. Case; courtesy Tongass Historical Society, THS 77.1.5.849.

blouse," described in *The Wrangell Sentinel* (May 3, 1940: 1) as a "colorful peasant blouse," or be charged an extra admission fee for the Saturday night dance. Tourists, government officials, and native guests from other communities were invited for the unveiling of the totem poles, ceremonial dancing, sports events, banquets, and the launching of an old war canoe. A contemporary report conveys some sense of the dramatic proceedings:

> The ceremony began with a fifty foot war canoe approaching Shakes Island. It was manned by Natives dressed in ceremonial garb who came into the landing, singing and chanting. As they came near, the Natives on shore who [sic] replied with chanting and songs of welcome.
> Stepping from the canoe Kudanake [Charley Jones], attired in the ceremonial chieftain's robes acknowledged the welcome of his people.[34]

Potlatch organizers actually hoped that the celebrations would become an annual event, making Shakes Island a popular tourist destination. Guests were energetically assured that Wrangell was the best place to see authentic native art and ceremony. The program for the 1940 celebration, for instance, lauded the event, emphasizing that it was worked out with the complete approval of Chief Kudanake, Charley Jones himself. *The Wrangell Sentinel* had also published many enthusiastic announcements (April 12, 1940: 3; May 3, 1940: 1) during the period prior to the potlatch in an attempt to inspire the interest of future visitors, who were told to expect "the genuine article" in this town, events orchestrated according to historical precedent:

> Wrangell has its original Wrangell people who know how to put on a genuine potlatch. We don't have to depend on build-up and phoney representation as is too often the case in ventures of this kind. In Wrangell we have the real thing; we can give the visitor value received—a real old time Potlatch. (March 29, 1940: 1)

The Sentinel announced that the Wrangell experience was sure to remain unique and traditional. Informative announcements about points of interest and the demography of the town called it the "Only genuine Indian Town on [the] Inside Passage that is a regular port of call." [35]

Despite these pronouncements, potlatching, the ceremonial validation of important Tlingit clan crests, has not continued in Wrangell today. A few native ceremonies and performances by a local dance troupe, the *Shx'at Kwaan* dancers, however, have been staged in the Shakes house.[36] A dedication ceremony was held there in May of 1972, for example (*The Wrangell Sentinel*, April 7, 1972), to mark the completion of a successful renovation project meant to preserve the house; it included the rebuilding of the wooden foundation, the installation of new flooring, and the replacement of half of the hand-split cedar shakes on the roof. Festivities to open the Grand Camp Convention of the Alaska Native Brotherhood and Alaska Native Sisterhood took place in the house in 1973, an occasion for much singing and dancing and a baby-naming ritual, according to *The Wrangell Sentinel* (Nov. 14, 1973: 1, 4). Celebrations also marked the completion of the 1984 carving project that will be described below.

Interestingly, the consistent maintenance of the potlatch tradition by the Shakes line would be considered by some individuals as essential, or the very hallmark of authenticity for the building as a traditional Tlingit tribal house. Yet somehow the historical prominence of the clan, as memorialized by the house, survives despite this lack of ceremony. This phenomenon has been commented on by Tlingit carver Nathan Jackson, who emphasizes that the Nanya.ayí have sufficient reason to be proud, based on their history. Many native people in Southeast Alaska still associate the house with the high status of the Shakes name, which was gained along with important crest privileges through dramatic warfare with the Nisga'a. Jackson has suggested that the modern people of Wrangell have been unable to pursue a more traditional route because their interests instead turned to "citizenship, equal treatment in school, and education is very important." To some extent, he associates the work of the Alaska Native Brotherhood and the Alaska Native Sisterhood in the Wrangell community with this greater emphasis on civic life and a strong dedication to Christian values. As one consequence of these choices, "a lot of the old ways were set aside" (August 31, 1992: interview). Potlatching and the clear identification of prestigious family affiliations are no longer practiced at Wrangell. Early assimilation to non-native ways of life, conversion to Christianity since George Shakes's time, and the increased immigration of outsiders to this town since the first half of the nineteenth century has compromised its completely native identity. This has also resulted in the lack of sovereignty status, a condition now being contested by some members of the local native population (Ockert, Byrd, Stokes 1992: interviews).

In other Southeast Alaska locations, much of contemporary Tlingit ceremonial life takes place in community centers. Perhaps ironically, potlatches are frequently held in the meeting halls of the Alaska Native Brotherhood (ANB) or other western-style buildings. These ceremonies may even take place in conventional split-level houses as long as knowledgeable people are present and appropriate representatives from the other clans are invited as witnesses (Jackson Aug. 31, 1992: interview). Nora and Richard Dauenhauer, for instance, have published (1990: 39–40) a seating chart for a 1988 Chookaneidi memorial (*ḵoo.éex'*) that they call typical, and which took place at the Hoonah ANB hall. This seems to indicate that the presence of proper joinery and other architectural devices that refer to past form, the "classic building blocks," are not required for traditional practice.

Contemporary conditions have indeed engendered the loss of some ceremonial practices at Wrangell, at least for the time being, but have selected for the preservation of other important art forms. The public display of representative Tlingit architecture and important clan carvings has been maintained by both native and non-native residents active in civic affairs; however, these formal devices are not used for the clear maintenance of traditional social divisions.

Artistic Restoration of the Chief Shakes Community House (1984)

In 1984, another major restoration project was administered by the Wrangell Cultural Heritage Committee, a designated committee of the Stikine Native Organization. This time, the restoration of Wrangell's particular artistic treasures was on the agenda. Native representatives active in the affairs of the Alaska Native

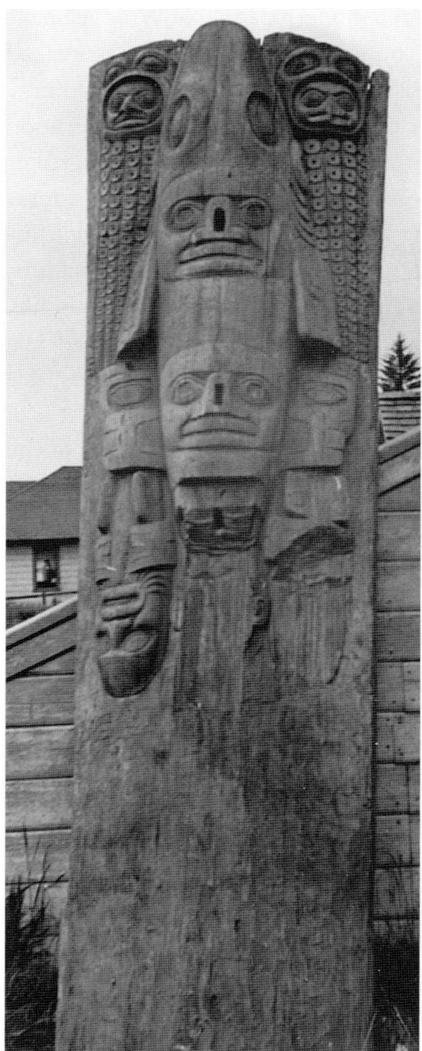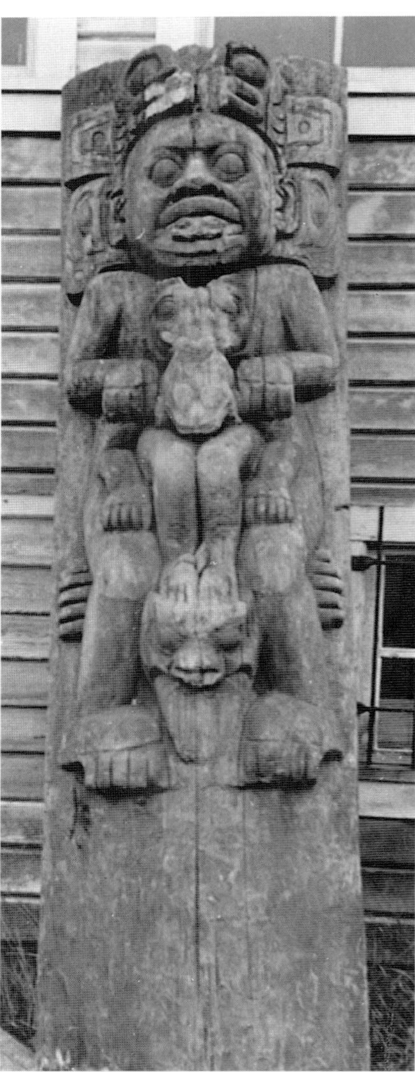

1.7–1.10 The old Shark posts placed outside the Chief Shakes house, c. 1939. Photos: Linn A. Forrest. University of Washington Libraries, Special Collections, nos. 3712, 3713, 3714, 3715.

Brotherhood, the Alaska Native Sisterhood, and the Stikine Native Organization worked together with non-native personnel from the Wrangell Museum to renew the four famous house posts, which were extremely deteriorated by this time (Figures 1.7–10). They were to be removed from the Chief Shakes Community House for conservation, and four replicas were commissioned along with copies of six of the totem poles on Shakes Island.[37] Steve Brown, an experienced

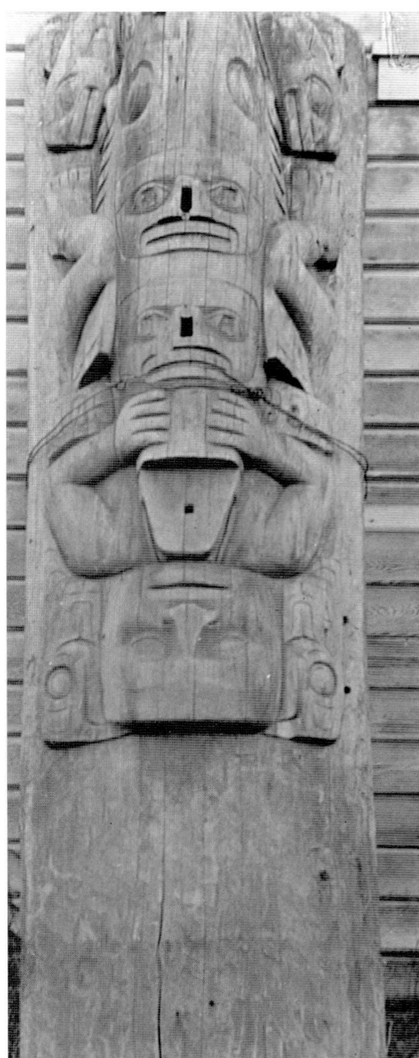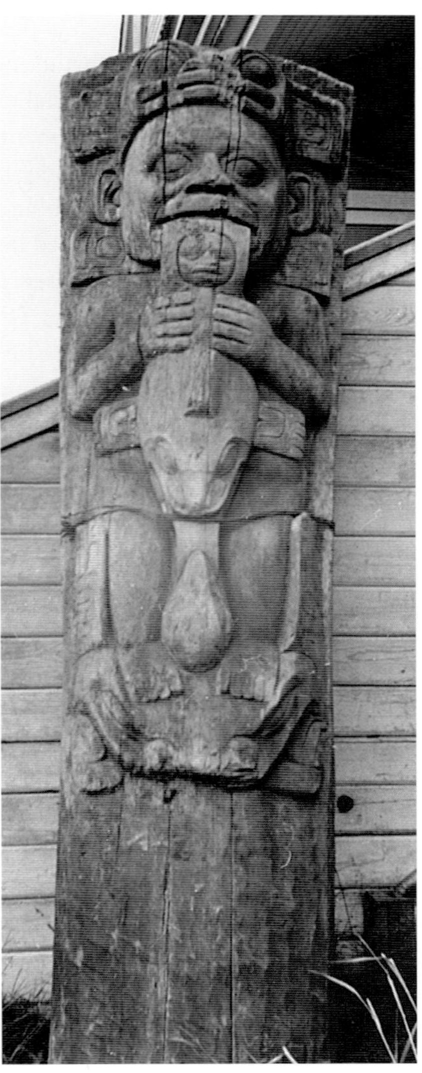

and skilled non-native carver who later became Associate Curator of Native American Art at the Seattle Art Museum, was hired to duplicate these carvings together with Wayne Price, a Tlingit carver from Haines, Alaska, and their assistant Will Burkhart.

Unerring faithfulness to the historical models was required of the carvers, according to their contract, which stipulated: "The finished product must appear as close as possible as the original pole looked when freshly carved when erected at its original setting," and furthermore, "The contractor will refrain from imposing a personal style or personal touch."[38] This feat was accomplished by the carvers through careful measurement, the use of cardboard and wood templates, and special tracing tools they made (Herem 1990: 50). Not only was this criterion for the proper execution of the house posts developed in relation to an homage for the past, as had been expressed in the era of the Civilian Conservation Corps (CCC), but on this occasion it grew as well from a new reverence for these particular carvings as masterpieces of Tlingit fine art.

Linn Forrest's project had also been based upon an historically accurate reading of older models. However, in 1940, the carefully reconstructed architectural monument had been surrounded by a selection of totem pole carvings that are considered "uneven" at best as representations of the highly skilled fine art practices known from the Tlingit past. Both Edward Malin and Aldona Jonaitis, for example, have observed that many members of the CCC carving teams had insufficient training, both in technique and in traditional design principles, a deficiency resulting in somewhat crude totem pole reproductions that may not be considered "classics," according to strictly formal standards (Malin 1986: 174; Jonaitis 1989: 244–45).

The replication of the Shark posts by the 1984 team, however, was approached in a different manner that drew upon insights of modern researchers and art historians. A report written for the Wrangell Cultural Heritage Association, for instance, claims: "The Houseposts belonging to Chief Shakes are among Alaska's most exceptional heritage materials. Aesthetically, they surpass [in] quality similar Northwest Coast art in American or European museums" (Ockert: n.d.). Bill Holm has also written about the excellence of the Shark posts, remarking that "There is nothing better anywhere in the collections of Europe and North America" (Herem 1978: 50). The Alaska State Museum has called the posts "national treasures" (Duff et al. 1969: 62). It is important to note that replicator Steve Brown, a scholar as well as a carver, has conducted extensive research on the original Tlingit carver of these outstanding works, now identified as Kadjidu.áx̱tc II, of the Kiks.ádi clan of the Stikine Tlingit. Brown suggests that a larger corpus of masterworks may be identified with this individual's hand, during a career that spanned the turn of the nineteenth century (Brown 1987, 1994). He writes: "This artist is a master of subtlety, all his work exhibiting soft hollows and bulges of fullness, sometimes where least expected." Brown is enthusiastic as well about the artist's ability to "move back and forth between stylization and pure naturalism at will," and further remarks that "The very attitude and expression of all the faces exhibit a most amazing quality of nobility and strength" (1987: 162).

This reframing of Tlingit antiquities as artistic masterpieces, together with Brown's own reverent attitude, resulted in the execution of these extremely skilled and sophisticated replicas of what may now be considered "classic" works of Northwest Coast art, at least according to standards for formal excellence (Figures 1.11–14). Brown has also been commended for the reinvention of certain missing parts of the posts—the shark fins for instance—based upon his careful study of other examples of the Tlingit artist's work (see Plate 2).[39]

The avid appreciation of professionals for the beauty of these works or the painstakingly acquired understanding of the art form should not be considered a unanimous sentiment, however. One woman, a biological descendant of the Shakes line, has wondered aloud why the house posts are so "ugly." She likes flowers or recognizable animals and regrets that there are so few of them in Northwest Coast art. She prefers a pole in the Wrangell Totem Park, not a Shark post, but one with an eagle atop it, a form she can more easily identify.[40] In this case, scholarship and artistic training were the qualifications required by those who arbitrated the authoritative representation of authentic Tlingit art in the 1980s. Clan affiliation and legitimate descent in the Shakes line is disputed today and is not in any case linked with connoisseurship.

Expedience and Classicism

The Chief Shakes Community House, along with the various prestige objects that have been associated with it over time, is a longstanding example of a corpus of artworks on the Northwest Coast that is best understood as a part of a series. It may be the oldest extant body of work that, together with archival documentation, serves as evidence for the habitual replication of crest art privilege as the basis for many generations of formal expression. In each instance, criteria for authenticity and canons of ideal form have affected the appearance of the house. Yet its significance to both native and non-native audiences has shifted over time and may at no point be considered uniform.

The various chiefs of the Shakes line who inhabited the house in the nineteenth and early twentieth centuries were concerned first and foremost with the display of chiefly prerogative and, when historical circumstances called for it, with the demonstration of prestigious affiliation and wealth in the white world. Photographers and collectors at the turn of the century sought out the masks and carved images that referred to the clan's past as evidence of authentic native life. The prestige of Shakes VI, however, depended as well upon his standing as a "modern American," on his letters, bowler hat, and printed posters. In 1939 the

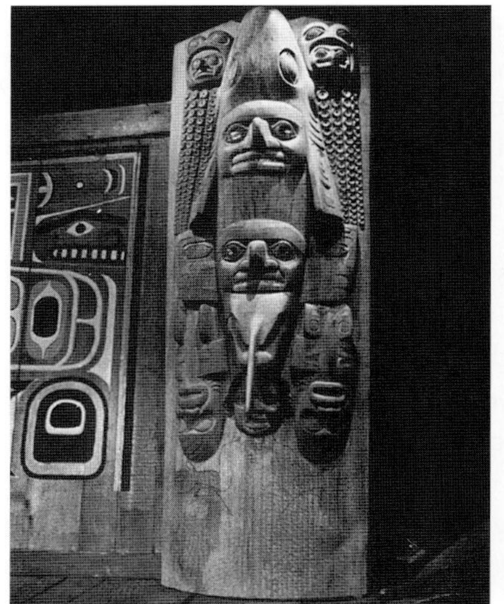
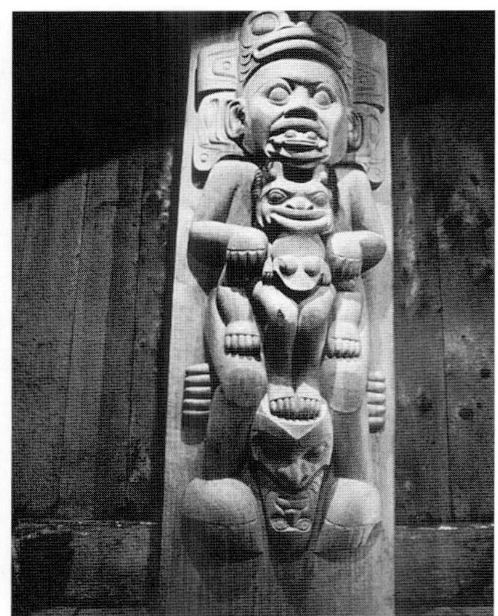

1.11–14 Replicated Shark posts inside the Shakes house. Photos: courtesy Steve Brown.

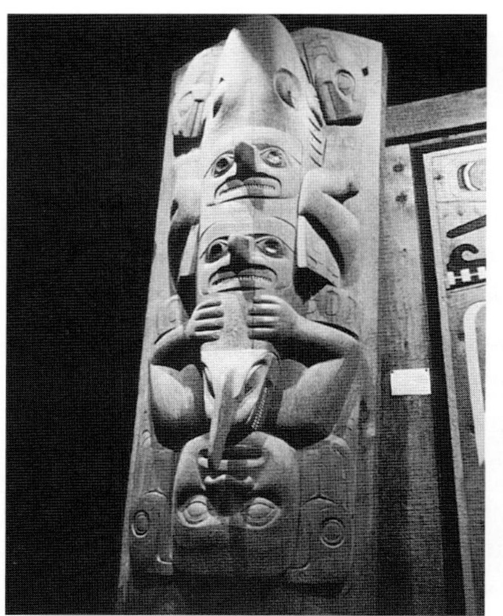
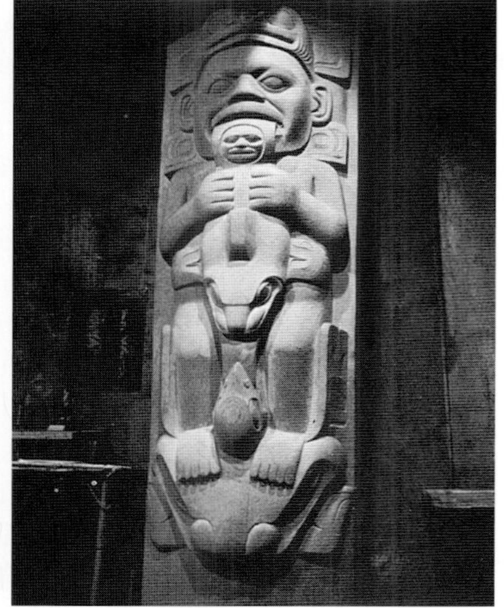

house was restored with the intention of preserving a glorious but disappearing history that would attract white visitors, probably avid museum-goers back home. Offered the opportunity to see real totem poles, a tribal house, and examples of native ceremony, it was hoped that they would travel great distances to contribute tourist dollars to a troubled local economy. Then in 1984, when the Shark posts were replicated, the house was renewed as an important tourist attraction in Southeast Alaska, but this time with an emphasis on the artistic quality of the carvings. Recognition of the virtuosity of the original Tlingit carver informed both the selection of the modern replicator as well as the attitude with which he approached the stylistic idiosyncrasies of the master.

This process of restoration and the continuing redefinition of the Shakes house and its treasures has been accompanied by the significant interaction of native and non-native collaborators striving to make effective representations of the past. The native history of both assimilation and resistance on the Northwest Coast is punctuated by a series of such opportunities, which are seized by some groups and individuals who are positioned on these occasions to express their strengths and their own points of view. Non-native collaborators, for their part, have used their resources to develop projects with Indian participants that meet needs of their own.

As early as Shakes IV's interaction with the Russians in residence at Fort St. Dionysius, for instance, the Nanya.ayí adopted considerable modifications in their lifestyle in order to make the best of the foreign presence in their territory. Later on, missionaries such as S. Hall Young identified George Shakes as an important person in the community, and he in turn made changes in his house and in the lives of people who responded to his authority. He was therefore able to legitimately take some part in the activities of the changing world around him. Native workers of the CCC in turn were gainfully employed by various non-native supervisors who, on their part, benefited from Indian participation. The Wrangell Chamber of Commerce, in fact, characterized Charley Jones's participation as an advisor as certification of authenticity for their project. In the 1980s, native people who were accustomed to being active in community affairs worked with non-native museum personnel who were more familiar with fundraising and bureaucratic procedures. Each of these projects that affected the appearance of the Shakes house parallels shifting relationships among native and non-native authorities who were influential in Wrangell over time.

Constructed to evoke the legitimacy of the antique in this manner, the form of the Shakes house has been adapted as each generation made a genuine effort to properly retell its life story. Each of these groups, even a community of a half-dozen decision makers, tells us as much about their standards for the display of classic Tlingit art and architecture as they do about the Chief Shakes house itself.

Their representations are both time- and audience-specific, and their authority must therefore be understood as being short lived. Unpopular opinions, a taste for pretty birds and flowers for instance, are temporarily left unexpressed. We do not know the criteria that will be applied by future generations to the form of the house. Therefore to insist now upon universal or unchanging standards—an excavated floor with stepped levels for instance, the traditional execution of joinery, or the evaluation of its graphic components according to principles of formline design—would decontextualize the constituent parts of the house, reducing them to mere "classics" that conform to a single reading. For as long as the house remains a significant place for both the Wrangell community and various interested parties around the world, such a final conclusion remains unlikely.

The Map and the Territory in the Grand Hall at the Canadian Museum of Civilization

DISUSED OBJECTS, ANTIQUITIES SEVERED from their places of origin, have customarily been recast for museum audiences by the directives of the Boasian tradition. Museum dioramas or "life groups," model totem poles, and field photographs are often made as visual aids, designed to help us think about the remote lives of people we cannot know at first hand.[1] When we are exposed to a plaster cast of a nineteenth-century Kwakwaka'wakw woman making a cedar bark mat and rocking her infant in a cradle suspended on ropes, for instance, or to film footage of a costumed Grizzly Bear dancer lumbering in the prow of a canoe as it approaches a beach, we have aspired to understand the mat or the costume as they were understood by their makers.[2] These desires, both to know and to teach, were conveniently mediated in these contextualizing displays by the glass front of the vitrine or the well-understood conventions and limitations of film-making practice. The effective nature of these constructed displays added authority to the didactic text on their meaning, but "virtual reality" had not yet become a well-known phenomenon. Therefore museum-goers never imagined that they were actually present on that beach or sitting on a blanket before the woman working with cedar bark. These images were taken as representative, not substitutes for the complex reality of the native lives that engendered the weaving technology or the dance costume.

Such representative objects and recorded images in museum collections, exhibited and stockpiled as schemata for native reality, may then be said to function as maps. They present items chosen as salient features of unseen territory, arranged to refer in a cogent manner to that larger reality. Ethnographic objects and the creative manipulation of their display have been organized to guide viewers and to encourage, by selective example, the conceptualization of a more complex whole.

A considerable body of scholarly works now documents criteria applied to the construction of museum collections and their further refinement for appropriate public display. These assembled objects now come to us laden with information that originates both from the study of their nonwestern cultures of origin as well as from recent analyses of provenance undertaken as tools for the explication of various art historical and curatorial programs.[3] In this manner, through the ongoing historical contextualization of nonwestern artworks, intended to mediate their presentation to the public, these objects continue in their mapping function by referring to larger issues. By way of contrast, the paintings, sculptures, and works of installation art found in the collections of fine arts museums are meant to stand on their own and be completely self-referential. This is particularly true of abstract works, hallmarks of modernity, for which contextualizing references are rarely provided.[4] Meyer Schapiro (1937: 187) referred to this inventive and self-referential nature of abstract art as characteristic of a so-called "pure art," supposed to be completely independent of historical conditions and furthermore, according to the Surrealists, "freed from the perversions of reason and everyday experience."

This decontextualization, exemplified in modernity by abstraction, has been analyzed, extended, and ultimately transformed by Jean Baudrillard in opposition to the process of mapping or the signing by discrete objects for more comprehensive realities. Baudrillard proposes "the generation by models of a real without origin or reality: a hyperreal [in which]. . . . The territory no longer precedes the map."[5] As a result of this reversal, "it is the map that engenders the territory," and practices of representation, already understood to be problematic, become more final and hallucinatory as acts of simulation (1983: 2, 11). Baudrillard proposes that this departure from external reality permits the generation of simulacra, "never again exchanging in itself, in an uninterrupted circuit without reference or circumference." This substitution, not of the part for the whole, but of a constructed reality for experience, suggests the loss of some more authentic awareness and therefore a process of prevarication. Although the conventions of representation also suppressed portions of reality, Baudrillard describes simulacra as more complete fictions, as though they were themselves works of art. Such simulacra in exhibition practice then, would be unlike the displays of the past. The aforementioned Bear dancer for instance, intended for representation, demonstrated only some gestures from his broader repertoire. The woman intent on weaving revealed nothing about those who wore furs. In the same manner the Chief Shakes Community House, described in Chapter One, has summarized for generations certain delineated high points of Tlingit architectural form suited to the requirements of specialized audiences. Its limited scope, intended for representation only, is evident. Shakes Island is positioned in clear view of the rest of Wrangell, a village of aluminum-sided, split-level houses and motorized fishing boats manned by native and non-native people who watch television and drive cars.

In Hull, Quebec, however, which together with Ottawa forms the capital region of Canada and is approximately 2500 miles from Wrangell, one enters a completely different Northwest Coast village (see Plate 4). Here in the Grand Hall of the Canadian Museum of Civilization (CMC), one is charmed, first by the sound of birds, particularly ravens calling. Then there is the unmistakable beat of Indian-style music, and perhaps most effectively, the sound of waves crashing on the beach. The stone floors are polished slick, in a band, to seem wet, and the darkened image of a Pacific Coast forest runs approximately 260 feet long and 30 feet high as a vast backdrop (LaForet 1992: 55). Before this perhaps "hyperreal" scenery, raised upon a platform, one section of which suggests a boardwalk with cylindrical pilings, are six traditional Northwest Coast style houses built in three dimensions and painstakingly elaborated with façade paintings, carvings, and various architectural details. The houses are situated among a collection of impressive totem poles, some on the boardwalk itself and others along the opposite wall, before huge windows. The view through these panes of glass, however, sabotages this "cultural mirage" by framing a postcard-perfect scene of the Canadian Parliament buildings and a portion of the Ottawa River.[6] Museum visitors know very well where they are. The view of the city outside and the presence of a great many props from contemporary life are not tampered with in the design of the hall. Black boxlike amplifiers that provide the environmental sounds are piled up near the "tidal pool" and faux fishing weir. Viewers have arrived in this village by way of a huge escalator, still visible behind them. Although there is no question that the museum audience is aware of the constructed nature of this extravagant village and the many special effects that will be described in greater detail below, they may believe in a great many of the more subtle illusions of authentic native history fostered here. Robert De Roos's anecdote (1994: 62) about a visit to Disneyland offers certain parallels:

> At the end of Main Street, faraway jungle noises made me turn to the left and enter Adventureland.
>
> I took the jungle river cruise aboard the sturdy river boat Ganges Gal, which chugged past menacing crocodiles, a ruined temple, and a group of bathing elephants. Gorillas and a tremendous African elephant roared from the tropical vegetation and the choked banks of the stream.
>
> There was some discussion among the passengers about the animals. Were they real? (They were of course animated.) But in Disneyland, it is sometimes hard to know where fantasy ends and reality begins. A little

later, I watched a pair of ladies peer intently at the live swans sailing on the moat of Sleeping Beauty Castle.

"They are not real," one lady finally said with authority.

In the Grand Hall, museum-goers know they are in Hull, Quebec, not in a nineteenth-century village on the Northwest Coast. Do they, however, recognize the differences between these carefully reconstructed houses on this immaculate boardwalk and the old buildings that they are modeled upon? Can they perceive the incongruity of this particular combination of houses and totem poles that come from the traditions of distinct ethnic groups, substantially separated in space as well as by cultural practice? Moreover, how important are these distinctions to their experience of this comprehensive exhibition, constructed according to contemporary concerns by native artists and elder advisors under the direction of non-native museum staff? These experts may have other educational goals in mind, apart from a faithful rendition of the past. They may be just as concerned to modify the past, to comply with the insights of new authorities.

Questions of authenticity and historical accuracy may be differentially applied at Disneyland to construct a glittering package of history, not as "it really was but as it should have been" (Fjellman 1992: 31). At the Canadian Museum of Civilization, however, conscientious workers went to great lengths to rediscover the correct appearances of the simulated houses within the limits of an exhibition hall environment. Yet the hall does not exist in an actual location where it has developed over time and in response to changing conditions. Therefore its historical accuracy may be considered quite good, but by necessity approximate. These particular approximations, however, educate viewers through extraordinary and persuasive means of display. Therefore this tableau, this map of nineteenth-century Indian life may indeed engender the territory, affecting the construction of Northwest Coast native history. An analysis of some of the key decisions and processes that affected the appearance of the replicated houses in the CMC Grand Hall, as well as their immediate environment, raises provocative questions about both historical accuracy and dissimulation in this project.

The Making of the Northwest Coast Village in the Grand Hall

The inspiration for the Grand Hall exhibit came from the existing collection of the Canadian Museum of Civilization as interpreted by museum personnel. George MacDonald, Executive Director of the CMC, recalls posing the question at the inception of the project, "What do we have that is world class?" which was quickly followed by his own reply—"totem poles" (Nov. 19, 1992: interview). The large and well-documented collection of totem poles at the CMC, as well as those conserved at many other museums in Europe and North America, may be traced to the efforts of Marius Barbeau who, during the first half of this century, is said to have "rescued [them] from the abandoned coastal villages" (MacDonald in Barbeau 1990: v).

MacDonald, known for his own work on Haida architecture and village plans of the Queen Charlotte Islands (1983), contended that totem poles could not be best understood when displayed in isolation. He suggested that the poles in the CMC collection be exhibited together with houses. Contextualized as key elements in a traditional village plan, as houses and poles in combination, "these forms [would] make a statement together" (Nov. 19, 1992: interview). House prototypes were selected for replication and display with the totem poles. These were originally envisioned as facades only, rather than as complete buildings in three-dimensions (MacDonald and Alsford 1989: 81). MacDonald, together with Art Price, a professional non-native artist, worked up a preliminary model for the hall, later modified and elaborated upon by architect Douglas Cardinal (Blackfoot) and exhibition designer Ian Gregory, a non-native.

The house prototypes selected for the hall were examples of Northwest Coast architecture known to have been in use during a hundred-year period spanning the late eighteenth and the late nineteenth centuries. Andrea LaForet, Chief of the Canadian Ethnology Service at the CMC, played an important role in this selection process. LaForet has commented that these examples were chosen, first of all, as appropriate companion pieces that would enable the museum to show off their most outstanding totem poles and other works from the CMC collection. Beyond this criterion, old houses were selected, for the most part, from historical photographs because they included especially dramatic forms or certain significant features that would be compelling when illustrated (Nov. 17, 1992: interview). The suitability of each house, according to these standards, can be readily observed in the hall and will be described here.

The village as a whole has been designed to represent native cultures during an even more specific time frame. In concept, the period has been collapsed to coincide with a single decade between 1880 and 1890 (LaForet 1991). The "Interpretive Plan," a document prepared by CMC staff during the development of the hall, explains: "It is from this period that the CMC collections come; it is about this period that most of the ethnographies were written; it was in this period that the dilemmas posed by the meeting of the Pacific Coast People and Europeans became acute. . . . To the visitor, who brings the twentieth century with him, this village is yesterday."[7] Here in the Grand Hall, then, is a museum-made town, generalized as the "past" or as that time period when non-native observers, many of them connected with museums or academic institutions, canonized late nineteenth-century native life as singularly authentic for cultural practice.[8] The "photographic period," for instance, delineated for the Shakes house described in the last chapter, is best known to scholars through visual and written records as well as the abundance of materials collected at that time. This same preponderance of evidence has enlivened and informed the public imagination, to a greater extent than any other, about the nature of the Northwest Coast native past as a whole. Therefore this period has come to "stand in" for all of native history in many public representations.

The houses and totem poles shown in the hall are organized according to geography, conceived of as a progression from south to north. They represent the traditions of six native groups, arranged in this order: The Coast Salish, the West Coast people (now known as the Nuu-chah-nulth), Central Coast people or Kwakiutl (Kwakwaka'wakw), Bella Coola (now Nuxalk), Haida, and Tsimshian. Three of the houses—the Nuu-chah-nulth (approximately 39 feet wide by 30 feet deep), Kwakwaka'wakw (approximately 30 feet wide by 30 feet deep), and Tsimshian (approximately 40 feet wide by 40 feet deep)—are full scale. The other three structures are the full width of traditional house fronts: the Salish house about 45 feet wide, the Nuxalk 30 feet wide, and the Haida house also about 30 feet wide, but these are only about 20 to 25 feet deep.[9]

Teams of native artists under the supervision of particularly knowledgeable project supervisors, also of native descent, built each of the Northwest Coast houses on display in the hall.[10] These individuals were instrumental as well in making adjustments, as required by actual building practice, that became necessary as the crews began to interpret the plans provided for them by the CMC design team. Some of these refinements were made through consultation with appropriate native elders, and others were worked out through the experience and practical expertise of the workers themselves. The entire construction project was supervised by Bill McLennan, a designer (not of native descent) for the University of British Columbia (UBC) Museum of Anthropology, whose own "Imagery Recovery Project" will be described. McLennan was assisted by both Lyle Wilson, a Haisla artist and Debbie Jeffries, a Tsimshian, also of UBC.

The houses were built in various locations. The Coast Salish, Nuu-chah-nulth, and Nuxalk houses were built on the Musqueam Reserve in Vancouver. The Haida house was constructed outside of Masset, on the Queen Charlotte Islands, and the Kwakwaka'wakw house was built in Alert Bay. Final assembly of the houses took place in the Grand Hall itself. Construction was carried out both with modern conveniences, as in the fabrication of planks by Alaska chain mill as well as with adzes and other tools of traditional design that were made especially for this project by the crews themselves.[11] The hall was conceived of by these workers as a contemporary project, and no native supervisor that I spoke with regretted the use of twentieth-century technology.

Environment and the Grand Hall

Some characteristics of this carefully constructed and landscaped village foster the experience of "environment"—of the setting as an integrated system of features that unfolds to the visitor moving or resting in the space as in an actual location. The houses, totem poles, and other works of Northwest Coast native art themselves create this effect because at least to the uninitiated eye of the casual visitor, they may seem unified in style. When the hall first opened in 1989, the display lacked labels or wall text to dispel this illusion of uniformity. George MacDonald wanted the viewers' impressions to be completely "experiential" at first. In 1990, however, he modified the plan to include lists of the native workers, labels that recorded the histories of the old totem poles, and some labels for modern works of art such as the bronze mask titled *Raven Bringing Light to the World*, by contemporary Haida artist Robert Davidson. These texts now indicate, to those who read them, that the relative ages of the carved and painted surfaces displayed here vary widely. Readers may also deduce the diverse tribal and family origins of these traditional works. The local histories of these carved and painted surfaces, or at least those of their prototypes, were deliberately affected by individual style as well as the selection of appropriate crest imagery that could legitimately be represented upon them. Without the label text, they might only be distinguished by the connoisseur.

The coherence of the streetscape is heightened further through strategically placed visual references to the natural environment of the Pacific Coast and to the traditional subsistence activities of its inhabitants. Four "environmental exhibits" contribute to this sense of place in the hall and to its significant appeal as a location for public gathering reminiscent of a grand courtyard lavishly planted.[12]

These ecological niches include a "tidal pool," situated near the Coast Salish house, which is built into a rocky outcropping. It is intended as an example of the pools of saltwater with small sea creatures such as mussels, chitons, and barnacles that are left behind by the receding tides and were traditionally exploited as food sources on the Northwest Coast (LaForet 1992: 26). A model of an estuary or river mouth has also been constructed further "north" in the hall, in the general vicinity of the Haida house. Here traps constructed with stones confine artificial fish. Driftwood and other debris are exposed on gray sand (Figure 2.1) (ibid.: 46). The forest is also represented in the hall, first by the moody scene reproduced by huge photographic prints on two layers of theatrical scrim that have been hung behind

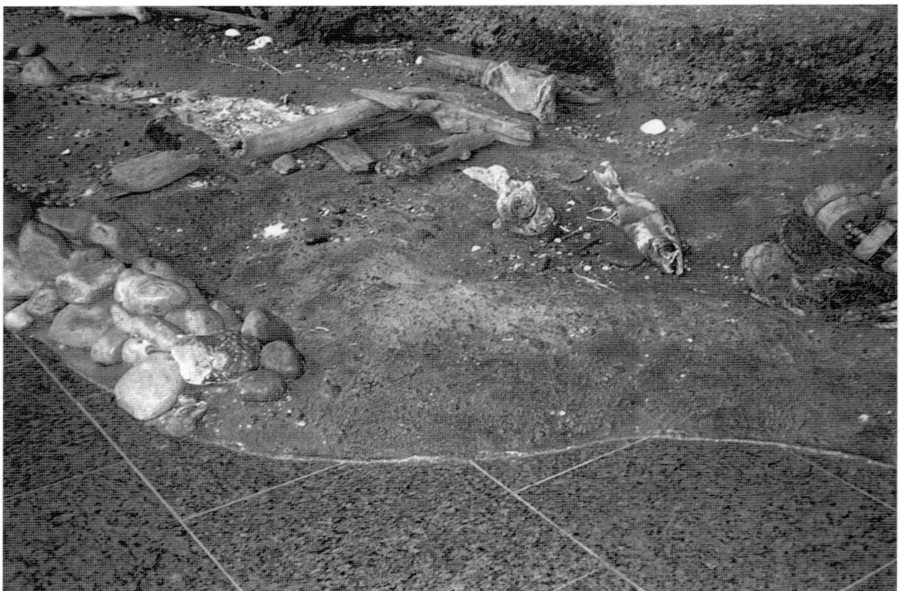

2.1 Estuary environment. Grand Hall, CMC, Hull, Quebec. Photo: Judith Ostrowitz.

the houses (ibid.: 55). In a small installation between the Nuxalk and Haida houses, some berries, ferns, and other products of the forest are artfully placed. The pebbly beach with shells and grasses as well as the boardwalk itself mimic features of the natural environment and places for the preparation of its products as food and for other purposes. These small but meticulously executed settings make handy environments for demonstrations by museum docents and native explainers.

One purpose of the hall, yet to be fully realized in practice, is as a type of "ambulatory theater" that would take these demonstrations of native culture—traditional food preparation, crafts, music and the like—one step further. Performances by native dancers, which illustrate traditional ceremony for instance, may in the future take place here with some regularity. Interestingly, ceremonial dedications, considered essential for the six houses by the native artists and advisors who worked on the project, have yet to be staged in this theatrical setting.[13] A new totem pole, however—a gift from the Royal British Columbia Museum and the Hesquiaht Nuu-chah-nulth people—that stands before the Nuu-chah-nulth house was formally dedicated. It was celebrated with song, dance, and speechmaking when the hall first opened to the public in October of 1989. Nuu-chah-nulth participants were originally asked to stage this event on the platform before the Nuxalk and Kwakwa̲ka̲'wakw houses, but they declined, insisting on the facade of their own house as the appropriate location for this event.[14] Similar issues of protocol, related to the discrete identity of each native group represented in the hall, will be discussed in great detail here as characteristic of the Grand Hall presentation.

Various other innovative performances, perhaps ones that dramatize legends, are also being considered for this location in the future. A slide show with some animated figures, for instance, may at some point be projected upon the surface of the forest scrim. It has been suggested that this presentation illustrate the Raven legends of the northern Northwest Coast with moving sculptures of supernatural creatures and special lighting effects. Suitable passageways and dressing rooms for performance artists have already been built behind the houses for these purposes, but the proposed productions are costly and have not yet materialized (MacDonald, Nov. 19, 1992; LaForet, Nov. 17, 1992; Gregory, Nov. 17, 1992: interviews).

The space is clearly suitable for the convincing enactment of ceremony and other dramatic productions. An illusion of coherence and unity throughout the village "scenery" is advanced by the detailed and life-sized works of art and architecture and is highlighted against a patchwork of pseudonatural phenomena. People come and go here, enjoying the ambience and perhaps catching sight of a docent engaged in an appropriate craft activity, basketmaking, for instance. The credibility of this historical scenario is most abruptly ruptured however, once the replicated houses are entered.

Although only one house interior, the Kwakwaka'wakw, may be considered complete with its permanent installation, none of the interiors are planned as replicas to illustrate the appearance of the inside of an actual nineteenth-century tribal house.[15] At present, the Coast Salish house has a display related to textile art in its carpeted interior and a slide show with images related to weaving. The Nuu-chah-nulth house includes two painted screens on display inside and a video that shows some images recorded in relation to the construction of the houses and the hall. The Kwakwaka'wakw house has a very elaborate interior, designed according to a clear "story line" that includes a slide show, the partial installation of a living room (modeled upon a photograph of an Alert Bay house of the 1930s[16]), a set of masks partly hidden behind a painted screen, and a bounty of potlatch goods stacked and piled about the room. These many objects refer to the nature of the potlatch, the dance practices so central to traditional Kwakwaka'wakw life.

Inside the Nuxalk house, an arrangement of masks is positioned below a large carved figure, originally from the interior of a nineteenth-century house in Qomqotes village. A panel with text on the opposite wall incorporates small video monitors that show a variety of masked dances. Above this panel is a photo mural of c. 1895 showing family members standing before the old house prototype. The Haida house contains a wooden partition screen and an old canoe set off and protected by velvet ropes. Various carved works are also on display inside the Tsimshian house, and a carpeted square on the floor marks a place that may be reserved for future performances. This location will eventually be altered, according to the Grand Hall floor plan (CMC files), to incorporate a central pit, as was typical in the construction of very prestigious old houses. All of these interior spaces, except for the Kwakwa̲ka'wakw, will be reworked over time.

The façades and other exterior details of the six houses are complete, however, and each has been elaborated in impressive detail. Ambitious processes were initiated for the fabrication of these architectural simulacra. Design and construction were accompanied by heroic efforts to retrieve certain forms and technical devices that were considered to be historically accurate. Simultaneously, some license was taken when historical information was lacking or when practical considerations were at issue.

The Coast Salish House

The term 'Coast Salish' has been generalized and used since the late nineteenth century to designate those speakers of fourteen related Salishan languages who inhabited different villages on the central to southern part of the east coast of Vancouver Island and the mainland opposite. Although members of these groups intermarried and were further connected through both economic and ceremonial practice, they were already differentiated by some cultural practices before contact (Suttles 1990: 14–15). Two types of houses were in use by the inhabitants of these villages, as noted by European observers. They have been categorized in the literature, first of all by roof type and also by the directional orientation of the hand-split cedar planks that made up their siding. The first house type, the shed or single-pitched roof examples, were found in much of the Georgia Strait–Puget Sound basin and on the shores along both sides of the Strait of Juan de Fuca. The second, or gable-roofed type, perhaps adapted from the form of dwellings seen in non-Indian settlements, were also observed on the southern coast. Waterman and Greiner (1921) as well as Barnett (1955) have suggested that the gabled houses were more common toward the north. In some areas, such as Sechelt, Squamish, and Musqueam, they may have been associated with the relative wealth and prestige of house owners. Both house types had frames of massive cedar posts and beams as well as curtain walls constructed from the cedar planks. The gable-roofed variety had planks aligned vertically and set into the ground at its base. Shed-roofed houses, however, were constructed with planks positioned horizontally, "lapped" or overlapping slightly, and tied with cedar withes between pairs

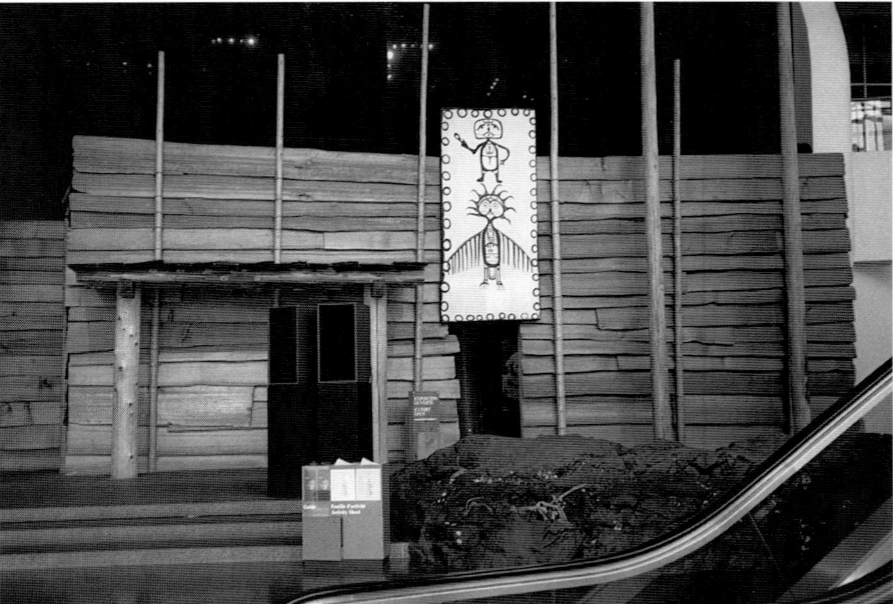

2.2 Coast Salish house. Grand Hall, CMC, Hull, Quebec. Photo: Judith Ostrowitz.

of vertical poles. The planks could be untied, removed from the polework, and loaded on canoes, to be taken along for use at summer fishing camps. Facade painting was not usual on these structures, perhaps because of the need to dismantle and reassemble these surfaces on a regular basis.[17]

The house that represents the traditions of the Coast Salish people in the CMC Grand Hall exhibit is of the single-pitched, shed-roofed variety and was modeled upon a specific house that stood in the village called Snanaimux, an early spelling of the village name Nanaimo, as it is presently known on Vancouver Island (Figure 2.2). Photographic evidence for the appearance of the house consists of three extant pictures dating from the 1860s (LaForet 1992: 23). Care was taken in the replication process to demonstrate both traditional architectural features and construction devices known from the original building and considered to be characteristic of the tradition.

The techniques illustrated here include post and beam construction, pole frame configuration, and hand-split lapped planking, sometimes cut in unequal lengths. Another such device, included to demonstrate the unique technical abilities of native Northwest Coast builders in the nineteenth century, are the cedar withes or ties used to attach the planks of the Coast Salish house (and the Nuu-chah-nulth house) to poles. Contemporary native artists, although well aware of this traditional building technique that suggests the "sewing" of the planks to the framework, were for the most part inexperienced in its application when they first arrived at Hull. During the construction process, the pieces of cedar, made from young, peeled branches, were soaked to make them flexible in the bed of the nearby Ottawa River. Both native artists and museum personnel were relieved to find that this time-honored technique for attaching planks could still be carried out today.[18]

Another feature of Coast Salish houses, known from both written and oral histories as well as from the photographic record, is the "potlatch platform," a wooden, scaffoldlike structure that was built for the Grand Hall house and stands to the left of its doorway. This elevated platform represents a structure used in the course of Coast Salish potlatching by the potlatch host, who gave speeches from it and then threw blankets down to guests standing below. The subsequent presence of such a platform before a house was prestigious, indicating that a potlatch had at one time been given there.[19] Wayne Suttles (May 25, 1995: letter) has commented however, that such platforms may not have been typical of shed-roofed houses, as the roofs themselves may have been used as the stage for these potlatch activities. Gable-roofed houses would have been more likely to have had such platforms.

The facade of the original Snanaimux building was also unusual. It had been elaborated with a carved, over life size figure, that the old photographs show positioned directly in front of the doorway, so that people entering or leaving the house would have to pass underneath its outstretched arms. A rectangular painted panel depicting a winged creature placed below a stylized human form was mounted directly above it. Exterior paintings and sculptures like these are not frequently seen in the historical record for traditional Coast Salish architecture. Figures, usually carved in the form of house posts and depicted in paintings, were more often known from the interiors of Coast Salish houses, and these are usually said to represent the supernatural helpers of the house owner. Barnett reported that exterior carvings at Nanaimo would have been unusual, and that certain examples may be attributed to the customary privileges of outsiders who had relocated there.[20] Michael Kew of the University of British Columbia has commented, however, that both "the painting and sculptured forms [in front of the CMC house] are solidly in the Central Coast Salish style." He explains as well that there are not many models of such houses to choose from "due to the early loss of such decorative features among the Salish and the lack of very early sketches" (Oct. 29, 1987: letter to LaForet).

Neither the nineteenth-century carving nor the old painted panel are known to exist today. For the final execution of the house in the Grand Hall, a replica of the painting was created by Coast Salish artist Shane Point, but the carving has temporarily been omitted from the design.[21] The large and striking painting, mounted above the doorway of the bare plank house, may add a certain visual interest to the structure, making it more accessible to a contemporary, largely non-Indian audience. Most visitors to the hall are more familiar with the figurative in art and have developed a sensibility that favors the decorative over the austere. Although extraordinary, this house model was selected to exemplify Coast Salish architectural tradition because of these dramatic embellishments.

Reproduction of the more spectacular features of Northwest Coast architecture was a priority in the planning of the entire hall. The addition of more characteristic elements and the representation of many historically accurate and more typical construction techniques seems, however, to validate the authority of these idiosyncratic examples. These unusual selections therefore may reveal as much about contemporary museum practice as they do about native buildings of the last century.[22] The combination of atypical but striking forms with impressively accurate examples of historical reconstruction will be seen repeatedly in the Grand Hall.

The Nuu-chah-nulth House

Like the Coast Salish house, the Nuu-chah-nulth building in the Grand Hall is an example of nineteenth-century post and beam construction with wooden plank siding fixed by means of cedar withes (Figure 2.3). Although the planks are not hand-split here, as in the Coast Salish example, the house was very carefully designed and constructed to illustrate the old building style in an accurate manner.[23] It is framed as a gable-roofed structure with a characteristic ridge pole at its center. The facade itself presents to the view of visitors strolling on the "boardwalk"[24] a rectangular surface of planks, attached to four vertical poles by the withes. To further illustrate traditional Nuu-chah-nulth technology, and not incidentally considerable "know-how," a plank on the facade with a natural split was visibly repaired by contemporary Nuu-chah-nulth artist Ron Hamilton in a time-honored manner. A patch of yew wood shaped something like a butterfly has been inserted at the weak point (LaForet 1992: 22).

The appearance of the Nuu-chah-nulth house is based upon a nineteenth-century example from the territory known today as Port Alberni on the west coast of Vancouver Island. The house belonged to the head chief of the Tsesha'ath people and was unusual in that it was built with its gable wall and entrance facing the beach, although most other Nuu-chah-nulth houses were positioned with the

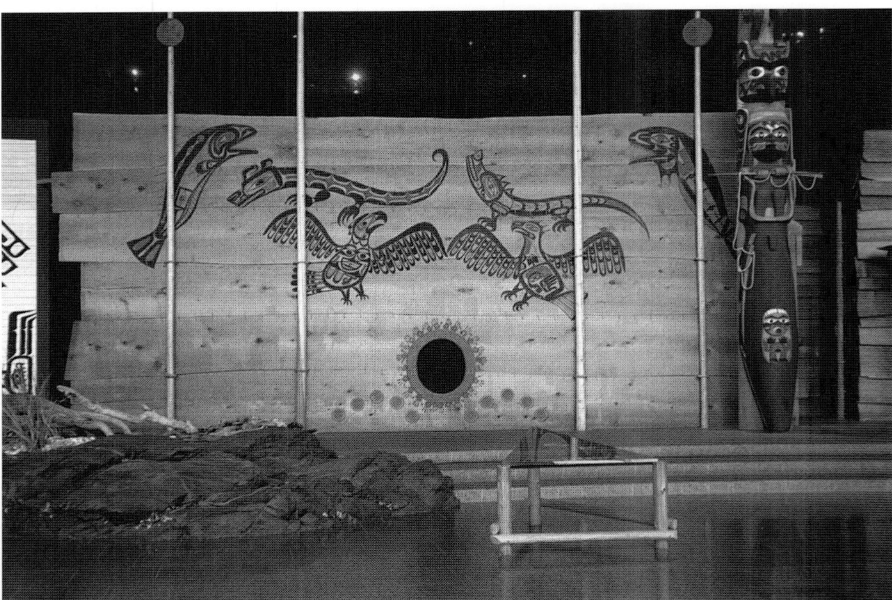

2.3 Nuu-chah-nulth house. Grand Hall, CMC, Hull, Quebec. Photo: Judith Ostrowitz.

long wall facing the shoreline (ibid.: 26).[25] One of the most fascinating aspects of the reproduction process for this particular house was the complete absence of any visual document to illustrate the old prototype. Instead of photographs, the complex of images on the facade was reconstructed on the basis of an account recorded in an unpublished manuscript by Edward Sapir. Sapir's notes on the appearance of the housefront, excerpted here, result from a 1913 interview with the man he refers to as "Tom":

> 10 nAx'As "round holes cut through boards" representing moons; 2 thunder birds facing each other; 2 He'il!ik' [Lightning Snakes, the supernatural servants of the thunderbirds] facing each other on top of each thunder-bird. Over nAx'As big round hole serving as door, at entrance of house, and at its upper sides were 2 tuckasoL!ik (big) cod-fish with heads towards each other.[26]

Based upon this description, the facade painting was created anew for the Nuu-chah-nulth house in the Grand Hall by Ron Hamilton, with the assistance of Haisla artist Lyle Wilson (see Plate 5). The Tsesha'ath house prototype had ceased to exist physically, long before the CMC project.[27] Hamilton was permitted to interpret the written description because of his expertise as an artist and because of his previous research on Nuu-chah-nulth painted screens. Perhaps his greatest qualification for the job was his own appropriate lineage and traditional affiliations.

Ron Hamilton was born at Ahaswinis, a reserve at the head of Barkley Sound, and is said to have the right to speak for the old head chief's family.[28] The contemporary chief and other members of the Tsesha'ath community knew which family maintained the rights to the story referred to by the old facade image, but no living individual knew exactly what the old painting looked like. Hamilton's version remains true to the description in Sapir's manuscript, but as Andrea LaForet has commented (Nov. 17, 1992: interview): "Ron Hamilton gave twentieth-century form to the description. If it is a little different from the nineteenth-century [version, I] don't worry about that anymore. . . . Although each house [in the Grand Hall] is an image of a house that existed in the past, [the CMC staff] found that the 'right to decide' (not the prerogative) had not passed out of the domain of Northwest Coast people." Here LaForet is referring to the rights of native communities to make decisions, not the privilege of individual families to display specific images.

This license, permitted according to the directives of influential native participants during the development process for the Grand Hall, functions throughout the exhibit. It exists, however, alongside historically based features and accurate details of construction technique that are said to duplicate past forms precisely. These historical elements help to validate the suitability of the more inventive designs. They imply both the reliability of rigorous research as well as the participation and consensus of knowledgeable native sources. Viewers may therefore assume historical evidence for decision-making in all cases. They may be generally unaware of the discretion applied by specialists. Hamilton, for instance, decided to invent four small circles, painted as phases of the moon, to be attached to the tops of the four poles that are integral to the facade structure. These are related, in his mind, to information from the old Tsesha'ath story in which the Codfish steals the moon (ibid.).[29] Similar adjustments in imagery are common in the work of traditional Northwest Coast artists, whose authority derives from their own considerable knowledge and prestigious affiliations. Therefore this may be considered "authentic" practice, but may not be justified by exact references to an historical model.

Other artistic elements in the hall result from the judgement of experienced artists and their own particular family and tribal traditions. The totem pole that stands before the Nuu-chah-nulth house, for instance, was a gift to the CMC from the Hesquiaht Nuu-chah-nulth people and the Royal British Columbia Museum (RBCM). Tim Paul, the senior carver at the RBCM at the time that this project was initiated, is a member of the Hesquiaht band. It was therefore logical that the figures on the pole derive from the traditional stories of that group and were further certified by the consultation of Hesquiaht elders. Tim Paul was assisted in this project by Kevin Cranmer, a young Kwakwa̲ka'wakw artist also employed by the RBCM, and Art Thompson, Ditidaht Nuu-chah-nulth band member, who was commissioned to carve the headdress worn by the figure at the top of the pole (LaForet 1992: 29).

This of course is not the first instance of collaboration among artists from different tribal groups and band affiliations on the Northwest Coast as a public project. An early notable example is the Bill Reid (Haida) and Doug Cranmer (Kwakwa̲ka'wakw) team that carved three exterior totem poles and one house pole, now on view immediately adjacent to the Museum of Anthropology at the University of British Columbia in Vancouver. Various artists, Kevin Cranmer among them, have worked on projects together at the carving shed on the grounds of the Royal British Columbia Museum in Victoria. These individuals descend from different tribes and bands of Vancouver Island—Richard Hunt, for instance, is Kwagu'ł Kwakwa̲ka'wakw, Tim Paul is Hesquiaht Nuu-chah-nulth. These circumstances, like the CMC project, have created opportunities to share knowledge and may even account for subsequent instances of stylistic change and hybridization in the various Northwest Coast traditions.

In the Grand Hall itself, certain forms and images have been combined as a result of this new type of work environment, arranged by outsiders who may be less concerned about the delineation of discrete social divisions. Art Thompson, for instance, has pointed out that the design on the front of the Nuu-chah-nulth house is not Hesquiaht, like the pole, but Tsesha'ath, and that this visual combination, derived from the tradition of two separate bands, would not be suitable in Nuu-chah-nulth territory. Participating artists came to terms with this collaboration, as it was arranged by the staff of the two museums who perhaps were unaware at first of the importance of protocol in reference to these territorial divisions. The artists, therefore, worked things out for themselves, making their own accommodations. Thompson says that those from other bands "stepped back," taking a lesser role when Ron Hamilton designed the Tsesha'ath painting and when Tim Paul carved the Hesquiaht pole, later dedicated by his elders. In the end, "this causes good cultural exchange," offered Thompson, but "after the fact" (June 10, 1993: interview).

In this case, native participants opted for a public display of unity but remained mindful of significant cultural divisions in their private dealings with one another. Such examples of cooperation can be seen throughout the CMC hall, although we should not generalize these combinations and joint projects as typical of Northwest Coast traditional display. Most important, there is no indication in

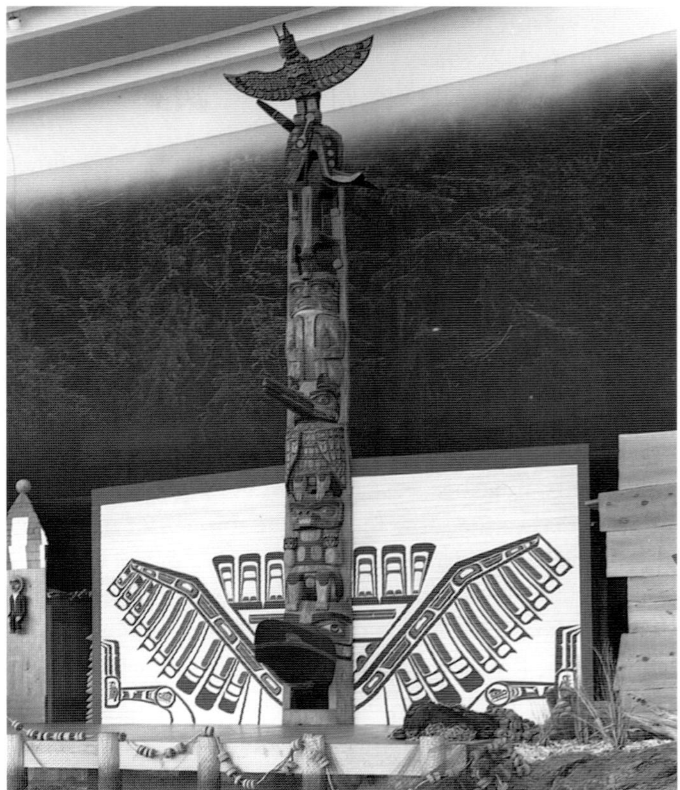

2.4 Central Coast or Kwakwa̱ka̱'wakw house. Grand Hall, CMC, Hull, Quebec; 92–39. Photo: courtesy Canadian Museum of Civilization.

the hall itself, for the information of the public, that such liberties have been taken. The museum audience believes that it is engaged with a very close approximation of past practice.

The Kwakwa̱ka̱'wakw House

The Kwakwa̱ka̱'wakw house in the Grand Hall is the latest recreation of the privileges of Chief Wakas of Alert Bay, British Columbia (Figure 2.4). Wakas was of both Oowekeeno (a non-Kwakwa̱ka̱'wakw tribe, located slightly north of Kwakwa̱ka̱'wakw territory on the British Columbia mainland) and Nimpkish ('Na̱mgis Kwakwa̱ka̱'wakw of Alert Bay) descent. His house, although it stood in Kwakwa̱ka̱'wakw territory, is identified in the CMC literature as the "Central

Coast House" because of this combined ancestry. The original structure existed from the 1890s through the 1930s, but the replica in the hall is modeled upon its appearance in 1900, based upon the photographic record (LaForet 1992: 32–33; LaForet n.d.: "The Wakas House").

Like the Chief Shakes Community House, several versions of the house, particularly the facade painting and the totem pole that defined the entrance to the building, have been restored over time under the aegis of both native and non-native commissioners. This has resulted in certain modifications of the elaborate housefront image. In the 1890s, when the totem pole was first installed in front of the Alert Bay house at the center of the facade, an archway through the lowest figure on the pole formed the entrance to the building, as may be seen in a photograph by N. B. Miller, now in the collection of the Smithsonian Institution. Five or six years later, Kwakwaka'wakw carver Dick Price elaborated this bird figure with the addition of a huge beak, as illustrated by A. J. Brabazon's photograph.[30] Price used a full-sized canoe prow to form the top half of this formidable beak and then carved the lower portion to match. The two pieces were rigged to open and close as a ceremonial entrance to the house, and a conventional rectangular door was also cut through the facade to serve as an everyday entrance. According to Doug Cranmer, the Kwakwaka'wakw artist who has worked on the replication and restoration of both the Wakas pole and housefront painting, the earliest version of the bird beak on the old totem pole included painted wings on its lower half. Around 1900, the wingspan, tail feathers, and clawed feet of the bird were painted on the horizontal wooden siding that now faced the house. Accordingly, the conventionalized forms made to represent the wings were then deleted from the lower portion of the carved beak.[31]

In 1928, the Wakas totem pole was purchased and removed from Alert Bay for reinstallation and public display at Stanley Park in Vancouver. There, exposed to the elements, the beaks of both the Huxwhukw and Raven figures deteriorated greatly. Routine maintenance by park personnel had also resulted in repeated and inaccurate repainting of the entire pole. In the 1960s, Doug Cranmer was therefore commissioned to restore the old pole and to replace the two beak sections (LaForet n.d.: "The Wakas Pole": 20).

In 1985, the pole was moved again and taken to the Museum of Anthropology at the University of British Columbia. In 1987, it was transferred to the Canadian Museum of Civilization for a loan period of thirty years. As part of the agreement, the CMC commissioned Cranmer, with the assistance of both Fah Ambers and Dickie Sumner, to carve a replica of the Wakas pole for replacement at the Stanley Park location. This 1987 replica, which stands outdoors among other totem poles and not in connection with any painted facade, has been painted again to include the conventionalized wings on the lower portion of the large, solid bird beak. Cranmer, this time with Bruce Alfred assisting, then restored the older Wakas pole for installation on the front of the Kwakwa̲ka̲'wakw house back at the Grand Hall. He recarved the Raven's beak and the entire Thunderbird figure and also painted the rest of the design on the housefront (LaForet 1992: 34–35; Doug Cranmer, June 20, 1993: interview).

Doug Cranmer, who now has quite a longstanding relationship with the pole, considers the accurate replication of old carved and painted works a personal challenge. Yet he believes that such precision is not at all important for museum audiences, who remain unaware of these efforts. In addition, in spite of extraordinary attempts at historical accuracy, he maintains that new versions are always a little bit different, either intentionally or by mistake, from the models on which they are based.

Because of his own long interest in the Wakas project, Cranmer became quite interested in the selection of the correct paint color for the border that surrounds the top and two sides of the housefront painting, as it appeared in the old photographs. Although he grew up in Alert Bay and saw the old house as a young child (he never went inside), Cranmer could not be sure of the original color of the border. Finally he was inspired to conduct an experiment. He painted a board with black, red, and green paints and photographed it with black-and-white film. The red paint looked like the same shade of gray that he had been studying in the historical photographs, influencing his final choice of red paint for the border on the Grand Hall facade.[32] Although modern photographic materials may record colors differently than did the films and papers available in 1900, this process was initiated by Cranmer with a strong intent to recover historically accurate information. Future generations will therefore know Doug Cranmer's color choices and full rendition of the Chief Wakas housefront and totem pole as an authoritative model, although they will have no inkling of how he arrived at it.

The Nuxalk House

All of the houses in the Grand Hall derive from relatively dramatic examples of architecture known from the native cultures of the Northwest Coast. The Nuxalk house, representing the traditions of the central coast people known until quite recently as the Bella Coola, is a particularly remarkable structure (Figure 2.5). This building is modeled upon an old house from the village of Qwemqtc (Bella Coola) that existed at the end of the nineteenth century. Its form was related to the legendary history of the family of Chief Clellamin. Clellamin's home was known as the House of Nusq'alst, a supernatural ancestor who came down from Nusmat'a, or the land above, shortly after the creation of the world. Nusq'alst

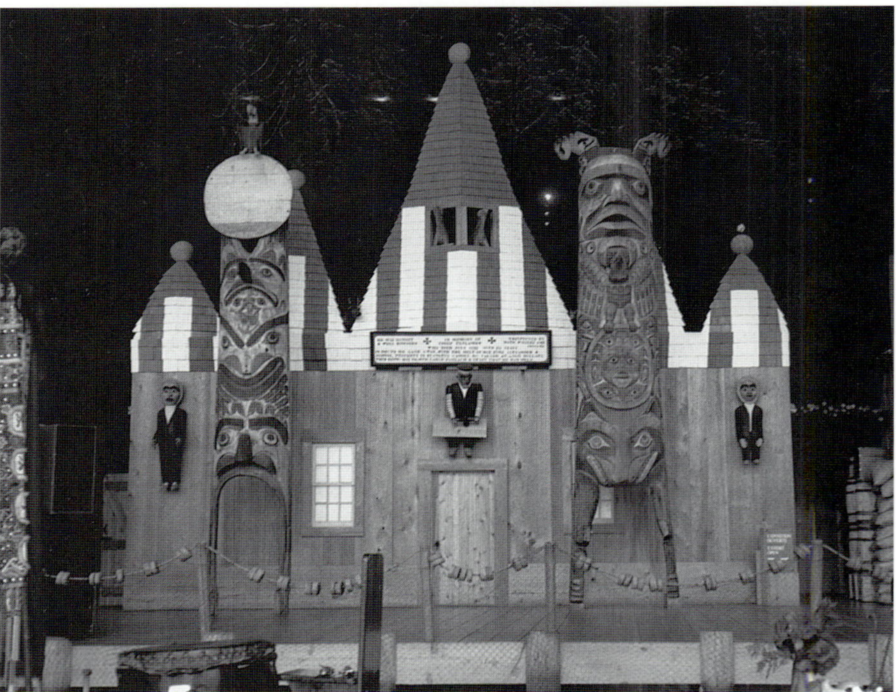

2.5 Nuxalk house. Grand Hall, CMC, Hull, Quebec. Photo: Judith Ostrowitz.

appeared as a man wearing a large hat with live snakes encircling its brim. He ultimately came to reside in the Bella Coola valley, where he transformed himself into a large mountain.

Above the facade, on the roofline of the house, Clellamin placed five spires faced with shingles and propped up by wooden struts. These spires displayed his exclusive privilege to represent the peaks of the ancestor-turned-mountain. Each of these tall points was surmounted by a carved wooden sphere that stood for the rocks at the top of the famous mountain to which the Nuxalk had tied their canoes at the time of a primordial flood. The legendary mountain scene was further elaborated by the presence of carved deer and wolves among the peaks and by two mountain goats, installed to gaze down from the two small windows built into the central and largest peak. These peaks, and perhaps some portion of the housefront itself, were painted with white stripes against a darker colored background, a scheme meant to mimic the pattern of snow in the crevices of the mountaintop. As with the Kwakwaka'wakw house, proper paint color was impossible to discern from old black-and-white photographs. In the exhibition, the deep ultramarine blue that is characteristic in Nuxalk painting was used as the background color on the shingled peaks (LaForet Nov. 17, 1992: interview).

The facade of this outstanding house also had the carved partial figure of a 'speaker' positioned over the front door. This wooden man wore the clothing and cap of a sailor and held a double-handled hammer in his two hands. The upper portion of the figure was rigged like a puppet so that the arms could be raised and lowered, causing the hammer to pound on a rectangular maple board at waist level. This figure was animated to announce a potlatch or feast (LaForet 1986; n.d.: "Nuxalk House"; La Foret 1992: 37).

Two additional humanlike figures, their faces framed by circular devices, were carved in wood and positioned at the right and left sides of the facade. Several coppers, shield-shaped prestige objects in Northwest Coast cultures, were also nailed to the original housefront, as was a large wooden sign commemorating the life of Chief Clellamin. This plaque recorded the chief's potlatch activities and described him as "honest and well disposed & respected by both whites and Indians." The sign, the original hammering figure, and one of the carved mountain goats are now a part of the CMC's Northwest Coast collection. Because of their age and fragility, these elements as well as a second mountain goat, the two wooden figures that flank the doorway, and both the wolf and the deer on the roof have been recarved as near-replicas by contemporary Nuxalk artist Glen Tallio (LaForet n.d.: "Nuxalk House"; La Foret 1992: 37).

The Nuxalk house in the Grand Hall is an exciting and theatrical structure but one that must be considered unusual within the tradition. More typical were simpler plank houses, some with carved "entrance poles" installed at the center of the housefront. In other examples, facade construction paralleled interior divisions that were conceived in three parts, resulting in a flat, tripartite surface. The crests of the house owner might be painted on all three parts; circular motifs were common. Some carved decorations for the gables of houses were also known, such as a single bird figure mounted on a pole (Vastokas 1966: 49–55; Nabokov and Easton 1989: 260; Kennedy and Bouchard 1990: 327).

The unusual house from Qwemqtc, with its spired roof line and multiple sculptural adornments, is thought to result, at least in part, from European influence. LaForet in particular has suggested that the animated figure of the hammering speaker and the carvings that were placed within the central windows or niches are reminiscent of large German clocks with moving figures that announce the changing of the hours. German models are also suggested because of the special exposure of a Nuxalk group to that architectural tradition. Beginning in 1885, a dance troupe from Bella Coola toured Germany for a year, a trip organized by Adrian and Filip Jacobsen. The dancers visited both Leipzig and Berlin, where their performances included the public exhibition of song, dance, games, and demonstrations with bows and arrows.[33]

In spite of the fact that the innovative Clellamin house was built in the late 1800s, at roughly the same time period as the tour of the dance troupe, project supervisor Glen Tallio maintains that it was not influenced by the European experiences of the 1885 dancers. Tallio concedes that "this is a very unusual house, but it comes from the story of the [mountain] peaks. . . . The yellow cedar balls come from the story of the flood. . . . This is a Bella Coola story and the Clellamin family was one of the first families after creation" (Mar. 23, 1993, interview). Here Tallio is privileging traditional knowledge over informed conjecture based upon the non-native historical record.

Tallio refers to a family history, or a *smayusta*, which relates the arrival on earth, from the land above, of the original ancestors of a particular descent group (McIlwraith 1948, I: 127). Images from such histories, those that belonged to different Nuxalk families, were displayed simultaneously in Qwemqtc by the end of the nineteenth century. Two houses away from Clellamin's, for instance, stood the house of Chief Qomoqua, whose ancestral stories described a supernatural undersea chief of the same name. A totem pole that refers to this history served as the entrance pole for Qomoqua's house.[34] Also living in Qwemqtc by the 1920s, was Captain Schooner, although the painted imagery on the front of his house is not easy to discern from the photographic record.[35] These important families came together or "amalgamated" in Qwemqtc in the 1920s. Smallpox had depleted the Nuxalk population to such an extent that like the Haida, various groups relocated to combine both their populations and resources (ibid.: 16).

In the Grand Hall, however, unprecedented liberties have been taken with the combination of these images derived from exclusive family prerogatives. The old Chief Qomoqua pole, for instance, has been installed directly in front of the Clellamin house, to the right of the doorway. Another entrance pole, collected in 1923 by Harlan Smith from the village of Tallio on South Bentinck Arm, has been installed to the left of the Clellamin doorway.[36] Inside the house, the current display incorporates a huge carved figure of a man with outstretched arms. This carving was originally a part of the Schooner house in Qomqotes village. These crest images, brought together for an elaborate and rich display in the Grand Hall, collage the exclusive crest privileges of different Nuxalk families in a manner that may be considered inappropriate according to traditional protocol.

As with the Nuu-chah-nulth, family privileges are still considered important by the Nuxalk. However, according to Glen Tallio, only a few people still know their proper hereditary crests. He feels that the unprecedented combinations at the CMC are not all that important to elders and other contemporary Nuxalk people because of their overriding desire to represent the strength of the community, rather than that of a particular lineage. "It's Bella Coola, not so-and-so's family," comments Tallio on the Grand Hall house. The magnificence of Nuxalk history is the issue here, and it is meant to shine in this environment. Members of the Nuxalk community have raised other issues related, for instance, to the great distance that this prestigious representation has been situated from "home," where the display might have been accessible to a greater number of Nuxalk people.

Some Nuxalk individuals have also expressed concern over the occasional proximity of a large Kwakwaka'wakw feast dish to their house, as positioned by museum personnel for display. The presence of this object on the boardwalk platform may confuse the proper presentation of Nuxalk group identity and may be a more sensitive issue to the Nuxalk, who are willing to tolerate the unusual combination of different family treasures.[37] It should also be noted here again that the Hesquiaht performers who created a presentation ceremony for the new totem pole before the Nuu-chah-nulth house rejected this same platform as an appropriate site when it was suggested as being the best place for their performance. They too were sensitive about the combination of their traditions with those of the Nuxalk, at least by implication. Yet they were also more accepting of the unification of Nuu-chah-nulth subgroups in relation to public identity, as evidenced by the Tsehsha'ath facade painting and Hesquiaht totem pole combination.

Andrea LaForet actually made numerous attempts to speak about these issues of protocol with community representatives and elders in each of the Northwest Coast groups represented in the hall. She relates that the descendants of Chief Clellamin were asked about their concerns and, in particular, about the proximity of the Tallio pole to the house. "The owner had doubts, but didn't fuss," she reports. "It was not a major concern. Anthropological categories are not always important."[38] Obviously, only those issues that seemed significant prior to the construction and ultimate opening of the hall could be discussed in advance. This naturally placed certain limits on the nature of the representation.

Ideals of strict historical accuracy and the proper display of traditional features were indeed strived for in the replicated Nuxalk house. The proper execution and placement of carved elements, according to photographic evidence for instance, was important. In a museum environment, however, some adaptations of traditional protocol were considered acceptable by contemporary spokespeople. Their concerns—to publicize their prestigious history and to inform a broader audience about their continued presence—fostered compliance with some museum objectives. Their choices result in the representation of a discrete but somewhat homogenous Nuxalk identity. This is demonstrated by the assertions of native workers who insist upon the completely Nuxalk inspiration for the old house rather than consider European influence. They also felt that the display of the Kwakwa̲ka̲'wakw carving nearby compromised the entity that these advisors had delineated as completely Nuxalk. Such selective compromises on the description of tribal identity in the hall will be seen again and again.

The Haida House

The six-beamed Haida house in the Grand Hall was constructed to accommodate the house entrance pole from the CMC collection known as House Waiting for Property, purchased by C. F. Newcombe in 1901 (Figure 2.6). According to Barbeau, the 45-foot pole, incorporating both Eagle and Killer Whale imagery and topped off with the figures of three Haida Watchmen, came from the village of Haina (New Gold Harbor) on Maud Island near Skidegate (1990, I: 288–89). LaForet's research indicates that it was earlier installed in front of a chief's house in the village of Chaatl (1992: 40). The house that one now enters through the ovoid belly of what is probably a Brown Bear at the base of this pole is not a reproduction of a particular structure known from the historical record. The CMC Haida house is however, stylistically correct or true to form, according to one of two traditional Haida construction formats.

The six beams of this Haida house type penetrate both front and rear wooden "plates," which are in turn supported by pairs of posts at the center, front, and rear of the house and by massive vertical beams at its four corners. They are slotted and notched to receive the ends of each plate in mortise and tenon fashion. A seventh central beam, split in the middle to leave room for the framed smoke hole, is not visible from the exterior of the house. The roof plates and bottom wall plates are grooved to receive the series of wall planks.[39]

A second type of Haida house in use in the nineteenth century had four roof beams not visible from the exterior, the two central ones supported by four interior houseposts. Prestigious houses of either of the two types were sometimes excavated to form a "pit" at the lowest level, with multiple elevated platforms extending around the perimeter of the interior space to serve as living and sleeping areas (ibid.). Although the representative house in the Grand Hall is constructed as a traditional six-beamed house, it does not include such an excavation or stepped levels. Instead it refers to the Haida past through the relatively smooth, subtly hand-adzed boards that make up its exterior walls. The house corners are mortised and tenoned and carved out as graceful U-shaped depressions at the top of the vertical members. Planks are inserted with precision into the grooved roof and wall plates. Not all characteristics of the house, however, even at its exterior, are consistent with traditional requirements. Like the other houses in the hall, its

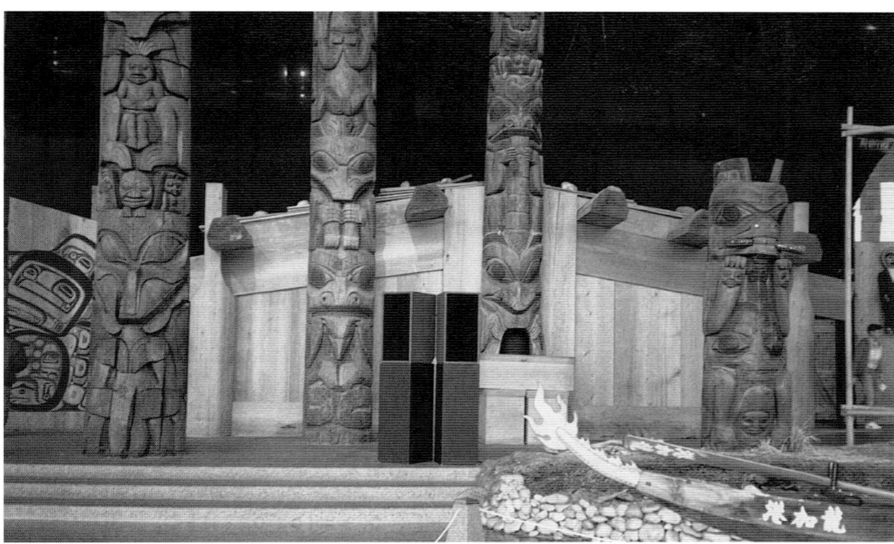

2.6 Haida house. Grand Hall, CMC, Hull, Quebec. Photo: Judith Ostrowitz.

structure has been augmented for strength by the addition of cement posts. The CMC house is also rectangular, slightly wider than it is deep, although the old houses were nearly square (MacDonald 1983: 18–19; Vastokas 1966: 27).

When project supervisor Jim Hart, a Haida carver from Masset, first received the plans for the house from the CMC, he proposed some changes in its proportions and an adjustment in the dimensions of the fascia boards to a slightly thicker dimension. His innovations were encouraged. Bill McLennan, construction supervisor at UBC, told Hart to incorporate these alterations that were meant to strengthen the house from a visual as well as structural point of view. "The building had to please your eye," recalled Hart. He compared his strategies to the vision of his predecessors. "Haidas overbuilt in the past, it was a visual thing" (McLennan, Mar. 22, 1993; Hart, Mar. 26, 1993: interviews).

The Haida house, like several others in the hall, is contextualized by a collaged display of old totem poles positioned directly in front of it. Again, poles are combined here that originate from the histories of different families from separate villages. An interior house post, originally from Chief Wiah's house in the village of Masset for instance, depicts a Beaver with a sculpin carved on its belly, and in its mouth is a stick inlaid with abalone. This pole is positioned to the right of the doorway. Another pole, this one from Kayang village, is an impressive 42 feet tall (MacDonald 1983: 58). A chief in an elongated ringed hat distinguishes the top of the pole that sits to the left of the entrance of the Haida house. Finally, the so-

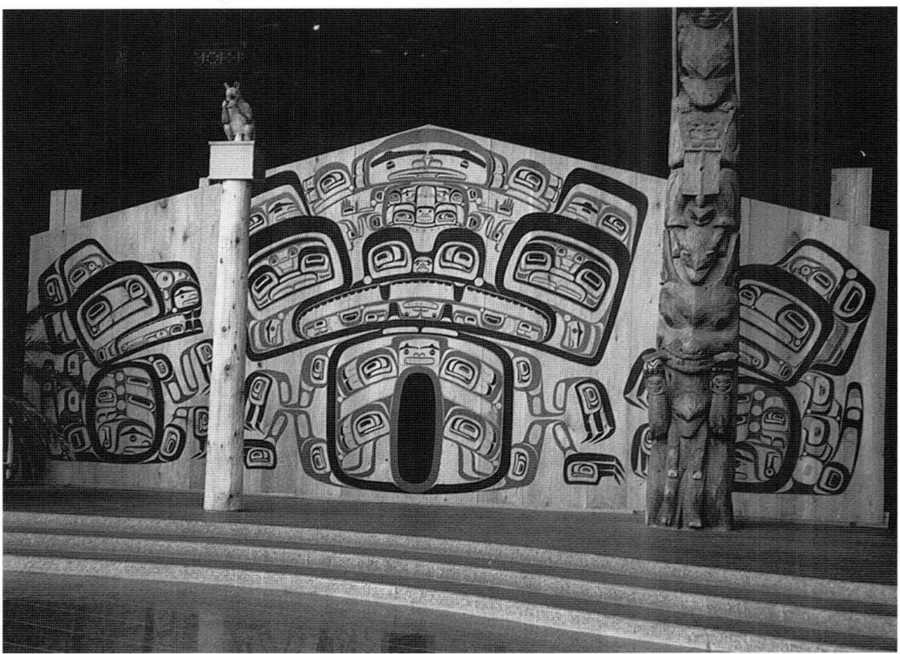

2.7 Tsimshian house. Grand Hall, CMC, Hull, Quebec. Photo: Judith Ostrowitz.

called Fox Warren pole (ibid.: 144), originally purchased at Masset, is positioned to the extreme left of the facade.[40]

This pastiche of privileges originating from the family histories of different chiefs at Masset, Kayang, and Haina, like other such generalized representations in the hall, are combined without explanation to the public. There is some difference however, between the improprieties permitted here and those seen in totem pole and housefront combinations at either the Nuxalk or Nuu-chah-nulth examples. Because the Haida house is generic, that is, an accurate stylistic representation of a nineteenth-century Haida house type with no specific owner, the breaches in traditional protocol refer in this case to totem pole combinations only and do not compromise the appropriate identity of the house itself. This subtle difference may not be that significant to native observers who profess to accept the replicated village on its own terms, at least as a museum display. They say repeatedly that such errors are inevitable, and that they are not that important in a non-native environment. Hart and his crew, for instance, have registered no objections. They claim that they are pleased with the house and insist that it is fine as an exhibition and therefore need not be completely traditional.[41]

The Haida group, like all the other native participants interviewed for this study have, for various reasons of their own, presented a sense of unity and satisfaction with the exhibition and equanimity about the breaches in traditional protocol seen there. They seem pleased to have been included in the project and insist that while these issues of appropriate representation are important back home, a museum is, after all, "just a museum." It is a place for outsiders to admire Haida artistry and to find out that the Haida are still very much alive and have a thing or two to say about the public presentation of their culture. This is not to say, however, that the works of art and architecture on display in the hall are completely unrelated to their traditional and even private concerns—recall that the Nuxalk group did not like the idea of displaying the elaborate Kwakwa̱ka'wakw dish directly in front of their house, nor would the Hesquiaht group agree to dance on the boardwalk in proximity to the crest representations specific to other groups. To some extent, insider concerns were undoubtedly considered by the Haida as well. One crew member, for reasons that remain obscure, concealed an eagle feather in the house during the construction process. Hart qualifies this gesture as a spiritual act, compromising his simplified definition of the house as "Just made for a show, not really traditional. It was made for a museum" (Mar. 26, 1993: interview). Houses made for show, strictly for the education and appreciation of outsiders, do not require spiritual acts in the process of their construction, particularly ones that are invisible to their audiences. These buildings may incorporate more than one meaning, thus making their definitions slightly more complex than they appear at first glance. Their significance may be specific to different audiences, and some information can be understood only by their makers.

The Tsimshian House

Like the Haida house, the Tsimshian house in the Grand Hall has been generalized to represent a type consistent with those structures observed in Tsimshian villages at mid-nineteenth century (Figure 2.7). The configuration of such gable-roofed houses included cedar post and two-beam construction with finely adzed plank walls, set outside of heavy corner posts, around the front, back and sides of the house. Central house pits with up to four or five levels were found in the interiors of some of the most important chiefs' houses. Such a pit may eventually be constructed for the interior display in the CMC house.[42]

The Tsimshian building made for the Grand Hall cannot be identified with the history of a particular family, but the crest imagery painted on its facade does have a specific origin. The housefront painting is a reconstructed image based upon the appearance of a particular interior screen, parts of which were

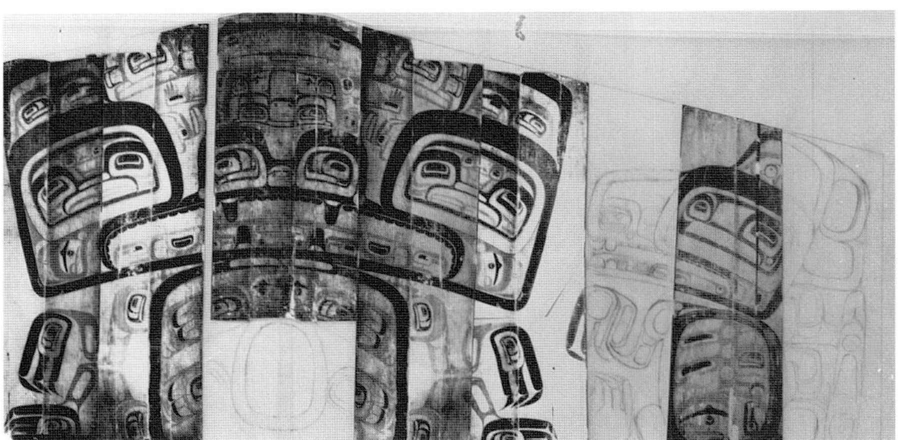

2.8 Interior screen from Port Simpson. Infrared image combined with drawing; used in the design of the Tsimshian housefront painting. Photo: courtesy Bill McLennan, Vancouver, University of British Columbia.

collected in the village of Port Simpson in the middle of the nineteenth century. A Dr. Raley, a medical missionary, found boards that made up a portion of the screen. These were already damaged by water. Unfortunately, any written records belonging to Raley, which might have provided additional information about the image painted on the boards, were lost in a house fire (LaForet 1992: 46–47).

Coincidentally, Bill McLennan, project coordinator for the Grand Hall, had been working for some time on the recovery of deteriorated images from carved and painted works of Northwest Coast art through the use of infrared photography. Working at the Museum of Anthropology at the University of British Columbia, McLennan has found that infrared film is sensitive to even small traces of paint or pigment that have been obscured by oils, soot, and other stains.[43] Photographed in this manner, the planks that Dr. Raley had collected revealed that the center section of the Port Simpson screen made up the conventionalized figure of a bear (Figure 2.8). Two smaller figures in profile had flanked the bear, but evidence was insufficient to completely identify these creatures or to discern the exact manner in which they had been portrayed. Only the center section of the profile figures remained intact, showing a part of the creatures' heads and torsos but not the snouts, backs, or tails—exactly those features that might have helped to identify the species (McLennan, Aug. 22, 1991; Mar. 22, 1993: interviews; LaForet 1992: 47).

McLennan, who had photographed many other painted objects from the Northwest Coast for his "Imagery Recovery Project," knew of a Tsimshian box

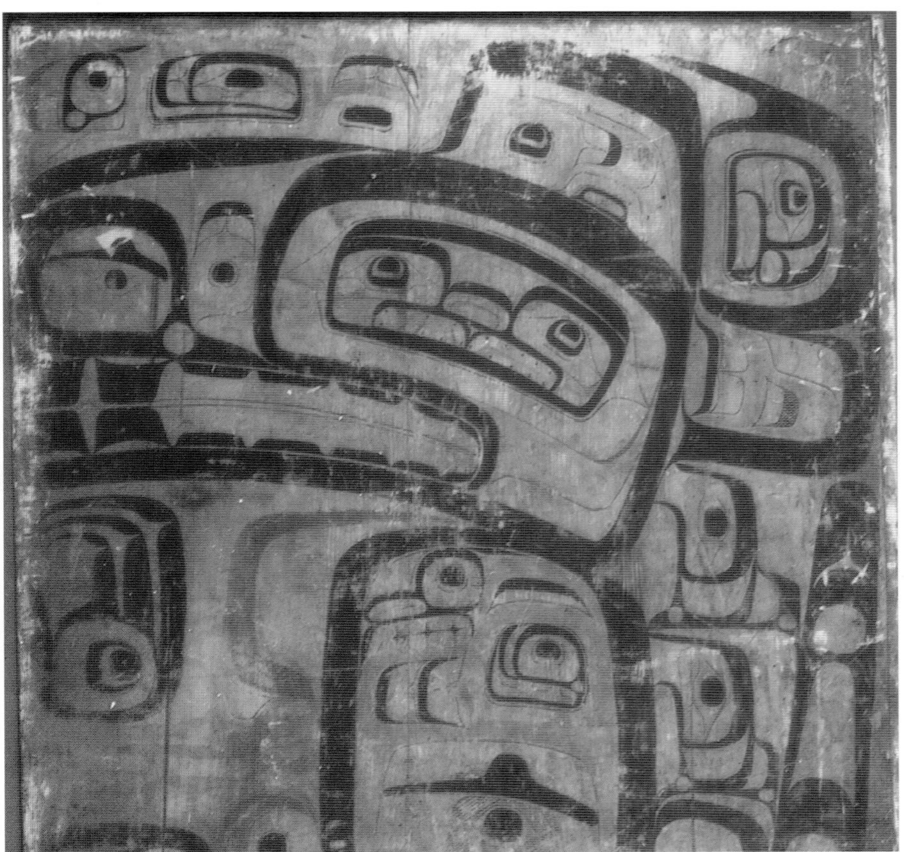

2.9 Panel of a box drum. Infrared image also used in design of the Tsimshian housefront painting. Photo: Bill McLennan. Chicago, Field Museum of Natural History, FM 78864.

drum in the collection of Chicago's Field Museum of Natural History (cat. no. FM 78864), which had been painted with the profile figures of two similar creatures and was visually compatible with the Port Simpson screen (Figure 2.9). The design on the drum was also painted with the same traditional vermilion color. Lyle Wilson, a contemporary Haida artist also employed at UBC, helped McLennan to develop a drawing for the flanking figures on the CMC housefront by referring to the box drum. He combined characteristics still to be seen on the remaining planks from the old interior screen with parts of the profile figures known from the drum.

Concurrently, Andrea LaForet was conducting field research with the Port Simpson band, attempting to find the family that had been associated with the screen. Alice White (now deceased) claimed that this crest image related to the privileges of Nieslhkomiek of the Giludzau Gispewudwade, her great-great-grandfather (LaForet 1986: "Report on Fieldwork . . .": 3). Mrs. White believed that the central figure in the painting was supposed to be a mother bear and that the two flanking figures should be bear cubs. In working out the details of the two profile figures from the Chicago box drum, however, Lyle Wilson designed the profile "bears" with different attributes. Small ovoid forms with eyes inside them are aligned along these creatures' backs; they may be interpreted as fins. Terry Starr, the Tsimshian artist hired to paint the finished design on the new housefront, has suggested as well that the tails on the animals may qualify them as wolf cubs (McLennan, Mar. 22, 1993; Wilson, Mar. 22, 1993; Starr, Mar. 25, 1993: interviews).

Starr, echoing Jim Hart's statements about the Haida house, concedes that "for that environment [a museum exhibit, the painting] is okay." Had it been Starr's responsibility, however, he might not have made the drawing as a representation of wolf cubs. Starr reports that information was lacking: "Elders with knowledge were passing on just at that time. There are fins [on the profile figures that] refer to sea creatures. Few people know the difference, or no one knows anymore" (Mar. 25, 1993: interview).[44] Bill McLennan comments on this case as well, adding that it is more important to First Nations[45] people today to identify appropriate spokespeople than to demonstrate connoisseurship related to crests. "The rupture in the tradition makes visual knowledge a long way off" (Mar. 22, 1993: interview).

As native leadership is designated anew and traditional knowledge is reconstructed from the vestiges that remain, some communities place less emphasis than do others on historically accurate crest displays. As noted, there is relatively little controversy about the totem pole combinations before this and other houses in the Grand Hall. The Tsimshian display also includes, for instance, a pole from the Nass River village of Angidah, once owned by Chief Kwasuh of the Neesles'yaes Wolf phratry; it has been placed on the right side of the new facade. Another pole from the village of Gwunahaw, which originates from the history of the lineage of 'Arhtimenazek, is called the Bear's Den pole; it stands on the left side of the house. Between them, to the right of the Bear's Den pole, is the White Squirrel pole from the Nass River village of Gitlakdamiks. The figure of the Squirrel on this pole comes from the traditions of the Eagle lineage. It has been combined with a newly carved pole structure and box form for the contemporary display.[46]

These combinations are particularly interesting in light of Margaret Seguin's observations on traditional Tsimshian culture:

In traditional Tsimshian thought, each village "was held to be a world apart, distinct in history, custom and law; to enter the territory of another village (or even of another lineage segment) was to enter a foreign land, whether a nearby one which shared the same language or a more distant Haida or Tlingit one." (Seguin 1985: 1; Halpin and Seguin 1990: 7: 267)

Clarity in the identity of Tsimshian villages and divisions, however, is definitely compromised in the CMC setting. This exhibit is not the first occasion on which these boundaries have been obscured for the public. 'Ksan village, for instance, located in Hazelton, British Columbia, the traditional territory of the Gitksan people, is a "craft village" for tourists as well as the location of the Kitanmax School of Northwest Coast Indian Art. This constructed site includes seven buildings that approximate the appearance of traditional houses through a combination of images and devices. These are executed with far less attention to historical accuracy and traditional protocol than those made for the CMC project. In one building, a woodworking shop, a facade painting by Tsimshian artist Vernon Stephens was combined with an interior screen painted by Nuu-chah-nulth artist Ron Hamilton (Nabakov and Easton 1989: 284–85).

In settings designed for museum audiences and tourists, the combination of images from different native groups and the conglomeration of their various divisions may now be typical. In the Grand Hall at the CMC, the Tsimshian house was made to stand for the composite identity of all four major divisions of the people who, as a group, are called Tsimshian. The Nisga'a of the Nass River, the Gitksan from the Upper Skeena, the Coast Tsimshian of the Lower Skeena and the adjacent coast, and the Southern Tsimshian from the coast islands are all represented by this section of the display. Perhaps the combination of crest art, particularly the totem poles installed in front of the house, permits a greater representation of these different traditions. Combinations like these may not be acceptable "at home," on the reserves, but if they continue to appear as a matter of course in the public domain, they may come to be considered standard by both native and non-native audiences.

Port Simpson residents have already responded positively enough to the CMC exhibit to have initiated their own similar project. Native representatives requested building plans from the CMC and have begun construction of a house based upon this design. The structure is small, around 35 by 40 feet, and originally intended as a "meeting place for chiefs," but it is presently unoccupied. At some point in the future, it may be used as a place to teach carving to young people. In this project initiated by native people, the crest images yet to be painted on the facade will have to be approved by local chiefs. Terry Starr has suggested as well that ultimately, an entire traditional "village scene" may be constructed at Port Simpson; if funding can be obtained, that would include adequate space for a museum and perhaps a restaurant (Starr, Mar. 25, 1993; McLennan, Mar. 22, 1993: interviews).

Tsimshian people have recognized that historical reconstructions attract tourist dollars. At the same time, such projects may serve as appropriate contemporary settings for traditional cultural events and Indian business, transactions that are enhanced when conducted among images referring in a positive manner to Tsimshian identity. At some point, the criteria developed by non-native museum personnel for the appropriate delineation of native images may affect the representation of the past in native locations as well. It is conceivable that this influence may exceed the development of building plans and come to include adjustments in the delineation of appropriate crest display.

Art of the Coherent Map

Simulation may exceed representation in museum display by degree only. The Northwest Coast village in the Grand Hall at the Canadian Museum of Civilization is, upon close examination, still a type of map that alludes to the vast territory of native history in this part of the world. It is a logical development from the representative displays in most museum halls that have, almost without exception, distributed their collections of artifacts among glass cases with label texts that refer to the traditional practices of native cultures. Like the discrete house units in the Grand Hall, these have been categorized according to circumscribed geographical regions, the selective delineation of tribal groups, or defined, according to their use, either as objects of technology or as the regalia of ceremony.

The authenticity of the Grand Hall display and the cogency of the information embedded in its presentation, however, has been significantly amplified, far beyond typical museum representation and by expert means. The strategies of native artists, for instance, generated meticulously crafted examples of Northwest Coast architecture for the exhibition. In the course of the Grand Hall project, workers became well versed in time-honored construction techniques, and in some cases, their enthusiastic immersion in their work resulted in extraordinary demonstrations of skill. The Coast Salish team, for example, hand-split every plank for the facade of their house in the traditional manner, with wedges, and then carefully lapped and tied each board on with cedar withes, resulting in the handmade character of what they considered a "real old house." Nuu-chah-nulth artists also learned to tie withes and to demonstrate traditional repair patches on their housefront. They also mined the past to create two new works of dazzling art, a facade painting and a totem pole, executed in historically correct style. The Kwakwa̲ka'wakw group scrupulously searched for paints of the correct hue. Their efforts resulted in the seamless combination of the restored entrance pole with a dramatically painted new facade. The production of the elaborate Nuxalk house required an extensive carving program to replicate the complex of human figures, carved animals, and painted signs that appear on the housefront and roof. The six-beamed Haida house is also masterfully constructed in the old way, with deftly carved mortise and tenon connections and the shallow, soft adze marks that pick up a glow of light as it moves across the planks of the facade. The Tsimshian house is also convincingly constructed, and the front is dramatically set off from the formidable and austere Haida example next to it by the house-sized red-and-black painting of the mother bear and her "cubs."

Both label copy and the explanatory literature that now accompany the Grand Hall display notify the public that the construction crews who achieved these effects were of appropriate native descent.[47] The names of elder native advisors are also incorporated into signs and texts. This understanding—that the house models have been crafted in great detail in a manner resulting from traditional knowledge—necessarily suggests the genuine. To the museum audience, these are bona fide examples of native architecture that quote the past in as accurate a manner as possible. The authenticity of the entire village scene is certified by this participation, and therefore tacit endorsement, of living First Nations people.

The resulting combination of impressive houses in the Grand Hall village, although derived from an unprecedented blend of native traditions, has the effect of a plausible if fantastic street scene. Reminders of nature, evocative sound effects, and the ambitious scale of the entire undertaking create a complex environment that functions as a weighty teaching tool. A recent analysis of Walt Disney World by Stephen Fjellman considers the significant enculturative power of such sophisticated historical and geographic reconstructions. They may be categorized as components of a more comprehensive "scholastic programme," of the type identified by Antonio Gramsci as being necessary to the assertion and maintenance of hegemony by influential parties.[48] Cultural theorist Pierre Bourdieu has also addressed the mechanics of more formal educational systems that ensure the "reproduction of the culture of the dominant classes," recognizing power relationships imposed with what he has called "symbolic force." In a manner that exceeds such practice in school systems, ". . . [In] symbolic products such as works of art, games, myths, etc.—[symbolic force]exerts by its functioning, particularly by the use made of it, an educative effect which helps to make it easier to acquire the dispositions necessary for its adequate use" (Bourdieu 1977: 217n40).[49]

Successful inculcation, in the case of the Grand Hall on the subject of Native

Canadian history, may depend on "symbolic force"—on the excellence and credibility of its symbolic representation, and on the authority of its venue. Comprehensive multimedia environments legitimized by the rigors of scholarship and the participation of native craftsmen may be even more influential than dioramas and display cases in the selective education of the public. Therefore information about the native past presented here may foster, in Baudrillard's terms, the influence of the map upon the territory. As George MacDonald himself has suggested, "[The] Grand Hall may begin to penetrate the Canadian psyche" (Nov. 19, 1992: interview).

MacDonald is correct. This exhibition is an extremely influential work of art. Yet despite the enormous efforts of all parties, it is not a completely accurate representation of history; no display could be. As in all exhibitions, the examples may be set either to generalize about the past or to specify and thereby omit alternate choices. As previously discussed, the Coast Salish House was selected as a representative model, even though the exterior display of elaborate carved and painted images, while legitimate, may illustrate an unusual practice. The Nuxalk house, elaborated to the extent that a European model has been suggested to explain its departure from the standard, may also skew the viewer's sense of history. The matter of inappropriate combinations of crest art, at least according to traditional nineteenth-century protocol, must be mentioned here again; these collages affect the scrupulous reconstruction of history that is presented here to the "Canadian psyche." These are the Nuu-chah-nulth house and totem pole complex which, like the unprecedented combination of poles from different native groups before the Nuxalk, Haida, and Tsimshian houses are displayed without explanation to the public.

Other selections made with great care—for instance the paint color for the border of the Kwakwaka'wakw facade and the invention of circular elements that surmount the poles on the Nuu-chah-nulth house—may be based upon the sound advice of knowledgeable artists of appropriate descent, though they may not be explained on the basis of historical accuracy. These works of art and architecture result instead from the complex circumstances that accompany a significant twentieth-century encounter between native and non-native collaborators pursuing goals relevant to twentieth-century lives. Therefore in some ways the Grand Hall is a self-referential work of art, significant to those who composed it and only partially known by those visitors who are educated by the convincing "hyperreality" of this setting.

The resulting representation in the hall, as an exhibition, is dedicated to a plausible coherence and an embracing illusion of totality. This illusion, the "real without origin or reality," need not dismay the viewer on the basis of the lost past, to which this fantastic landscape may only refer indirectly. As David Lowenthal has provocatively observed: "Restorations and reconstructions need not always strive to be wholly authentic: even a patently altered or brazenly contrived past can have its uses" (1985: 408). Perhaps the contrived past may be best used to demonstrate more current social realities. As the appropriate contextualization of native cultural materials becomes increasingly problematic, perhaps only the overt installation of these works as components of a constructed past, even as "installation art" projects may emerge as the most scrupulous and useful demonstrations of subjectivity. These would indeed be simulacra, but their fabricated nature need not be presented as representative historical reconstruction.

Such installations would have to be quite explicit or they would only cause more confusion. On opening day at the George Gustave Heye Center of the National Museum of the American Indian in New York, for instance, two visitors were heard commenting on the parodied installation of American Indian kitsch in the diorama-like setting of a living room in a slightly offbeat reservation house. One woman remarked, "This is just how they live, you know," revealing that she missed the "art," the element of satire here due to her extreme familiarity with contextualizing ethnographic display. Viewers are accustomed to equating museum displays, particularly elaborate scenes or installations, with earnest and accurate attempts at historical representation. Undoubtedly visitors to the CMC judge the Grand Hall as objective and historically accurate as well. It may come to function as the "map-as-logo," as described by Benedict Anderson for the post-colonial "popular imagination," as "Pure sign, no longer compass to the world" (1983: 175). Audiences will no doubt be deeply affected by the identifying characteristics or discrete iconic units designed to identify "types" of Northwest Coast native people in this exhibit.

In museum display, the invented map has always influenced the territory. Because it is impossible to reconstruct the past with complete accuracy, the designation of appropriate decision-makers, those who mediate and construct the past for the public, has become central. In the Grand Hall, native consultation was an important component of the development process; however, the project was orchestrated on the whole by non-native museum staff. The resulting exhibition is not a coalescent representation of native thought. Neither is it limited to the simple expression of goals set by museum professionals; they too were constrained, to some degree, by the effects of collaboration as well as by practical concerns such as budgetary limitations and deadlines. The version of history conveyed with such force here represents a combination of concerns, the results of which could not have been completely foreseen at the outset of the project. These were concerns not only about the appropriate portrayal of the past, but about the right to participate in the construction of ideas presented here.

One theme, repeatedly conveyed in the Grand Hall, is the cooperation and unified identity of the various tribes and cultural divisions on the Northwest Coast. The creation of expedient icons (or "logos"), in this case the architectural facades, for the transmission of general information is typical of museum practice. This strategy generates concise identities for native traditions that are in reality far more complex. These practices are not typical of native concern on the Northwest Coast, however, which is to continually define by visual, ceremonial, and political means, discrete identities and affiliations down to the micro-level.

Olu Oguibe (1993) has written on the designation of Modernism, as it has been denied to Africa and to other cultures outside the West, as the product of such unifying narratives, as conceived by outsiders. He extends his discussion on the reclaimed authority to "correct" history: "To correct is merely to reconfigure, to counter-distort." For Oguibe, to problematize the "formulation of a singular African 'identity'" is to complicate the discourse once again. Those who update the presentation of social divisions as well as alliances do more than correct or err, they too legitimize the territory and describe a map for the incontrovertible reception of outsiders. The newest map, or museum exhibition, will also be constructed according to the vision of current authorities.

The generalizations about identity in the Grand Hall at the CMC are acknowledged as improprieties by native consultants, yet, on the whole, they seem to be accepted as inevitable in an exhibition environment. As Bill McLennan, who supervised the construction process has noted, "[Traditional] visual knowledge is a long way off" (Mar. 22, 1993, interview). The loss of some knowledge about crest art display may indeed have been a factor here, as was the enticement to participate in a prestigious display of cultural heritage at the Canadian capital. In addition, the opportunity for gainful employment should not be overlooked as motivation for tacit accord. Perhaps native collaboration in the construction of this illusion of unity may be accounted for by the necessity of an authoritative public image. Factionalized "tribal" communities that vie with one another for power are regarded as disorganized and impotent in their dealings with dominant cultures. Today's protocol, to appear as a force to be reckoned with and sought after for its imprimatur, in full view of the Canadian Parliament buildings, may have encouraged the participation of native representatives in this display of constructed history made for the Grand Hall.

Making Dance History: Kwakwa̲ka̲'wakw Performance Art at the American Museum of Natural History

THE FLUIDITY OF NATIVE PERFORMANCE on the Northwest Coast accommodates the requirements of unique new audiences in diverse settings and demonstrates certain criteria for protocol, acceptable to contemporary participants. Standards for propriety, renewed by each generation, may be exhibited through the thoughtful construction of repertoire, the ordering and length of dance, and the selection of accompanying masks and other items of regalia. The analysis of native theatrical presentations therefore reveals relative standards of authenticity for both form and content—standards which depend upon the relationships that exist between certain performance artists and their audiences and which have developed as a result of local historical precedent for the display of dance privileges and accompanying oratory. What will count as ceremonialism, or even as the appropriate display of traditional dances for theatercraft, depends upon the interpretive strategies of these various arbiters of propriety in dance, whether they are the elder members of a native community, as is customary, or whether they are among the many non-native scholars who have described specific performances for the written record and have therefore established canons of the traditional for succeeding generations.[1]

The Kwakwa̲ka̲'wakw of Vancouver Island, for example, have established themselves as heirs to the "enduring potlatch," the continuous practice of which links them with the dance traditions of their ancestors, it is said, since time immemorial. Although the Nuu-chah-nulth, Gitksan, and other groups claim an unbroken history in the execution of their performance traditions, despite the concentrated efforts of non-native religious and secular authorities of the nineteenth and twentieth centuries to discourage and outlaw these practices, it is the Kwakwa̲ka̲'wakw who have taken up this hard-earned continuity as their particular banner (Cole and Chaikin 1990). Features of Kwakw<u>a</u>ka'wakw public identity and position of authority may therefore depend upon some aspects of this historical continuity. For this reason, it is significant to examine not just the relationship between the composition of modern dance presentations to similar ones recorded at the turn of the century, as has frequently been treated in the literature,[2] but also to explore what is said by twentieth-century native choreographers and dance witnesses about the manner in which they perceive this connection to the past, and about the relative importance of historical accuracy itself, among other features, as a formal device to signify this continuum.

In October of 1991, for instance, a delegation of Kwakw<u>a</u>ka'wakw people from various villages and cities of British Columbia convened on the Upper West Side of Manhattan to construct a formal beginning for the exhibition *Chiefly Feasts: The Enduring Kwakiutl Potlatch* at the American Museum of Natural History. Following an elaborate presentation of performance art at the opening, a dazzled viewer approached one of the dancers, Mrs. Ethel Alfred of Alert Bay (Plate 7), to express her appreciation. Mrs. Alfred, who wore a headring and sequined button blanket, had just glided through a number of traditional dances, demonstrating both her skill and ancestral prerogatives. "Oh, we always do this back home for the tourists," she replied modestly. The viewer was rather disconcerted by this comment, which appeared to sabotage both the historicity of this event and the authenticity that she had sensed in the dances. Her disappointment may be compared with Dean MacCannell's evaluation that tourism can promote "the restoration, preservation and fictional recreation of ethnic attributes." Similarly, Nelson Graburn has coined the phrase "secondary" ethnicity, which by implication is not "original." Viewers are therefore cautioned by this term that they are not witnessing a genuine expression related to the social reality of the native community (van den Berghe and Keyes 1984: 349; MacCannell 1984: 377; Graburn 1984: 411). These observations on the representation of ethnic identity for outsider audiences depend on a strict division between expressions of long-standing native concern and any accommodation that they may choose to make in artistic treatments suitable for non-natives, especially for those events considered to be "tainted" by financial transaction.

The dance history of performance art or "reenactment" made for tourists and other non-native audiences indicates, however, that many elements of extreme significance to "insiders" (those who have created the performance) may indeed be included in such productions.[3] The authenticity of these events depends not only upon correct protocol evaluated according to precedent, but may also be related to a certain internal coherence and the new expression of timely concerns, the purposes of which may be more meaningful for practitioners, who continue to authorize the form of their own presentations, than for observers. Interviews with native participants in the *Chiefly Feasts* ceremonies and newspaper accounts of similar "dances for entertainment," designed by their immediate predecessors in the 1950s and 1960s, may be cited to indicate that dance displays for outsiders may follow selected traditions and express information significant to the native community, even when not of antique provenance.[4] It will also be useful to recall here that what we know as "traditional" or "authentic" for Kwakwa<u>ka</u>'wakw performance is usually limited to the descriptions of particular dance privileges recorded by Franz Boas in *The Social Organization and the Secret Societies of the Kwakiutl Indians* (1897), a work generalized by later scholars as canonical.[5] Although formal aspects of Kwakwa<u>ka</u>'wakw dance may vary, the appropriate display of crest privileges and the contemporary authority to designate their performance, as well as significant modifications in their presentation, remain the essential points in all dance productions.

Although unprecedented in New York City in 1991, Northwest Coast native people have for some time created dramatic displays of song and dance for non-native audiences and continue to do so with some frequency. As mentioned in the preceding chapter, a Bella Coola (now Nuxalk) troupe was assembled by Adrian and Filip Jacobsen in 1885 to tour Germany. Other performances for entertainment include those staged by a Kwakwa<u>ka</u>'wakw group for the Chicago World's Fair of 1893 and the St. Louis Universal Exposition of 1904. In both those cities, the performers emphasized sensational, and to western eyes, some gory aspects of their famous *hamat'sa* dance. These included bloody and frenzied demonstrations of feigned cannibalism. In St. Louis, for instance, Bob Harris represented the behavior of a *hamat'sa* dancer by pretending to kill a pygmy performer, a visitor from a neighboring exhibit. He used a model of the man, made of mutton, and then concealed inside it a bladder filled with blood to create a vivid "special effect."[6]

These lively portrayals of potlatch dancing for outsiders were then discouraged for about fifty years. When Bill 79 — the revised Indian Act that deleted the anti-potlatch law from public record — passed in Canada, staged presentations of native identity became popular again as a form of public entertainment in British Columbia. Early in this period, for instance, Mungo Martin, renowned artist and teacher of traditional practice, who was at the time employed by the British Columbia Provincial Museum, inaugurated his ceremonial house in Thunderbird Park, Victoria. The house was dedicated in 1953 with a lavish traditional potlatch, a portion of which was open to the general public.[7]

Alert Bay Dance History

Of particular interest here is the adaptation of traditional dancing for public presentation in Alert Bay, British Columbia, during the 1950s and 1960s. Some of the elderly participants in the *Chiefly Feasts* ceremonies were active in these productions, as were the parents and grandparents of several others. 'Y<u>a</u>lis, as Alert Bay is known in Kwakwala, has also been a strategic location in much of Kwakw<u>a</u>ka'wakw political and artistic history of the middle of the twentieth century. Therefore organized displays of native life for outsiders constructed by some residents of the period, those who were (not coincidentally) extraordinarily active in the civic life of the community, were quite influential.

This unique village on Cormorant Island first attracted Kwakw<u>a</u>ka'wakw workers from the Nimpkish ('N<u>a</u>mg<u>i</u>s) tribe on Vancouver Island around 1870, when a salmon cannery was established. By 1887 an Anglican mission led by Rev. A. J. Hall relocated to Alert Bay from Fort Rupert and was soon followed by the Kwakewlth Indian Agency. A sawmill was also built there in 1888, and in 1894 an Industrial School for Boys was established in Alert Bay by the Department of Indian Affairs (Codere 1990: 363).

By mid-twentieth century, Alert Bay had become quite a hub of Kwakw<u>a</u>ka'wakw life. The Anglican Church was an important force in this process, offering land to those Kwakw<u>a</u>ka'wakw whom they termed "progressive." To be so defined, residents had to be alumni of the Anglican school in the Bay and married under the auspices of the church. Perhaps most significant, these "modern" Indians were required to renounce the potlatch and had to promise to try to live what was called "a good clean life." The church, and some native residents, envisioned a new type of reserve where native people ran businesses and lived in conventional western-style houses (Spradley 1969: 128, 135). By around 1950, a plan for what was called "amalgamation," the incorporation of Kwakw<u>a</u>ka'wakw from various other bands into the 'N<u>a</u>mg<u>i</u>s reserve, was taken up. The cooperation of people from the different Kwakw<u>a</u>ka'wakw subdivisions was supposed to be a factor in this proposed advancement among like-minded people. Some families did leave the old, isolated villages for Alert Bay to work for greater financial security and to educate their children in the non-native manner (ibid.: 139–43; Cole and Chaikin 1990: 23).

Some members of this community of Kwakw<u>a</u>ka'wakw people managed to retain a strong identification with traditional practice even while dedicating themselves to this new form of progress and a greater participation in Canadian life. As one consequence of this unique combination of ideals, Alert Bay became the location of several new performances designated "Indian Dances," composed for outsider audiences that were meant to highlight both the time-honored artistic abilities of these people as well as their up-to-date organizational skills.[8]

These Alert Bay public performances were based upon the potlatch itself, known from childhood and still practiced by some residents. They were shortened by the selection of songs and dances considered by organizers to be entertaining and appropriate to the interests of visitors. Furthermore, the meaning of these performances was carefully interpreted for non-native consumption by certain key historical figures of the period. Some were community-minded individuals, many concurrently active in various programs designed to restore native rights and self-determination. Many were also instrumental in the construction of new theatrical conventions for social dancing. Both the dances themselves and public commentary about them, as expressed in explanatory speechmaking and local newspaper reports, framed these events as high entertainment; the public was duly informed that they were planned and produced with extraordinary effort and consummate skill by the modern native population of Alert Bay.

James Sewid's autobiography, recorded by James Spradley (1969), notes that in the spring of 1951, the native people of Alert Bay were invited to participate in the public life of this part-white, part-Indian village in a novel way. Sewid, the chief councillor of the 'N<u>a</u>mgis band, was asked to apply his recognized expertise in the development of various business and cultural projects to the efforts of the "Hospital Week Committee." For several years the white community had been involved in fundraising efforts to support St. George's Hospital, which still provides health care to residents of Alert Bay. Sewid, the first native person ever to be included, was elected chairman of the committee. It was his idea to produce an Indian Dance and charge admission to the guests or "witnesses," rather than have the host chiefs give away property in the traditional manner. This proposed adjustment would lead to a series of financial and cultural victories for the Alert Bay community (see Plate 8).[9]

There was some initial resistance to this key modification in the purpose of potlatch dancing from the native community. Until this time, the dances were performed and witnesses paid solely as a means to display and to legitimize the prerogatives of chiefly families. Sewid eventually worked closely with other prominent men like Willie Seaweed, Tom Dawson, Herbert Johnson, Harry Mountain, Mungo and Spruce Martin, Billy Wilson, Herbert Martin, Dan Cranmer, Sandy Willie, Joe Johnny, Tom Hunt, Herbert Cook, Ed Whannock, and others who also became convinced that this new type of event would serve the community and highlight the native contribution (Spradley 1969; Holm, Jan. 24, 1994: letter). It should be noted that these men came together in an unprecedented manner from the different Kwakw<u>a</u>ka'wakw tribes, which traditionally displayed their prerogatives as exclusive and discrete. Now they were organized for the good of the entire Kwakw<u>a</u>ka'wakw community.

William Scow, the president of the Native Brotherhood, acted as master of ceremonies for this fundraising event and eventually for several other dances like it.[10] Scow's new role was adapted by this group of native stagewrights for the interpretation of these proceedings to what was largely a non-native audience. On

May 24 and 25, 1951, according to *The Pioneer Journal* (May 30, 1951: 1), the local newspaper, this crowd was packed into the community hall. Scow introduced the performances, referring to them as a form of diversion practiced by his forebears. He announced that "This was the Indian culture the way they entertained themselves and forgot their cares on the long winter evenings before the white man came." He also went on to explain the behavior of the *hamat'sa,* the unruly performer who was inspired by the Cannibal Spirit to search high and low for his "food." The dance, performed by Herbert Martin and Charlie Matilpi on this occasion, was explained simply as a device used in days gone by to frighten the children as a way of making them obedient.

The newspaper account also played down the more intimidating aspects of the famous *hamat'sa* dances, distancing the native participants from the more threatening or antisocial aspects of the "man-eater's" performance as it had been known at fairs and expositions at the turn of the century. Historically, the violence of the dance had been very closely associated with the Kwakw<u>a</u>'wakw potlatch, until recently legally denied them by Canadian law. Instead, these performances were introduced as simple "diversion," an interpretation guided by native petitioners for rights in their dealings with outside authorities since the end of the nineteenth century (Cole and Chaikin 1990: 27). Dan Cranmer made sure to explain in his speech to the crowd, for instance, that "they were just playing." (*Pioneer Journal,* May 30, 1951: 1).[11]

The 1951 performance was constructed to center instead upon the grace and artistic qualities of what appears to have been an *atla<u>k</u>im,* or Dance of the Animal Kingdom:

> Trained ballet dancers or adagio dancers with their names in lights and their praises in press notices could not thrill us more than Billy Wilson's portrayal of the grouse as he danced and swayed around the simulated log fire in the middle of the hall and literally flew to the entrance to admit another bird or animal. (Ibid.)

A *tuxw'id* dancer also conjured up a war canoe that evening, and Willie Seaweed and Dan Cranmer had a great time presenting what was termed a "comedy routine," pretending to be in a boat lost in the fog. The entire production was a big hit in Alert Bay, and more than nine hundred dollars was raised for the hospital.[12]

On May 23, the success of the Indian dances was announced with pleasure in *The Pioneer Journal*:

> These are all indications of the way in which *our* [emphasis added]

Indian people are taking on responsibilities not only in their own affairs but also in the community around them. Indian leaders across
Canada have agitated for a long time for changes in the Indian Act that
would release them from their dependence on a paternal government,
and our Coast Indians, through their organizations [like] the Native
Brotherhood of B.C., have been in the fore front of this fight. This year,
when Bill 79 is passed in Ottawa they will see some results for their efforts. . . . they are moving toward the administration of their own affairs.
(May 23, 1951: 1–2)

Here the display of native art was associated with efficient organization and
skill, qualities linked with civic responsibility. The success of the event was considered an indication of the ability of these Kwakwa̱ka̱'wakw people to function
productively in a larger sphere. Consequently outsiders began to think it was appropriate that some native rights be restored.

James Sewid remained the chairman of the Hospital Week Committee for
three consecutive years. In 1952, his second dance production was specifically
directed to raise funds for new X-ray equipment for St. George's. Sewid with
William Scow, who was again the official master of ceremonies, now expertly
provided running commentary, interpreting the dances for the white and native
audience in English. Willie Seaweed performed again that year, appearing first as
a Grizzly Bear dancer and then as what the newspaper called the Cannibal. Four
maskers appeared following his section of the dance, one was called a Heron. This
was probably a *hamat'sa* dance, based upon the appearance of the man-eater and
characteristic call of the long-beaked bird.[13] Although considered suitable for
outsiders at this event, this presentation of the cannibal dance was not described
in detail in the public account (*Pioneer Journal*, May 22, 1952: 2).

A striking display of one woman's *tuxw'id* privileges was more prominently
featured at that event. The chiefs were asked to feign the bludgeoning of the female dancer so that she might demonstrate her supernatural ability to come back
to life. The first men who were asked to perform the deed backed off, handing the
undesirable job along from one man to another. Ed Whannock would have liked
to accommodate the woman but said that he "was afraid that the R.C.M.P. [Royal
Canadian Mounted Police] would get him." Chief Herbert Johnson finally gave
in, saying that he "had reached the age of 70 without being prosecuted but there
must at last come the time when he cannot avoid it" (ibid.). Here the chiefs
seemed to have a wonderful time, making light, in public, of past interferences of
the Canadian authorities with their dance practices. I believe that they were also
alluding to the very serious consequences, approximately thirty years earlier, of
Dan Cranmer's famous potlatch. Some participants at that event were arrested,

and this was very serious business to the Kwakw<u>a</u>ka'wakw. But in 1952, amiable relations with the Canadian government were highlighted instead and again implied when the entertainments of the week closed with the singing of "O Canada" by Chief Johnson (*Pioneer Journal*, May 28, 1952). Once again, the Indian Dances of Alert Bay were framed simply and positively as a successful adjunct to the many other Victoria Day Celebrations usually held in Canada at the end of May.

Over the next decade, native performances became de rigueur for the celebration of various community events. In the spring of 1958, *The Pioneer Journal* (April 30) gave an account of costumed native dancers assembled for the Alert Bay Centennial Celebrations. Ceremonies were also designed to welcome the Union Steamship *Catala* back into service that year. At those festivities William Scow spoke about the role that the ship had played in the early progress of isolated Indian communities (*Pioneer Journal*, May 28, 1958: 1).

By 1958, the Kwakw<u>a</u>ka'wakw of Alert Bay had developed distinct ideas about the proper presentation of authentic native life to non-native audiences. They had chosen to "historify" certain elements of their own dances for the Indian Celebrations, events held in Victoria on June 21 at Thunderbird Park. By doing so they distanced their own modern identity, to some extent, from the "picturesque" arts practiced by their ancestors. For instance, no fixtures of modern life were permitted to undermine the authenticity of the morning parade in which an "Indian Princess" was transported by four bearers in a sedan-type chair. No cars were included in the procession, and participants were asked to conceal their modern clothes under button blankets and other native costumes. Elders were asked to search their attics and basements for the masks and regalia of "by-gone ceremonial dances," and among the amusing activities of the day, *The Pioneer Journal* (June 11 and June 25) described an Indian version of a game, compared in the press to baseball, that was supposedly played many years ago.

Selections called "happy dances," that included a Peace or Feather Dance, adapted from the *tła's<u>a</u>la* section of the traditional potlatch, were also displayed that year to Princess Margaret of Britain, who was visiting Courtenay at that time. James Sewid and Reg Cook presented her with two totem poles on behalf of the Native Brotherhood and "all the Coast Indians." Dr. Peter Kelly, a Haida leader active in the Native Brotherhood (Cole and Chaikin 1990: 165), was present as the keynote speaker for this event. He thought it significant to observe that the Coastal Indians had "proved their loyalty to the crown in two world wars" (*Pioneer Journal*, July 16, 1958: 1). Progress, loyalty, creativity, contentment, and public service were the qualities of Kwakw<u>a</u>ka'wakw life extolled most often in the public record during this period. In addition, their identity as a group capable of effective team efforts was put forward once again. For these public events, the tribal identities of the various subgroups or individual chiefs were not announced.

By the time Queen Elizabeth and Prince Phillip visited Nanaimo in 1959, James Sewid and Herb Cook were experienced hands at organizing representative displays of Indian culture to outsiders. Sixty-five dancers and ten singers were assembled for the trip down-island, and they rehearsed frequently to polish up their presentation before they left Alert Bay. The older people trained the young ones, who had little experience in the art form (Agnes Cranmer, June 23, 1993: interview; Spradley 1969: 209). Sewid insisted that the group present itself properly again, telling them that "if they didn't have any regalia they weren't going to go down. We were going to provide transportation for them but we weren't going to have them go down to Nanaimo as white men" (Spradley 1969: 209).

More than 1000 people gathered to see these ceremonies presented by the various native tribes of Vancouver Island. A large field in Nanaimo had been transformed into what was called a replicated Indian village, which included a "simulated 'long house'." Arts and crafts were demonstrated, most notably by Mungo Martin, who carved a totem pole at the site. Some native groups demonstrated basketmaking, and the Cowichan people knitted sweaters. After various speeches, one an address of welcome by James Sewid (*Pioneer Journal*, Dec. 31, 1959: photo caption), the Kwakwaka'wakw representatives performed their *hamat'sa* dance from the *t'seka* or red cedar bark series as well as a Feather Dance for "peace" from the *tła'sala* (Spradley 1969: 209–10; *Pioneer Journal*, June 24, 1959: 1). Representative selections from both of these sections of the potlatch had, by this time, become routine in performances for entertainment.

These opportune demonstrations of traditional arts were delivered along with a clear and public statement of the intent to obtain native rights. In their speechmaking before the Queen, the chiefs, as interpreted in English by Herbert Cook, took the opportunity to mention the impending journey of Robert Clifton, then president of the Native Brotherhood, and Peter Kelly, chairman of the Legislative Committee, to Ottawa. These two men would present a brief to the Committee on Indian Affairs, "laying out the rights and privileges that they expected from the government" (*Pioneer Journal*, June 24, 1959: 1–2). It seems that all of the events of the day were perceived as an effective and cooperative effort by the natives of the province. The entire production, speeches included, was well received by the audience and in the press. Just a year later the native people of Canada, now known for their artistic talents and industrious participation in such important public events, were awarded the right to vote in federal elections (Spradley 1969: 210).

As displays of traditional life and social dancing became established art forms, the "cultural activists" of Alert Bay went on to recognize the potential that existed to earn tourist dollars as a local industry and concurrently to preserve their artistic traditions. In 1963, the 'Namgis Village council set aside some land near their ball field for the construction of a traditional style "big house" where potlatches, public presentations, and the sale of native crafts could take place on a regular basis. The Kwakwala Arts and Crafts Organization[14] was established to coordinate this project and to regulate future representations of Kwakw<u>a</u>ka'wakw culture (see Plate 9).[15] Residents of native descent were recruited for membership in this group and asked to contribute a one-dollar fee. James Sewid, again at the center of an ambitious community project, composed a letter inviting all the different tribes to participate. Again a group effort was called for to promote Kwakw<u>a</u>ka'wakw arts and direct them to benefit the native community. Sewid's letter appealed to potential members and recommended that they establish collective ownership of their cultural tradition and their sole right to authorize its formal expression in the public domain. He wrote to the chief councillors:

> If we do not take a firm stand now, we shall lose our dances, carvings, etc. to the non-Indians as well as to the other Nations. These people know the great demand and value of our Arts for they have already begun to learn and produce them. These are ours and our people should be the people to benefit from them. Let us not lose our Arts like we did our lands, for if we do we shall regret it. (ibid.: 241–42)

The Kwak̓wala Arts and Crafts Organization went on to complete the "Community House" in 1965, which was inaugurated with a potlatch hosted by Chief James Knox of Fort Rupert. It officially opened, however, in 1966, on a date selected to coincide with the British Columbia Centennial Year when the lieutenant governor was due to return to the 'N<u>a</u>mg̱is band the rights to the Alert Bay foreshore. The successful conclusion of this suit to claim land had been under negotiation for some thirty years (ibid.: 245–56).

It is likely that the public face of these performances of the period, some of them described here, was constructed to be compatible with the broader political goals of this generation of Kwakw<u>a</u>ka'wakw people. The rhetoric that accompanied their performances continually alluded to the modern and hardworking ways of the native people of the Northwest Coast. Ceremonies were no longer presented as the exotic preoccupations of pagan Indians possessed by dangerous cannibal spirits. The dances were instead characterized as the harmless pastimes of days gone by, now comparable in their skilled execution to ballet and theater, the epitome of high culture in white society. The Indian dances were also frequently conflated with the national holidays celebrated by all citizens of Canada, some of whom responded with pride and admiration to the accomplishment of "their Indians." Some of these events were also eventually associated with highly charged political statements in which influential groups pointedly asserted their rights to land and to a public voice.

The big house, the site of many potlatches, also became the location of regular presentations of dance to the "summer visitors" or tourists, by the Kwak̕wala Arts and Crafts Organization with some assistance by the local board of trade.[16] Cruise ships were contacted, the *Princess Patricia* en route to Alaska in particular, and passengers were treated to quite a show. On board, they were offered a printed program for a fee of $1.75, illustrated with a Killerwhale crest by Henry Speck. This price included tickets for admission to the dances as well as convenient round-trip transportation between the big house and the dock (Agnes Cranmer and Ethel Alfred, June 23, 1993: interviews; Spradley 1969: 245, 253–58). The small pamphlet promised "a look into the past with authentic Indian dances and music of the Kwagutl Nation." It announced that visitors might expect to see selections from the Red Cedar Bark Dance, such as the "Nimpkish ('Na̱mgis) Dance of Welcome," the *hamat'sa* or Rebirth of Man, "Se-kwa-latl" or Paddle Dance, "Ya-wum" Ladies' Dance, "Na-na-la-latl" Swan Dance, "Mai-za-wi-su" Salmon Dance, "Ya-wi-le-nuk" Professional Dance, "Glu-gla-kwa-la" Wolf Dance, "Ma-dum" (now spelled *mada̱m*) from the sea or mountains, and the "Tuk-wid" or Retreat. Selections from the Feather Dance (*tła'sa̱la*) would also be included, beginning with the Chiefs' Dance and accompanied by the display of treasures received in marriage or as gifts from other native groups.[17]

Interestingly, some of the selections made by this heterogeneous and determined group, such as the *hamat'sa*, the Paddle Dance, the *mada̱m*, the Ladies' Professional Dance (in which women skillfully follow the changing beat of the music), and the Chiefs' Dances have become standard selections for public entertainment, and these were chosen for display at the *Chiefly Feasts* opening ceremonies (Figure 3.1). It is not surprising to find that several of the women active in the Kwak̕wala Arts and Crafts Organization, such as Agnes Cranmer, Ethel Alfred, and Margaret Cook, were also advisors and dancers in New York. Dora Sewid and Daisy Sewid Smith, the daughters of James and Flora Sewid, were also important *Chiefly Feasts* participants.[18] Although less celebrated in the literature, these women, from various tribes or bands and with considerable knowledge of Kwakwa̱ka̱'wakw tradition, had played a significant role in the organization of staged dances in Alert Bay.[19] They were among the decision-makers who instructed the young people in dance, were also tireless organizers of salmon barbecues, produced baskets that were offered for sale, and supervised the many essential details that accompany public performance.

In this light, the reference to tourist dances in Ethel Alfred's reply to that appreciative viewer of the *Chiefly Feasts* ceremonies (p. 87, above) takes on new meaning. The fundraising and tourist dances of Alert Bay at mid-century are legitimate antecedents to various contemporary native performances. Furthermore, just as the dances of the 1950s and 1960s were composed and presented in a manner consistent with the broader goals of that generation—to appear as a

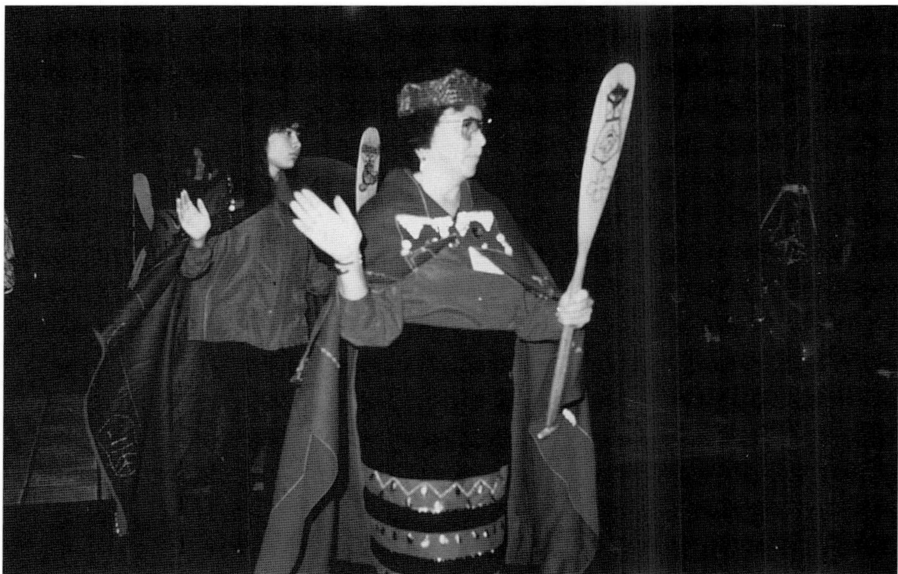

3.1 Irene Hayman leads a line of Paddle dancers at the Chiefly Feasts *opening ceremonies, 1991. Uncatalogued photograph, AMNH; courtesy Department of Library Services.*

group of cooperative citizens qualified to take charge of their own affairs—the present generation has adapted these historical precedents to construct displays of native identity according to their own up-to-date requirements.

Kwakwaka'wakw Response: What will count as ceremonialism?

The New York dance repertoire was designed entirely by Kwakwaka'wakw participants in 1991 at preperformance meetings in Alert Bay and in a hotel room in New York City. It may have been based in part upon earlier productions that originated in Alert Bay. Bill Cranmer, the master of ceremonies for *Chiefly Feasts*, has added that the program, like many other dances for outsiders, including those produced for tourists, was affected by its nature as a communally hosted event. He claims that the event, like many public presentations before it, was not designed to glorify the reputation of a single chief, as is customary at a potlatch, but was structured instead to meet a twentieth-century need, the public expression of a larger group identity. Performers had been assembled in New York from different families, each with their own prerogatives. These circumstances made standard dance selections more convenient and, I surmise, more diplomatic. According to Cranmer, certain dances are simple. Many people today know how to do Ladies' Dances and the Paddle Dance. Elaborate productions, however, like the Dance of the Animal Kingdom or the Undersea Kingdom, are owned by individual chiefs, and only large dance troupes exclusively composed of family members know exactly how to perform them.[20] They are usually performed to express prestigious and exclusive affiliations back home on the reserves. In New York, it was significant to the Kwakwa̲ka̲'wakw that the dances selected for display be legitimately claimed by at least one *Chiefly Feasts* guest, according to insider standards of propriety for such an occasion (Bill Cranmer, June 21, 1993: interview). It is interesting to observe the long-standing regard of the Kwakwa̲ka̲'wakw for some show of exclusivity in dance display, even when performances are constructed for non-natives. Bill Holm has noted that even Edward Curtis's famous photographic subjects "declined to perform dances to which they were not entitled or to distort them for the camera" (Holm 1977: 7; Curtis 1915: 155–243; reprint, 1973).

At the beginning of the opening ceremonies, on the morning of October 18, 1991, the delegation of Kwakwa̲ka̲'wakw visitors from Vancouver Island made their way by boat up the Hudson River. Singing and dancing, they arrived wrapped in the Chilkat robes and button blankets that bear the crests they are entitled to wear according to individual ancestry. At the 79th Street Boat Basin, Chief Adam Dick began by speaking in Kwak̓wala on behalf of all on board. He asked permission of a group of local native people from the American Indian Community House in lower Manhattan, also invited as honored guests to these festivities, to be allowed to come ashore. Chief Dick asked that the Kwakwa̲ka̲'wakw be permitted to "eat apples in your house," an imaginative reference to the New York territory as "Apple City" or the "Big Apple."[21] This invented introduction was based upon standard practice. Visitors approaching a village for a potlatch in the Northwest would also ask for permission to land, but using the nickname of the city, treated here as if it were its crest, was a playful approach and amused those "in the know."

Following a translation, the local native community greeted the Kwakwa̲ka̲'wakw and granted them permission to land on what had been called "their territory." Museum personnel, the general public, and the news media also welcomed the Northwest Coast visitors, and speeches were briefly made on the dock in their honor before the entire group moved on to the Hall of Ocean Life at the American Museum of Natural History. There speechmaking by both non-native hosts and native visitors continued, and much was made of the inestimable value of the legacy of George Hunt and Franz Boas, the collecting team that had assembled most of the Kwakwa̲ka̲'wakw art on display in the exhibition.

Mourning songs by three chiefs, singing in order of their relative rank

among the Kwakw**a**ka'wakw, opened the performance section of the program
(Figure 3.2).[22] A line of women sat still before them, just as they would have at a
potlatch, their eyes cast down, their features expressing concentration and an attitude of respect (Figure 3.3). Such a presentation would necessarily be greeted
with some puzzlement by a New York audience prepared for a dazzling theatrical
display, especially at the outset of the performance. This sequence was also the
longest section of the ceremonies, a telling choice by the native composers of the
event, many of whom are international travelers and all of whom own television
sets, which made them quite familiar with the conventions of non-native entertainment. It was outstanding for its gravity, length, and its lack of spectacle, when
evaluated from a non-native perspective.

Chiefly Feasts participants later explained why the prolonged mourning
songs were indispensable, even in this venue. They had been included to honor
the memories of important ancestors, those who had contributed to the preservation of artifacts in the AMNH collection. Tony Hunt commented, "We owe it
to those chiefs who went to jail . . . to make sure we never lose it. They paid the
price."[23] The chiefs that went to jail were those arrested following Dan Cranmer's
potlatch. Here the arrests were referred to gravely, an approach that was not yet
possible, or even desirable, in the Canadian performances of the 1950s.

Bill Cranmer also noted that "The events in New York were important because the old people worked hard to hold on to the culture and history. Also
George Hunt's work [was important . . . The ceremonies were] to recognize their
work and to put some life to these things that have been stored for such a long
time, these things that are a part of the *Chiefly Feasts* exhibit" (June 21, 1993: interview). It is important to understand that many of the New York dancers, including Bill Cranmer and Tony Hunt, are actually George Hunt's descendants,
which perhaps explains their particular desire to commemorate his contribution
and associate themselves with his well-known achievements. Although lengthy
and perhaps inexplicable to the many schoolchildren in the audience, this portion
of the performance was treated with respect and met with silence by all viewers.

These mourning ceremonies, the "wiping your eyes before you start things,"
was brought to a close when the women rose to their feet and "shook out the sadness" with the delicate hand gestures typical of Kwakw**a**ka'wakw female dancers.
Then George Hunt and Kevin Cranmer (respectively great-grandson and great-
great-grandson of Boas' colleague) commanded the attention of the large audience as *hamat'sa* dancers, followed by the appearance of two Cannibal Birds,
snapping their improbably long beaks and crying out for the hushed crowd. Then
the 'N**a**mgis Sea Monster dance was performed by Kevin Cranmer, who wore an
unusual mask carved by Tony Hunt Jr. (see Plate 10).[24] Its large eyes closed periodically, revealing copper lids, as the dancer paused dramatically at certain points

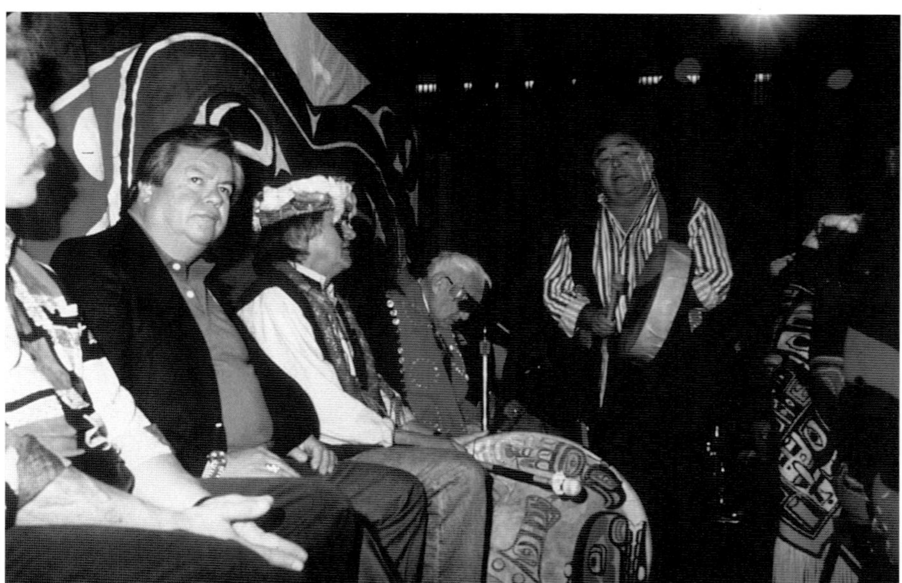

3.2 *Mourning songs at the* Chiefly Feasts *opening ceremonies, 1991. L. to r.: Art Thompson (in profile), Tony Hunt, Bill Cranmer, William Hunt, Adam Dick with drum. Uncatalogued photograph, AMNH; courtesy Department of Library Services.*

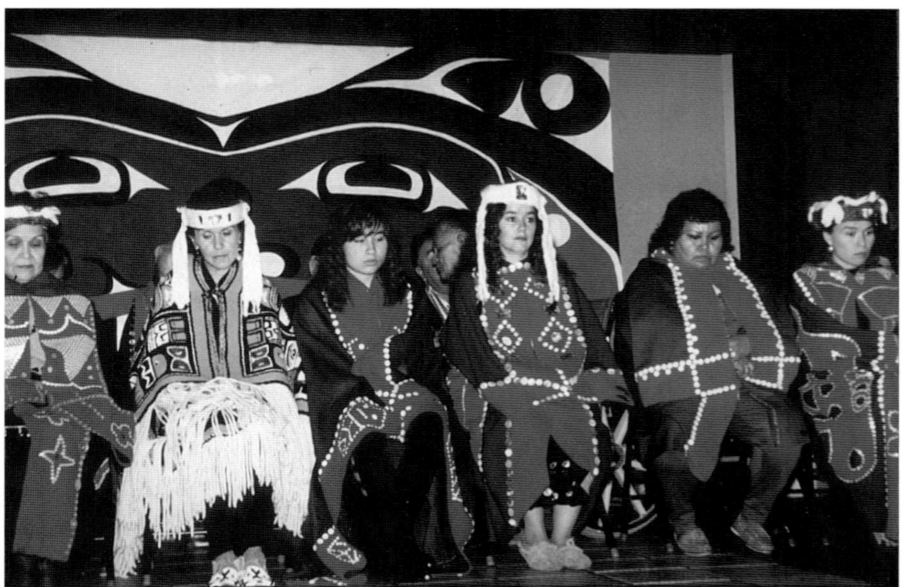

3.3 *Women seated for the mourning ceremonies at the* Chiefly Feasts *opening ceremonies, 1991. Uncatalogued photograph, AMNH; courtesy Department of Library Services.*

around the dance floor, just as he would in the corners of the big house. Then a hidden flashlight illuminated a large quartz crystal that had been fixed to the forehead area of the mask.

The women performed the Ladies' Professional Dance, demonstrating skill in adjusting their gestures and steps to the changing beat of the accompanying drum. Then came the Paddle Dance, with much whirling around the dance platform with painted paddles and the "bailing out" of an imaginary canoe with Dixie cups. Three young women displayed the quivering movements of the *mad<u>a</u>m*. With these dances the *t's<u>e</u>ka* section was completed, and the Kwagu'ł song to remove cedar bark was sung.

For the *tła's<u>a</u>la* portion of the performance, the chiefs, dressed in Chilkat blankets and ermine headdresses, performed the Peace, or Feather dance. Later one of the chiefs was heckled by an attendant, as is customary, causing him to leave the floor, to be replaced by a treasure or *długwe'*. The treasure was an Echo mask with changeable mouthpieces that were attached in turn, transforming the dancer into various animals, wolf and eagle among them, as was demonstrated by his appropriate gestures. Interestingly, this very mask, owned by Agnes Cranmer, had been used in some of the tourist performances staged in the 1960s by the Kwakwala Arts and Crafts Organization (Gloria Cranmer Webster, June 22, 1993: interview).

Closing speeches were accompanied by gift giving, by both visitors and host, and the proceedings ended with a so-called Fun dance, in this case one that had been given by the Nuu-chah-nulth to the Kwakw<u>a</u>ka'wakw, appropriately accompanied in song by Nuu-chah-nulth guest Art Thompson. Members of the audience, invited to get up and join in, filled the dance floor.

Just as the lengthy mourning songs had displayed the authority of the Kwakw<u>a</u>ka'wakw to compose the performance according to their own concerns, there were other indications that the ceremonies had been constructed to meet certain additional requirements of insiders. For example, performers expressed the necessity for the correct execution of their dances and songs. The regulation of performance as well as the policing of proper potlatch behavior has a very long history among the Kwakw<u>a</u>ka'wakw, and any mistakes must be acknowledged with the distribution of payment.[25] At the *Chiefly Feasts* ceremonies, this same concern was demonstrated in the form of a song, presented by Adam Dick and Bill Cranmer, thanking the Creator, that the *hamat'sa* ceremonies had been carried off without any mistakes or problems. By accomplishing this, the *Chiefly Feasts* exhibition was said to be "brought to life" (Bill Cranmer, June 21, 1993: interview).

According to Tony Hunt, accuracy in the speechmaking of chiefs, even in a museum context, is also crucial. Those who make mistakes demonstrate to other

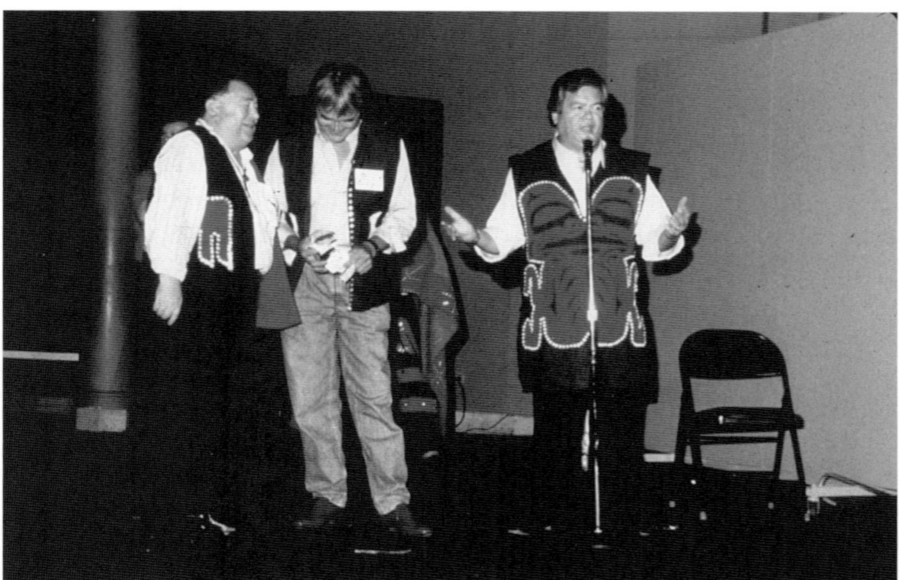

3.4 Tony Hunt speaking at the Chiefly Feasts *opening ceremonies, 1991. To his left are Adam Dick and Bill Cranmer. Uncatalogued photograph, AMNH; courtesy Department of Library Services.*

chiefs that "they don't really understand," a critical error for the bearer of oral tradition and for maintaining credibility within the Kwakw̲ak̲a'wakw community (June 8, 1993: interview). In his welcoming speech (Figure 3.4), Hunt had directed to those who understood the Kwak̓wala portion of his address the reminder that they "carry out tradition as it was set out in the past . . . to walk on the straight path of our ancestors so what we do is never lost."[26] Speakers at this event demonstrated their command of language and tradition to each other, but the importance of correct performance and public speaking was lost for the vast majority of outsiders, who conceived the formal speeches to be part of the customary prelude and closing to the "real entertainment."

The selective designation of these public speakers and the inclusion of other guests at this event may have been even more central to the concerns of the Kwakw̲ak̲a'wakw. Their sensitivity about appropriate and equitable representation, even before viewers incapable of discerning the individual identities and group affiliations of these people, was evident. These choices resonated in conversation among the Kwakw̲ak̲a'wakw tribes for some time beyond the events of the day. They serve as a strong indication that museum-sponsored events, even those that display unity to the public, confer some individual authority and support ongoing alliances.

Tony Hunt, for instance, in his presentation later the same week at the American Museum of Natural History for a symposium entitled *Tradition and Innovation in Northwest Coast Indian Art*, spoke of his own role in preserving Kwakw<u>a</u>k<u>a</u>'wakw tradition. He expressed significant disappointment, however, that many other great "artist-chiefs," those bound to resent such a slight, had not been included in the events of the week. As Hunt suggested, "The chiefs that own the pieces in *Chiefly Feasts* deserve better representation. There are knowledgeable people that will be speaking after I do. They will do justice to the exhibition but I think that the people that made those pieces and the people that are alive today should have been here to speak for them."[27]

Curator Aldona Jonaitis, also Vice President of Public Programs at the museum at the time, was advised by two exhibition consultants, Peter Macnair of the Royal British Columbia Museum and Kwakw<u>a</u>k<u>a</u>'wakw co-curator Gloria Cranmer Webster, to include specific dancers, speakers, and other Kwakw<u>a</u>k<u>a</u>'wakw guests in all of the opening festivities associated with the *Chiefly Feasts* exhibition. Earlier, in 1990, a team of elder advisors had been assembled for an initial visit to New York to offer their insight, during the research process, on artworks to be included in the exhibition. Selected by Jonaitis, Macnair, and Webster, this first set of guests represented the villages from which these artworks were collected. From the village of Fort Rupert, where many of these objects originated, Tony Hunt and George Hunt were invited to consult. Adam Dick represented Kingcome, Alice Smith came from Gilford Island, and Tom Willie and Elsie Williams traveled to New York from Hopetown (Jonaitis, May 4, 1995: interview).

When Jonaitis, Webster, and Macnair convened again to determine the guest list for the opening, they invited these elders who had consulted on the show and other direct contributors. Calvin Hunt, for example, the artist who had replicated two very old works of art for the exhibit, was invited to travel to New York. Jonaitis also hand-delivered invitations to leaders and chiefs of all the Kwakw<u>a</u>k<u>a</u>'wakw bands, and twenty of these individuals came to New York at their own expense, some raising funds for the trip by holding bingo games (ibid.).

These guests traveled far from home to be associated with this major public presentation of Kwakw<u>a</u>k<u>a</u>'wakw history. As previously mentioned, the Hunt family, including many descendants of George Hunt who now have different family names, took this opportunity to validate their prestigious affiliation with the American Museum of Natural History. Other guests wished to be present, and they too were included in this display of Kwakw<u>a</u>k<u>a</u>'wakw public image, as constructed for non-natives. Among these were Dora Sewid and Daisy Sewid Smith, both Lekwiltok Kwakw<u>a</u>k<u>a</u>'wakw from Cape Mudge. None of the pieces displayed in *Chiefly Feasts* had been collected from their home village, and therefore they had not been included in the original 1990 group of advisors.

James Clifford has written about certain past conflicts between the Cape Mudge visitors and the same Alert Bay group. The history of their differences of opinion is related to the correct public representation of the potlatch hosted by Dan Cranmer back in 1921. Again, participation in this potlatch resulted in the confiscation of important items of regalia by Canadian authorities. This historical event, significant for all of the Kwakw<u>a</u>ka'wakw, is still often cited, as indicated in this study, on public occasions. Most of the regalia was eventually repatriated through the hard work of active members of both the Alert Bay and Cape Mudge groups. Therefore, as Clifford has suggested, it would be misleading to overemphasize rivalry between them. In addition to the famous repatriation case, they share a long history of cooperation in regard to larger issues of Kwakw<u>a</u>ka'wakw identity and political activity (Clifford 1991: 246–47).

In traditional Kwakw<u>a</u>ka'wakw culture, both legitimate authority and any claim to correct the public record are expressed before an audience, through the right to tell stories and dance in honor of historical events. Perhaps the New York gathering served to transfer some contested aspects of Kwakw<u>a</u>ka'wakw position into the halls of a non-native institution. If so, it was carried out well below the surface of an event that seemed cohesive, at least to outside viewers uninformed about these issues. Greater rivalries might ordinarily be settled through the dynamics of potlatch protocol, ceremonial displays in Kwakw<u>a</u>ka'wakw territory. Here, at the American Museum of Natural History, the ceremonies were significant events, but despite possible undisclosed lobbying for appropriate representation, they did not constitute a true potlatch. Some "business" related to prestigious social position was conducted here, but it did not "go on the copper" or bring honor to any individual chief, nor was a copper's history or the story of a particular family the subject of oratory (Tony Hunt, Bill Cranmer, Gloria Cranmer Webster, Art Thompson, Ethel Alfred, 1993: interviews). Therefore, crucial payments to witnesses and various others, which validate the claims of such a host, were not strictly called for here.

Some privately owned dances and the masks that accompany them had been used for the ceremonies, however, and their owners individualized their contributions to these events by making small symbolic payments. The 'N<u>a</u>mgis Sea Monster Dance, for instance, is the property of the Cook family of Alert Bay, and young Sophie Cook, the current owner of this privilege, was asked to stand during that portion of the performance. Her grandmother, Mrs. Margaret Cook, had some crocheted doilies and "loonies" (Canadian dollars) distributed to certain guests to show her "good will" (Bill Cranmer, June 21, 1993: interview). Other cash payments, made so unobtrusively during the ceremonies that the average viewer might not have seen any money change hands, were made to the chiefs who sang mourning songs. Song leader Adam Dick also paid Gloria Cranmer Webster after she recounted the story of the 'Na̲mg̲is Sea Monster. These customary occasions of payment in traditional dance could not be completely omitted, even in a museum setting.

Dancing for Entertainment

Although they met certain ceremonial requirements, the *Chiefly Feasts* opening ceremonies were said to be constructed for entertainment. It may be helpful to compare this event and other historical productions prepared for "diversion" with the tradition known as the "play potlatch," recorded since Boas' time.[28] Like other dances organized for outsiders, these events were modeled upon the potlatch itself but were intended to amuse and educate the audience, rather than directly validate the rank of important participants. The term *gwomiasa*, used for the play potlatch, has been recorded in reference to the first potlatch once given for a child of aristocratic birth at the age of ten months; it is also called the ochre potlatch (Boas 1921: 994, 825, 1425; Codere 1956: 343).

Women also created events that mirrored the form of actual potlatches, and these too were called play potlatches. Humorous references, often made about the husbands of the participants, were a part of the festivities, and small gifts were distributed. Codere (1956: 343) published descriptions of the play potlatches of women, affairs that the men did not attend:

> The women had their own songs for it, and they took positions according to their husbands' positions and then proceeded to mock the business of singing insulting songs and giving insulting speeches while they distributed things like wooden dishes in the earlier days and similar types of manufactured items later . . . the insults were all for fun.

Play potlatches for boys, also modeled upon actual potlatches, were conducted with a more overtly businesslike intent. Charles Nowell suggested that they were "just like teaching us what we should do when we get grown up and give real potlatches." He also reported that competitive gift-giving, sometimes in the form of "little canoes," took place on these occasions, sometimes to set straight the quarrels of the boys, animosities that could otherwise last into adulthood (Ford 1941: 86). Important messages about public standing were thus conveyed, even while the guests enjoyed themselves.

As Bill Holm has written, these parodies of potlatch behavior—the taking of humorous names and the "burlesqued" speeches at play potlatches—were not meant for the legitimate or official display of privileges (Holm 1983: 32). Generally lighthearted events, they involved a wider participation, not quite so exclusive as displays of privilege at a potlatch. Tony Hunt explains: "Play potlatches are fun, but they get everybody involved. The potlatch is such a heavy, heavy statement. At play potlatches everybody dances whether they own that dance or not. It doesn't matter who makes speeches" (June 8, 1993: interview). These descriptions present the play potlatch as a time to enjoy oneself, perhaps with a less select group of players. It is also a time to practice or demonstrate the salient features of the art form.

A reference to this form of entertainment, then, may be helpful to contextualize an event like the *Chiefly Feasts* ceremonies. The dances were not supposed to validate the name of a single high-ranking host. They were intended to be diplomatic, a communally sponsored event requiring a public display of cooperation among various Kwakw<u>a</u>ka'wakw people from different families and villages. The program was meant to give the audience a good time, but it also provided an abbreviated model for idealized potlatch protocol to nonnative observers, functioning in a didactic manner for the public presentation of contemporary, and in this case unified, Kwakw<u>a</u>ka'wakw identity. For instance, the ceremonies showcased the persistence of traditional practice among living people, and like the productions of the 1950s and 1960s on Vancouver Island, the performers advertised their considerable abilities. Unfamiliar creatures such as sea monsters and Cannibal Birds as well as sedate and perhaps incomprehensible mourners demonstrated that native guests had the authority to compose their own display, without very much "creative control" by museum personnel. Through their speechmaking, the *Chiefly Feasts* dancers validated as well their claim to a direct line of cultural descent from the generation that had created the carvings and regalia that this institution exhibited.

Authenticity in Public Places

At this public event, a heterogeneous audience assembled with high expectations. Although these proceedings unfolded far from the big house of Alert Bay, observers were rewarded with the grand spectacle of Kwakw<u>a</u>ka'wakw theater. Yet they remained largely unaware of insider concerns—the issues of privilege, rank, and appropriate representation discussed here—the same motivating forces expressed through dance display in the nineteenth century. Native arbiters of form, by virtue of their participation, also implied their certification of these events. They produced a bona fide display of contemporary native identity for these spectators, not despite the precedent set by tourist dancing, but perhaps because of it. The ongoing challenge to assert competence and authority in the world beyond the home village has fostered a number of formal solutions in the course of the twentieth century, none of which may truly be considered "fictional."

The Kwakwaka'wakw continue to demonstrate the authenticity of their dances to the public by their conscientious orchestration of these events, and to one another by their continuing insistence upon the exclusivity of crest privilege display, the execution of proper form, appropriate oratory, and the desire to insert references to important ancestors. They continue to distribute small payments, symbolic of the legitimacy of many of their ceremonial acts, even before an audience unfamiliar with the conventions for such procedures. These productions also contain significant references to historical events and follow some conventions established by culture-bearers of the recent past. Embedded within the cohesive display of group affiliation staged for outsiders, issues related to band membership and family privilege, which are central on the reserves, continue to operate "behind the scenes."

To mount a show that includes these elements in the late twentieth century, just a couple of miles from the home of the "Broadway show" and the Metropolitan Opera House, is a great challenge. These performers had a mandate to meet the requirements of tradition and to establish themselves, once again, as the appropriate arbiters of dance protocol, even in New York City. Interestingly, this generation, when invited to validate the undertakings of non-native institutions by their presence, still looks to historical precedent to inspire them and to verify the propriety of their performances.[29] Their most potent statement of identity may be even more closely associated however, with their sole authority to arbitrate necessary modifications, consistent with their own concerns, yet suitable to the constraints of venues so far from home.

False Cognates: Looking Backward at the Latest Thing in Contemporary Northwest Coast Art

IN A SHADOWED GLASS CASE of the Northwest Coast hall at the American Museum of Natural History, an intricately constructed wooden rattle from the Clayoquot tribe of the Nuu-chah-nulth people from the west coast of Vancouver Island has been installed for many years. Dozens of small flat fish are tied by raveled cords to this boxlike contraption, and set to jiggle and bob in bunches within gridded compartments that combine to resemble a cage or trap. This display is just one among many that may be viewed by visitors to the hall, who have a vast number of equally compelling discoveries to make in this room full of enigmatic treasures. Since 1988, however, the rattle has been singled out for special consideration; it was selected for illustration against a pristine white backdrop in Aldona Jonaitis' book *From the Land of the Totem Poles: The Northwest Coast Indian Art Collection at the American Museum of Natural History.*[1] Clearly silhouetted against the page, it may now be admired as much for its sculptural form as for its function as part of a complex of ceremonial devices once designed to attract salmon.[2] Like the Zande hunting net pointedly recontextualized to suggest a minimalist installation piece in the *Art/artifact* exhibition at the Center for African Art in New York (also in 1988), it may now be known by museum-goers and art book readers alike as a unique object with considerable visual appeal.[3]

Back on the Northwest Coast, the rattle has also received new attention, although here it is not so highly individualized. During the last couple of years, several new versions of the rattle—quite similar but not identical to the nineteenth-century piece—have been created by contemporary native carvers for the art market and appear here and there in the art galleries of Victoria and Vancouver on pedestals, stands, and artfully suspended by monofilament in display windows. Beau Dick, a Kwakwa̱ka̱'wakw artist, Art Thompson of the Nuu-chah-

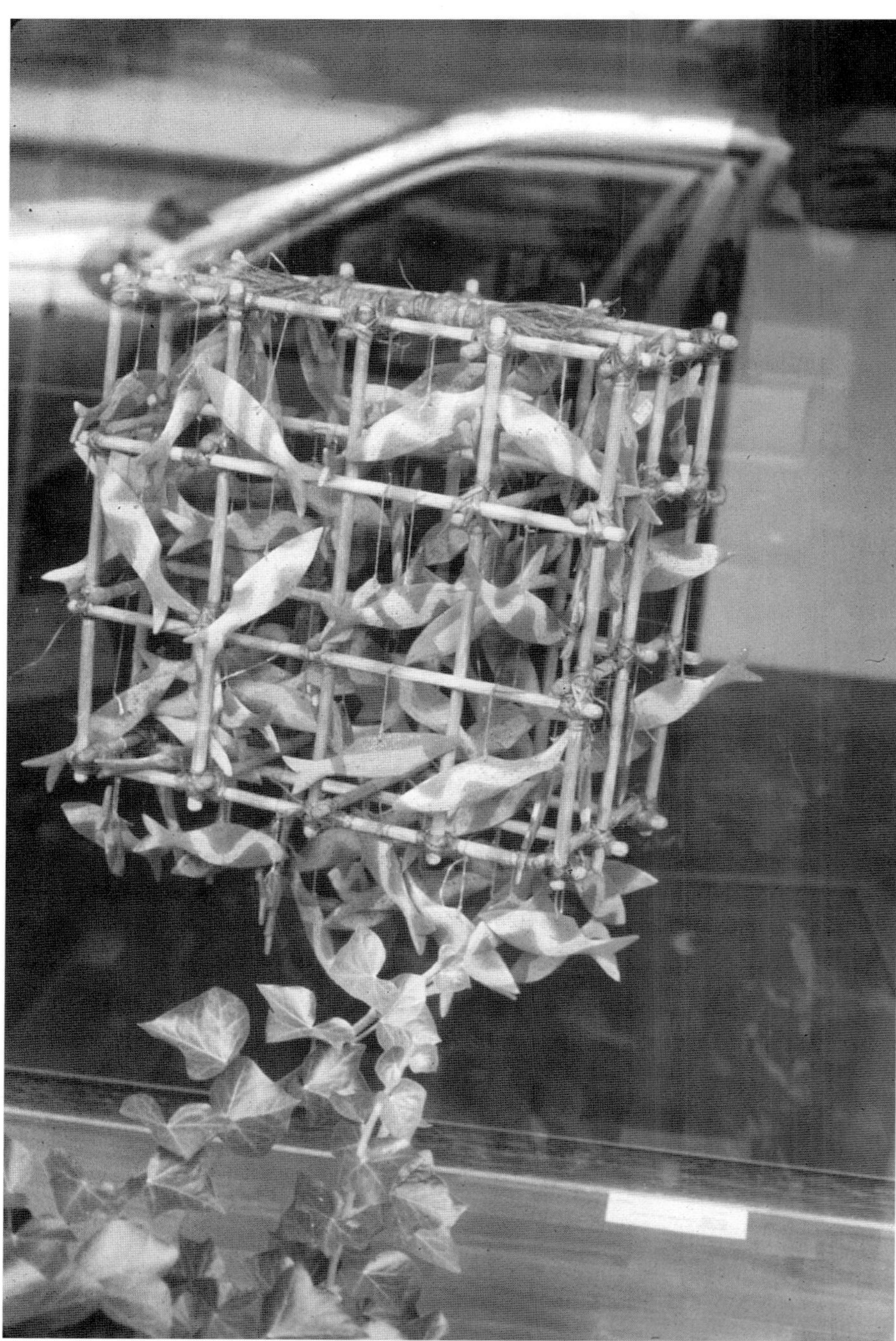

4.1 *Rattle by Beau Dick, c. 1991. Photo: Judith Ostrowitz; courtesy Beau Dick.*

nulth Ditidaht tribe, and Matthew Esquega an Ojibway (not a Northwest Coast group) are among those artists who have produced creative translations of this work, ranging from near-replicas of the old rattle to oversized take-offs decorated with metallic glitter (Figure 4.1). The origin of these carved works, derived from an example of native art in a major museum collection, may in fact enhance their "authenticity" and increase their value in the marketplace. One gallery director implied as much when I, as a former AMNH employee, was invited informally to verify the origin of this rattle design for potential buyers.[4]

This phenomenon, the adaptation of imagery from Northwest Coast art of the nineteenth century by contemporary native artists, was first noted by Margaret Blackman (1982, 1990). It has been facilitated by the publication of many illustrated volumes on native art—books that are found frequently on the shelves of carvers' studios all over British Columbia and Southeast Alaska. Indian artists consult these books and peruse major museum collections for ideas, although their new works are rarely, if ever, exact replicas of the old pieces. Now, in the 1990s, the ongoing success of this modus operandi is confirmed by the abundance of masks and other works of native art displayed in commercial galleries, their forms traceable to historical models.

A great many examples of these artworks that quote the past may be specifically named.[5] A Bella Coola (now Nuxalk) Sun mask collected in the nineteenth century, for instance, with rays in the filigreed form of stiff-fingered hands, was illustrated on the cover of Jonaitis' 1988 book and has since inspired several new works, including a close copy by Art Thompson[6] and a more fanciful "glowing" version by Glen Tallio (Plate 11). Tallio was born and raised in Bella Coola, B.C., and is a direct descendant of hereditary chiefs of South Bentinck and Nuxalk. He acquired his ability to create such airbrushed special effects, however, by painting novelty designs on cars (Glen Tallio, Mar. 23, 1993: interview). Similarly, an often-admired Octopus mask from the AMNH collection with expressive tentacles rigged to move like the limbs of a marionette (Jonaitis 1988: plate 76) was re-invented with great imagination by Kwakwaka'wakw carver Wayne Alfred (Plate 12). Alfred used flexible rubber tubing for the tentacles, which undulate appropriately if the mask is danced. Gene Brabant (of Cree descent, but highly trained in several Northwest Coast carving styles) and innumerable other carvers have created versions of a well-known *atlakim* grouse mask quite similar to the one attributed to Willie Seaweed in Audrey Hawthorn's *Kwakiutl Art* (1988: 136, Fig. 237). This type of mask may almost always be seen in the galleries and shops of the Northwest along with a ready supply of Gitakhanees masks, again inspired by illustrations in the Hawthorn book (pp. 226–30), with bright white faces and energetic feathered tufts springing from the center of their foreheads. Both Walter Cox (Kwakwaka'wakw) and Art Thompson (Nuu-chah-nulth) have carved new versions of another Sun mask from Kingcome Inlet; its dramatic semicircular superstructure unfolds when danced to become a series of rays that surround the face (ibid.: plate 23). Beau Dick has created a masterfully constructed Bear mask. Covered with real bear skin and provided with metal ball-shaped eyes, it resembles the very famous Nanya.ayí Tlingit Bear mask which, according to legend, is an "original" made from the skin of the creature that led that clan to safety from a primordial flood (see Plate 3).[7] Dick, like many other Northwest Coast artists, does not copy the old masks and other works that he sees in books. Instead he claims that he "gets a feeling, inspiration. It puts you in the mood that the older carvers were in. It puts you in their frame of mind" (Mar. 26, 1993: interview).

Countless examples of this phenomenon—the reproduction of antique form for the art market—could be mentioned. Interestingly, such works are also routinely produced for contemporary ceremonial life, as I will illustrate here. It has therefore become essential that the significance of this widespread practice, this seeming conservatism on the Northwest Coast, become the subject of greater analysis. The positive reception of these many near-replicas might easily be glossed as the overvaluation of a grander and longed-for past by both art audiences and potlatch practitioners alike. These products may be better understood, however, when they are specifically contextualized within the unique circumstances that affect their making and use as recreations of form and self, and thus deemed fit for specialized consumption.

This interpretive process must now be considered a cross-cultural project, not only because these objects have become a part of the non-native art environment, but because contemporary Indian artists are almost always quite familiar with international culture and art traditions. Some have traveled widely, visit museums and theaters, and regularly read specialized art publications. Those successful in the art market may spend part of their time in the cities of Victoria or Vancouver, returning periodically to the reserve for visits and ceremonial occasions. A few contemporary Northwest Coast artists have formal art school training as well. All of these artists, even those who stay closer to home, have substantial exposure to the media—television, movies, video games, newspapers, and even the World Wide Web. Thus we must understand that their choices are well informed and based upon a broader exposure to non-native art traditions than those known by artists of their parents' generation. The purposeful selection of historical subject matter by these artists, who may or may not wish to address a global art community, is therefore even more significant.

Most native artists are well aware that in the idiom of the West, replicas, or even artworks that more loosely quote the past, have until recently been characterized at best as reproductions and under some circumstances as fraudulent. Doug Cranmer quips, for instance, "All Northwest Coast artists do is make copies" (June 20, 1993: interview). Bill Reid, perhaps the most widely known Northwest Coast artist of his generation, called himself an "artifaker, meaning a creator of pastiches—pieces in nineteenth-century Haida style that are themselves originals" (Duffek 1986: 41). An aspect of modernist critical heritage that continues to affect non-native sensibilities, and apparently those of many native artists as well, insists upon a certain equation of new invention or unique artistic vision with authenticity. As a correlate, recreations imply some degradation of the tradition.

Curiously, the appropriation of historically based form has also emerged among the contemporary strategies of western artists. However, new works of postmodern art, recast in composite form from various art historical traditions, by the hands of highly individualistic white artists, are well received. Such works are indeed positioned by contemporary art audiences and the influential institutions that speak for them as original and crucial signs of the current moment.[8] But new works by native artists that draw from the past are certainly not viewed as such timely statements. Although encouraged through non-native patronage, they remain significant largely as the relics of vestigial ethnic groups.

These historical references, expressed by Indian artists through formal transcription, are very likely misapprehended by western audiences. Long-standing criteria established for the derogation of "copies," an art practice that appears to be similar to this Northwest Coast phenomenon, may be misapplied. This type of speculation on the significance of works that refer to past form results in their being categorized as "false cognates." They may be imagined as being discontinuous with cultural dialogue, or mere curios, historical documents disengaged from the circumstances of modern life. This native art practice derives from enduring historical precedent; however, it survives tenaciously because it is a part of contemporary life, both in ceremonial practice on the reserves as well as through the exigencies of the current art market. Northwest Coast artists do not apply these historical citations in either a random or uniform manner, but align themselves in a variety of ways with issues of local, and on rare occasions, global importance, as will be described here. Yet the apprehension of these practices as homogenous and antiquated contributes to the circumscription of Indian art as a phenomenon peripheral to the concerns of the "art world."[9]

Therefore these postcolonial artists on the Northwest Coast, who are generally encouraged by the art market and by non-native scholarship that identifies them by means of their heritage, are nonetheless excluded from contemporary art discourse. They appear to converse in an idiom that is timeless, at least to the untutored eye. Their works, currently on view in museums, art galleries, through the printed media, and in film, are considered perennially premodern and imagined as static in an international art environment driven by invention. This "art world" continues to define the concerns of these artists as incidental to the life of the mainstream and excludes them from participation in centers of cultural power.

The Discourse of Originality

The pervasive celebration of originality in western art, signaled by considerable praise for invention, some tolerance for the eccentricities of the avant-garde, and the continuing glorification of highly individual "artist-personalities," is a feature of the modernist's belief in the certainty of progress. Frederic Jameson (1991: *xi*) has observed that the modern notion of this advance may be characterized as one "in which each genuinely new work unexpectedly but logically outtrumped its predecessor." This conception of art history as a chain of inventions has also been effectively critiqued by Hans Belting (1987: 8ff) as a "single, unidirectional process" understood since the Renaissance by comparison with a biological model of "growth, maturity and decay," the apex of this cyclic movement corresponding with the designation of classic form.

Even the avant-garde, attempting to break with this inexorable stream of tradition and the delineation of canon, understood their unique alternate vision as the manner in which art was still to be brought forward, "paying for this privilege [ironically, a type of inclusion in a decision-making cultural elite] with the stigma of the outsider" (ibid.: 12–13). Consequently innovation through the hand of an inspired master (idiosyncratic but visionary) continues to suggest to modern audiences a sense of this advance, and therefore such individuals have been awarded great prominence as art professionals.

Our ongoing preoccupation with authorship and identity in art making, even as modernity is problematized, remains significant. Recently, in an acid test for unique vision, the work of contemporary white artist and master of marketing Mark Kostabi provoked considerable discourse among baffled audiences struggling with a continuing redefinition of both originality and artistic merit.

Kostabi, a young man of flamboyant personality, is said to "paint by proxy," hiring a team of assistants to execute his pieces at a factorylike workplace called "Kostabi World"—as did Warhol and other artists before him. Sometimes he goes a bit farther by having his employees develop concepts for new pieces, which he then legitimizes with his signature. Straining publicly and legally accepted standards of authenticity to the limit, Kostabi accused his former public relations agent, Andy Behrman, of profiting by the Kostabi example. He claims that Behrman applied forged Kostabi signatures to certain works executed in Kostabi style, which he then sold.

Issues raised by Kostabi's lawsuit challenge our regard for the "artist's hand" and suggest a breakdown in the romantic concept of this individuality that is believed to move history along. The case (or performance) resulted in some agitation among viewers. Paintings that include Kostabi's typical "generic figures" are easily replicated or "forged," but legal definitions are difficult to establish here when the artist himself paints placards with "Kostabisms" such as: "Most artists steal their ideas—I pay for mine," and "Amateurs Imitate Professionals Steal" (Kaplan 1994: 28–34).

In the case of this artist-performer, the trickster or provocative exception to modernist sensibilities, the propriety of the "readymade" is exceeded as the authorship of that appropriation becomes less individual and more difficult to establish. Traditional definitions of authenticity become largely detached from artistic vision in such instances, becoming instead a matter of recognizable personal identity. Value and the mark of the artist are then interchangeable, like the signature on a check, or the autograph of a movie star. The general public is offended by the Kostabi case because the idiosyncratic creation of form remains a sensitive subject for western audiences.

Ironically, many powerful individual creators of contemporary art now forage through the visual storehouse of the past or the characteristic images of other communities. Indeed, their familiarity with exotic images, including those from nonwestern cultures, may be associated with the timely pluralism of the postmodern agenda (see Jencks 1992: 11–12). A number of cases in point were on view in the exhibition *Magiciens de la Terre* in 1989, in which transcultural processes were celebrated. Although it was fascinating to see the works of African, Native American, and prominent European and American artists considered on common ground, this new "internationalism" actually obscured the major differences that account for the range of forms seen in these works. This exhibition's agenda was, in fact, comparable to the strategies used to put together the much-critiqued *'Primitivism' in 20th Century Art: Affinity of the Tribal and the Modern* show at the Museum of Modern Art, New York, in 1984. In any case, the wide-ranging appropriations and casual comparisons drawn among works in *Magiciens* certainly did not suggest that they were forgeries.

David Harvey has observed that the "active intervention" of such pioneering artists of postmodernism defines their undertaking, and these orchestrations of adapted imagery actually legitimize their projects. David Salle, for instance, is considered a leading American postmodern painter. One journalist, reflecting upon his work following an interview, astutely commented that Salle's "jarring juxtapositions of incongruous images and styles point up with special sharpness the paradox on which this art of appropriated matter is poised: its mysterious, almost preternatural appearance of originality" (Harvey 1990: 54–56; Malcolm 1994: 50–68). Such "archaeologists of the visual past" recast their finds outside the logic of chronological history, and through an intentional recycling of images assert their own identities, and most importantly, their unique authorship (Harvey 1990: 54–56).

Representation of past form among native people on the Northwest Coast does not usually signal a similar recontextualization or elevate their works to "the cutting edge." This is the case even when innovative touches—the introduction of enamel paint, the use of rubber tubing for tentacles, or the inclusion of tape recorded sound effects in dance performance—suggest formal invention. Instead, their recast images, both those conserved for ceremonial use and those created as prizes for the white collector, still speak for the most part to tradition and the continuing issue of crest prerogative, even when the constituency of the privileged group has changed over time. Yet formal variation of these privileged representations occurs, as will be noted, referring both to the artist's contemporary alliances with local traditional communities as well as to the complex of criteria established for contemporary art in the marketplace.

Postmodern appropriations by western artists do not often refer to similar matters of group affiliation. Instead they signal a certain discontinuity and the authority to establish the universal availability of all images for purposes of individual expression. The exclusive claim to legitimately represent key elements of the past as a sign of membership in a prestigious group is, however, the central concern of Northwest Coast native artists, at least according to ideal protocol. Therefore it is over this issue that cross-cultural dialogue fails, even in the most cosmopolitan of venues. In light of the ongoing association between the singular and the authoritative for white audiences, and more recently for art cognoscenti of native descent, how may Indian art that incorporates these references to older works, already valued by outsiders for their historical significance, be evaluated in a world of experiments conducted, for the most part, by contemporary non-native artists?

Locating the Individual in Native Art

Both art historians and anthropologists have made some efforts to reconcile modernist criteria for the identification of individual great artists and their unique masterworks with actual native art practice. Franz Boas in his 1927 work *Primitive Art*, for example, discussed at length the variations in form produced by non-western artists within the strictures of highly conventionalized art styles due to differences in technical skill and imagination:

> The highest type of artistic production is there, and its creator does not
> know whence it comes. It would be an error to assume that this attitude
> is absent among tribes whose artistic productions seem to us so much
> bound by a hard and fast style that there is little room for the expression
> of individual feeling and for the freedom of the creative genius. (155–56)

Boas explained that the mental operations and innermost thoughts and feelings of the individual were involved in this creative process and furthermore that they do not take place in "the full light of consciousness" (ibid.). Not surprisingly, Boas's student Ruth Bunzel, in her famous study of Pueblo pottery, took up the same theme, exploring the manner in which the "hands of gifted individuals" were capable of carrying traditional pottery styles forward. "Characteristic forms" by certain makers were, "with but few exceptions, entirely unconscious" (1929: 87). Interestingly, both analyses refer to unconscious forces, relying on some knowledge of psychology, a modernist's tool for interpretation which was used by these scholars to explain individuality. Processes associated with the intellect, however, long associated with non-native artist-personalities, were not discussed.

The characterization of these gifted individuals as outstanding "artist-geniuses" within native art traditions, and the relatively recent identification of masterpieces that can be attributed to their hands, may now be compared with the strategies of historians of western art. This interest in known personalities and questions of attribution, exemplified by the study of works by historical figures such as the Master of the St. Francis Cycle and the Master of Flemalle (now identified as Robert Campin), has recently been adapted to provide important data for nonwestern studies. Often a personal style rather than a signature, or a characteristic selection of subject matter configured in a particular way, identifies the work of these artists among extant artifacts. This level of connoisseurship has been cultivated in African art history, for instance, since the acknowledgment of a corpus of work produced by the "Buli Master" of the Baluba people by Olbrechts, another of Boas's students, in *Plastiek van Kongo* (1946). Perhaps the most notable research in this regard was carried out by William Fagg in reference to Yoruba art; he identified the hands of several master artists with descriptive names that reference their styles and frequently used subject matter, including The Master of the Aquiline Profiles and The Master of the Cascade Coiffures. Along with these identifications, Fagg was influential in contributing the idea of the individual African artist of note to a much larger discourse about nonwestern art history.[10]

Since the 1980s, groundbreaking studies by scholars of Northwest Coast art such as Bill Holm's *Smoky-Top: The Art and Times of Willie Seaweed* have also identified the unique styles of individuals of native North American descent. Peter Macnair of the Royal British Columbia Museum has said that Haida artist Charles Edenshaw created a "personal version of that tradition [which] because of its innovative qualities is difficult to compare . . . with that of his contemporaries and even his traditional forebears" (Jonaitis 1993: 11). Similarly, Steve Brown (1994, 1987) has isolated the unique hands of several outstanding Tlingit carvers, including one he has called the "Fort Wrangell Master." Robin Wright (1983, 1985, 1993) has also recognized the stylistic idiosyncrasies and configuration of particular creatures habitually represented by the provocatively named Master of the Long Fingers, a Haida carver of argillite who worked in the middle of the nineteenth century. More recently, Wright has identified the stylistic attributes of works by John Gwaytihl and Simeon Stilthda, also nineteenth-century Haida sculptors (1998: 42–57, 106–107). Today individual Northwest Coast artists of renown are featured in solo art exhibitions. The Vancouver Art Gallery, for instance, first assembled *Bill Reid—A Retrospective Exhibition* in 1974, and has updated its focus on the individual Indian artist of note with the installation of Robert Davidson's show *Eagle of the Dawn* in 1993. Other prestigious exhibitions are sure to follow. These non-native interventions have been motivated by the desire to further distinguish native tradition, but according to the criteria of outsiders.

This sympathetic application of the European art historical project to non-western art, the identification of superior vision and ability, may be useful in establishing discrete markets for non-western art and for the application of accustomed scholarly processes. It may not serve us well enough, however. For example, it may not be helpful in properly contextualizing recent developments in the appearance and function of contemporary native Northwest Coast works—either those carved for the art market or those created for traditional ceremony—as they are understood by Indian artists and audiences.

On the Transpersonal: The Social History of Replicas

For the casual viewer, elements of personal style remain difficult to discern in contemporary works of Northwest Coast native art. Even connoisseurs, more familiar with the conventions of tradition, regional style, and the characteristic approaches of individual artists, will note frequent repetition and be able to recall some of the historical pieces that new works are modeled upon. The existence of works in such "series," then, may encode some indispensable information more central than the delineation of unique authorship. In commercial works, the relationships among these pieces may even function as a type of "subtext," or as the purposeful allusion to the works of known artists of the past as well as to important pieces from major museum collections. This may enhance their significance and therefore their value to informed buyers. Certainly the artists themselves are aware of these references to the lineage of their works. Kevin Cranmer, a Kwakwaka'wakw artist, for instance, remarked to me on the relationship between his recently carved Sea Monster mask (Fig. 4.2), displayed in a prestigious Victoria art gallery, to one carved just a couple of years earlier by Tony Hunt Jr. that had been danced on the occasion of the *Chiefly Feasts* opening ceremonies (see Plate 10). Cranmer's mask is by no means identical to Hunt's, but it does in-

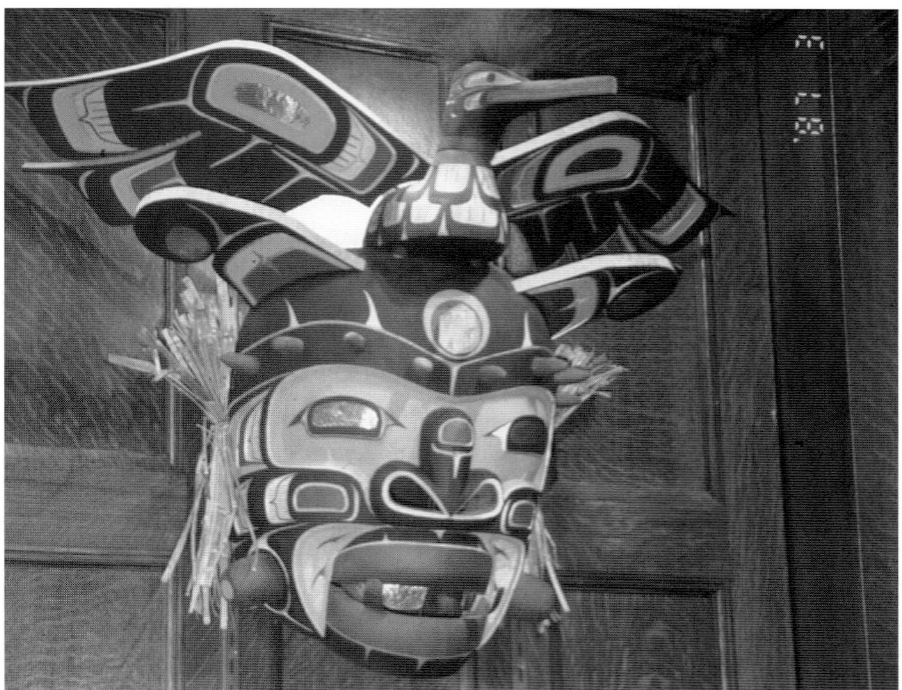

4.2 Sea Monster mask by Kevin Cranmer, c. 1992. Photo: Judith Ostrowitz; courtesy Kevin Cranmer.

clude a large quartz crystal embedded in the forehead area and certain other conventionalized elements that refer to this same creature. Sophie Cook, in turn, who owns the contemporary right to show this mask in ceremony, has commented to me that Hunt's mask itself is based on another very old Sea Monster mask, now on display at the RBCM, though she confided that it does not look all that similar (Kevin Cranmer, June 9, 1993; Sophie Cook, Oct. 1991: interviews).

This phenomenon of lineage, commonly observed in the galleries of the Northwest Coast, might be profitably compared with the "reuse of antiquity" as discussed by David Lowenthal (1985: 81, *xx*) for Renaissance artists and their high regard for the selective reworking of classical works: "The Renaissance painter or poet advertised his derivations from classical sources while consciously distancing himself from them, making the reader or viewer notice both his allusions to the past and his departures from it."

Contemporary Northwest Coast artists also make references to both the recent past and antiquity, while making their own adjustments in a manner that may only be noticed by those "in the know." This fosters an exclusive dialogue among themselves as well as with knowledgeable collectors and scholars in reference to the tradition as a whole, and in a lesser manner to their own authorship of contemporary pieces. The appearance of these carvings in the galleries are thus well-considered and astutely tailored, not just a matter of mindless repetition. Their particular subject matter has usually been selected and their forms elaborated to command both admiration among knowledgeable viewers and the highest prices in the marketplace, just as many non-native works of art are composed. This is accomplished both through references to history as well as to the contemporary social life of native people.

Contemporary appropriations by these same Northwest Coast artists for ceremonial use are just as selective. They are similarly modified and updated, just like the examples in the galleries, but their altered forms are not primarily constructed to recall the hands of their makers. Neither do these formal changes, composed to be stylish and impressive to a broad audience, suggest any definite changes in their meaning. Their significance in ceremony is affected to a much greater extent by the highly select context of their use, as props to support an individual or family claim to a dance privilege that must be publicly confirmed from time to time. They are meant to update the relationships said to persist between contemporary people and their ancestors. Visual affinity, or their resemblance to older artworks, is one manner in which this relationship to the past may be quoted and affirmed. More central to native concepts of historical accuracy, however, is the legitimately inherited and exclusive right to display some version of an old image, which must still be publicly validated on the Northwest Coast. The venue for such displays has traditionally been the potlatch, but other, less formal opportunities to claim high position and access to important works of art may now take place in new environments, under the aegis of non-native observers.

This point is well illustrated by the recent history or "cultural biography"[11] of a replicated Kwakw<u>a</u>ka'wakw painted screen, the various generations of its form adapted from a nineteenth-century dance apparatus in the collection of the American Museum of Natural History.[12] The old screen, from New Vancouver, is made up of two major components (Figure 4.3). One is a simple strip of cloth supported by wooden slats inserted at intervals. Its surface is painted with a series of conventionalized animal faces and paws or claws, all placed so closely together that they are difficult to distinguish as those of discrete creatures. The other major portion of this assemblage is also a screen of sorts, with a human figure on top. Its trunk and legs are painted on cloth, but its head, moveable arms, and two articulated dorsal fins above the shoulders are carved from wood and painted. The figure surmounts two square sections of cloth with conventionalized faces painted inside them, as if in boxes. This second major section is cur-

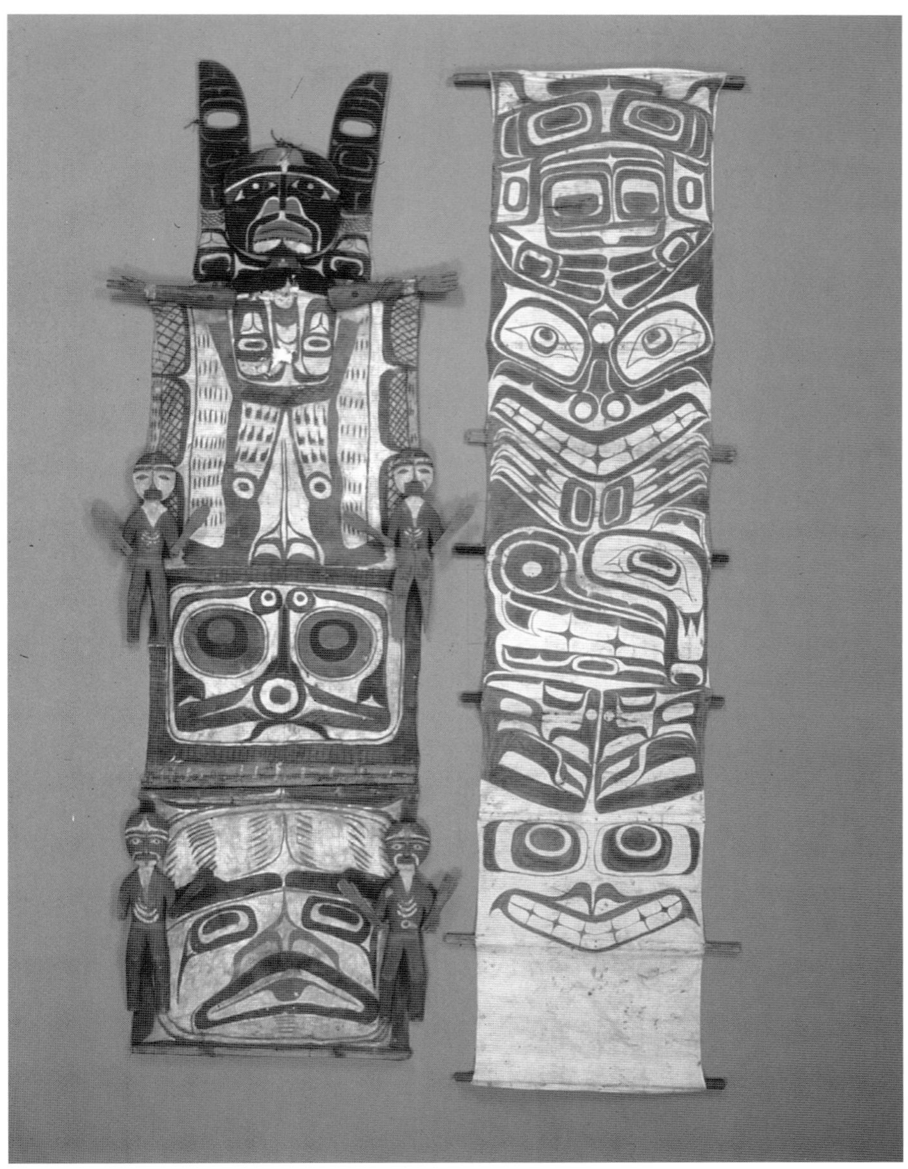

4.3 Kwakw<u>a</u>ka'wakw dance screen. New Vancouver. Cloth, wood, paint. H: 523 cm. W: 165 cm. AMNH 16/9584AL, neg. 4506; courtesy Department of Library Services.

rently configured so that four man-shaped puppets, arranged in two pairs, flank its sides. Certain stylistic differences among the various sections of this ensemble, however, and patterns of wear throughout the entire piece suggest that this work may originally have been intended for use in separate segments. In addition, the wooden figures or puppets appear to have been nailed to the screen at some point after the original construction of this work, perhaps after it was collected for the museum.[13]

Photographs and then the work itself, arranged in this provisional configuration, were submitted for the remarks of Kwakw<u>a</u>ka'wakw elders who were assembled as advisors to Aldona Jonaitis and her staff in the process of research for the 1991 exhibition at the American Museum of Natural History, *Chiefly Feasts: The Enduring Kwakiutl Potlatch.* Although this physical object was claimed by no individual, both aspects of its appearance and its Kwakwala name, *nuɬami'sta yelxts!ayo* (a term that defies exact translation to date), recorded by hand in the 1904 field ledger of George Hunt, Franz Boas's colleague and the collector of this work in the field, elicited suggestions by these elders on its former function.

Mrs. Agnes Cranmer of Alert Bay recognized the words *nuɬami'sta yelxts!ayo* as the name of a particular dance privilege she claimed to have inherited as a young girl from her aunt, Mary Johnson, George Hunt's daughter. She, in turn, had inherited it from her own mother, a 'Nak'waxda'<u>x</u>w woman.[14] Mrs. Cranmer also suggested that the AMNH screens are similar to ones that she used in her dance. Her childhood performance began with the appearance of a female dancer dressed in a blanket and wearing a piece of cedar bark on top of her head. She was endowed with the special ability to "throw supernatural power," which affected the behavior of her audience in an amusing manner. Entering the ceremonial house and circling left, she paused at each of its four corners. Each time she stopped she threw an intangible substance from the folds of her blanket, which caused the seated spectators to laugh hysterically in one corner, hug each other in the next, and scratch at an intolerable itch in the third. They were unable to stop these reactions until, with another gesture of her hands, she "took that supernatural power back." In the fourth corner of the house, Mrs. Cranmer reported that the screen would unfurl, rising up behind the performer toward the roof of the house.[15]

In 1990, when the entire group of elder native advisors visited the American Museum, Mrs. Cranmer demonstrated her dance, with great humor and theatricality, in one of the storage sections of the building. Peter Macnair, escort for the advisors and exhibition consultant from the Royal British Columbia Museum, distributed dollar bills as payment to those who had witnessed this display as well as participated as supernaturally affected audience members. Though this gesture was just a parody of potlatch protocol, nonetheless it referred to Mrs. Cranmer's legitimate claim. No visitor publicly questioned her right to the dance. Very discreetly however, some of these advisors from other Kwakw<u>a</u>ka'wakw tribal divisions suggested that the museum's screen may once have been the treasure of another female dancer, called a *tuxw'id*, who also possesses supernatural abilities.[16]

At the same time, the integrity of the physical object, not just the appropriate designation of its function, was in question. The cloth sections of the screen had holes in them and looked as though they were about to give way completely. Museum conservators were hesitant to allow this set of objects to go on display in this condition. Therefore in 1990, Kwakw<u>a</u>ka'wakw artist Calvin Hunt (George Hunt's great-grandson) was hired by exhibition curator Jonaitis to replicate the old dance apparatus for public exhibition in the "Women in the Potlatch" section of *Chiefly Feasts.*

Hunt modeled his replica upon the museum's configuration of these pieces as they had been arranged by museum personnel in the past and set out on tables by AMNH conservator Judith Levinson (1992: interview). He traced the various sections on paper and brought his drawing home to Fort Rupert, British Columbia, where he completed the work. His new version of the *nułami'sta yelxts!ayo* (Figure 4.4), which arrived in New York some months later, is a crisply painted and masterfully rigged mechanism that is true to the form of the nineteenth-century piece, except in some minor details. One of the profile faces of a creature, perhaps a wolf, on the simpler cloth strip section is reversed, its snout facing right rather than left, as in the older version. In addition, larger sections of off-white canvas, which may be conceived of as the "background" of the piece, have been left intact, giving the finished product more structural integrity.[17]

This new work of art has become another link in what is probably a series of props constructed for use by various generations of Kwakw<u>a</u>ka'wakw dancers. The nineteenth-century version may itself be modeled upon earlier works, and each one of them would, in all probability, have been made a little differently than the one before it. None of them would be considered less useful in ceremony because they derived from an earlier model. Similarly, we have no reason to believe that the AMNH set of screens represents a fixed form to be copied or followed slavishly for all time. Neither should Calvin Hunt's rendition of the screens be conceived as the last of its line, nor should its form be thought to dictate the correct appearance of all versions to follow. In fact Tom Hunt, Calvin Hunt's nephew who worked at Calvin's carving studio, was immediately inspired to create a variation on his uncle's work.

Both Calvin Hunt and Mardonna Austin-McKillop of The Legacy Ltd. Gallery in Seattle, Washington, encouraged Tom, a talented young carver, to try his hand at creating yet another version of this unusual apparatus (Plate 13) (Tom

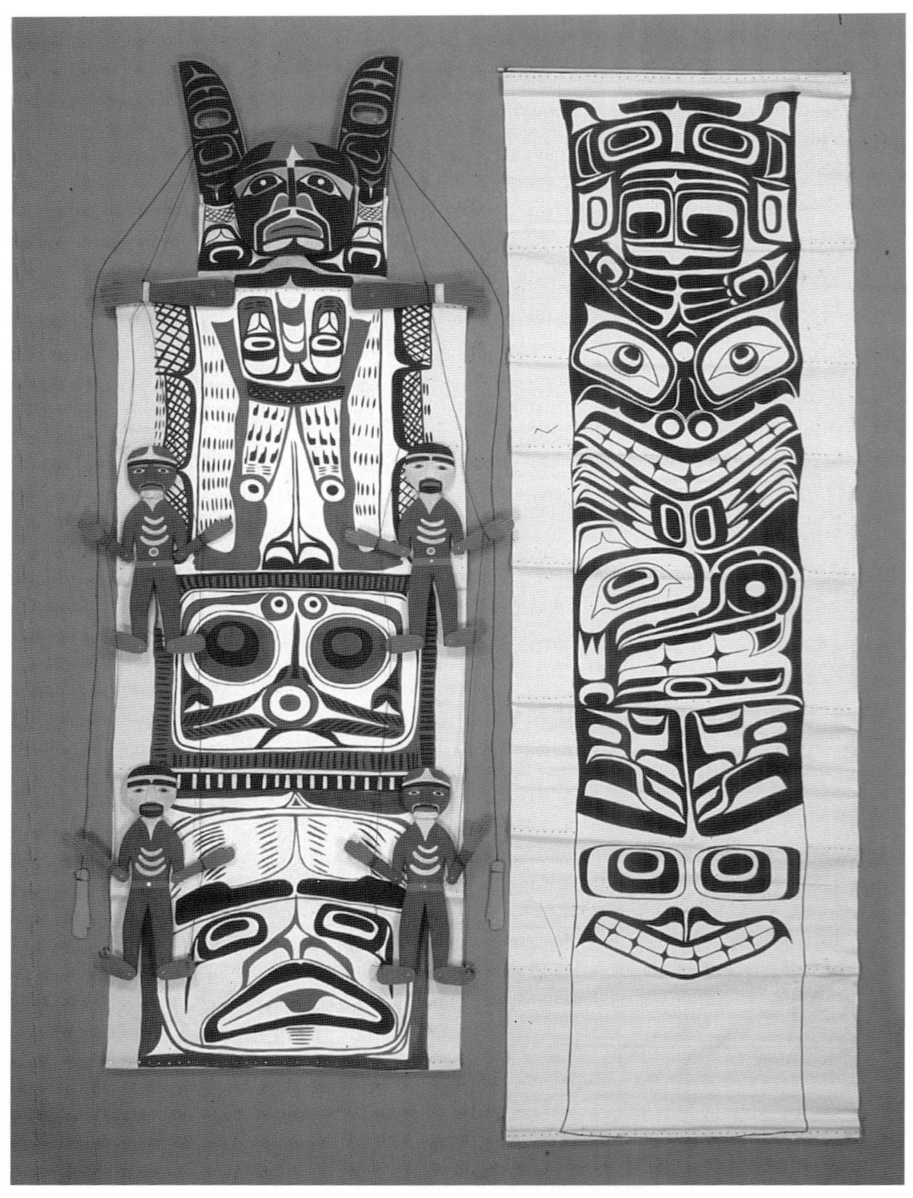

4.4 *Dance screen by Calvin Hunt, 1991. Cloth, wood, paint. H: 17 ft. 2 in. W: 5 ft. 5 in. AMNH 16.1/2630AB, neg. 4505; courtesy Calvin Hunt and Department of Library Services.*

Hunt, Sept. 1991; McKillop, Sept. 1991: interviews). He considers his version of the screen to be a similar "take off," not a replica of Calvin Hunt's piece. Tom understands his uncle's version to represent the mythological *sisiyutł*, a double-headed snake, but has translated the creature in his own work with the attributes of both a human being and a whale instead. He made this change because he thought that it would simplify the construction of the piece. Tom Hunt's polychrome version is also carved completely in cedar, not painted on cloth like the earlier examples, because of the durability of the wood. He has omitted the separate section with the graphic representation of animal heads and claws from the piece as well. Tom's version also varies from the older pieces by his inclusion of only two of the four puppet figures (Sept. 1991, interview). Ultimately, his unusual and striking piece was purchased by the Microsoft Corporation in Bellevue, Washington. In this case, it was not the crest image that remained stable over time, but aspects of the composition of the screen, a configuration that was perhaps invented at the American Museum of Natural History.

These modifications in the appearance of the dance prop were paralleled by repeated changes in its social function. Tom Hunt's grandmother, Mrs. Emma Hunt of Port Hardy, sang a *tuxw'id* song before the new sculpture at a reception in the Legacy Gallery in the fall of 1990 for the exhibition *To Dance*, associating its appearance with a dance privilege of her own. Simultaneously an attendant behind the screen pulled strings, causing the work to "come alive." The hands, feet, and dorsal fins became animated, and feathers were blown out through the creature's "blow hole." The sculpture and the song were so impressive that since that occasion, Mrs. Hunt had a new *tuxw'id*'s *długwe'* or "treasure" carved for some younger members of her family. It includes four puppets or "dolls like the ones carved by Calvin and Tommie," and she taught the younger women an accompanying dance to carry on the privilege and the visual legacy of the screen.[18]

The dynamic circumstances that influenced formal changes in these generations of the *nułami'sta yelxts!ayo* screens were accompanied by modifications in the social standing of certain Kwakwaka'wakw people displaying the accouterments of their rank on public occasions. These claims may have been accomplished at unusual locations and in collaboration with non-native patrons; nonetheless, each person associated with the screen made certain adjustments and subtle proclamations concerning their position in the Kwakwaka'wakw community. Different women, for example, have used a version of this object to affirm separate claims to dance prerogatives. More than one artist has established prestigious affiliations outside of the reserves—with museums, art galleries, and a major corporation—by carving or painting this image. Ultimately their claims may be questioned, as they were not validated at a potlatch, but not because they were accomplished with replicas or derivative works.

The reproduction of this screen, and its subsequent departure from its original representative function as an unspecified nineteenth-century dance prop, cannot be said to signal the end of its significance on the Northwest Coast. Instead, its replication under new circumstances has created a device for the renewal of its meaning. These "copies" function in contrast to the idealization of more "original" works by theorists such as Walter Benjamin. "Even the most perfect reproduction of a work of art," he argued, "is lacking in one element: its presence in time and space, its unique existence at the place where it happens to be" (1968: 220). These reproductions of the screen, certainly not true to the earliest known model and used in various unusual places and not where it originated, is an artistic phenomenon seen more and more frequently in the late twentieth century. Reproductions are commissioned in various new places as one consequence of the increasing interaction between native artists and non-native patrons, particularly in museum settings. As the requirements of outsiders continue to foster the revitalization of the artistic and ceremonial tradition, under unusual circumstances and in settings that demand considerable accommodations from all of the parties concerned, replicas become important adjuncts to the public statements and various assertions made by participants. This process of duplication may actually retrieve artworks from the decontextualization, the loss of the "first" symbolic order, posed by Jean Baudrillard (1983: 21).[19] It may instead be the well devised reworking of the symbolic order.

This is not a unique example of Northwest Coast art practice. Various generations of other carved and painted works, similarly related by crest or aspects of composition, have undoubtedly been reproduced over time to help demonstrate adjustments in the rank of their owners at potlatches. They too would have used whatever means were available to them to increase their reputations and spheres of influence. The study of such recreated works of art, each one just an installment in a series, remains difficult. Old pieces were discarded because they rarely survived repeated use and the moist climate of the Northwest Coast. Earlier versions may also have been given away to individuals in distant villages as gifts or sold to non-native collectors around the world. In any case, the historical relationship of these artworks to pieces made by preceding generations is not customarily a matter of record. Most significantly, the discovery of historically bound series is complicated by the appearance of the new "replacement pieces" themselves, which are not identical, as seen in the case of the painted screen, to their worn-out predecessors. As a result, important works of Northwest Coast art in museum collections are usually thought of as one-of-a-kind rather than new-generation pieces that build upon the prestige of earlier models.

In 1989 fortuitous research, again on the *Chiefly Feasts* artifacts, revealed another traceable link between two generations of Kwakwa̱ka̱'wakw artworks. Various consultants working on the exhibition recognized, through careful study of accession records, that a number of nineteenth-century masks and related artworks representing fantastic sea creatures had been collected, again by George Hunt under the direction of Franz Boas, as a set.[20] Hunt's field ledgers that record his acquisitions between 1901 and 1902 frequently refer to a being known as Nā'lanōkumē'g I lakwē ('Nalanukwame'gi'lakw) or Born-to-Be-Head-of-the-World, a title acquired by a boy whose original name, Siwidi (Paddled-to), was changed after he had been transformed by supernatural experiences (AMNH field ledgers Acc. no. 1901–32). These records were cross-referenced to manuscript pages later published as a story under the title "First-Beaver," from the traditions of the Gwawa̱'enux̱w people (Boas and Hunt 1906: 60–79).[21] These records confirmed that the set of masks, feast dishes, and other artifacts assembled by Hunt had probably been used at some point in the past to perform at a potlatch, demonstrating the dance privileges of the descendants of Siwidi.

To briefly summarize the native history: young Siwidi had angered his father by being lazy and not seeking out supernatural sources of wealth. "Oh Fool!" the father had abused him, "Don't think too much of sleeping. Look at your elder brother! He is all the time rubbing his body with hemlock branches" (a practice meant to prepare the young man for supernatural experiences). The young hero was shamed by his father's words and, contemplating suicide, he went off into the deep woods. Eventually he sat down on the shoreline of a lake where the waters rose mysteriously around him. A devilfish (the creature we know as an octopus) then appeared before him, and it grew and grew until it completely engulfed Siwidi, dragging him down to the fabulous house of K̲umugwe', the wealthy chief of the Undersea Kingdom. K̲umugwe' became the young man's benefactor, helping him visit the various tribes beneath the sea with the gift of a small canoe that transformed itself into a killerwhale and taught the boy how to spout water. This particular episode in the story is commemorated by a pair of Gwawa̱'enux̱w feast dishes in the AMNH set; they are carved as killerwhales with some human attributes. A small tube for dispensing liquid, probably valuable eulachon grease, is inserted in the area of these creatures' spouts. In all likelihood the killerwhale feast dishes were able at some point in the past to mimic the spouting actions of the creatures in the story.

When his voyages were finished, Siwidi returned to K̲umugwe', and the wealthy chief gave him a house called Sea-Lions-All-Over and several new names to mark his acquisition of supernatural power—including the title Born-to-Be-Head-of-the-World. Then, at the place called Monster-Receptacle, near his family's village, up floated Born-to-Be-Head-of-the-World, house and all, where he was spotted by his elder brother, First-Beaver. Each time that his family tried to approach him, both the hero and his house disappeared again beneath the waters.

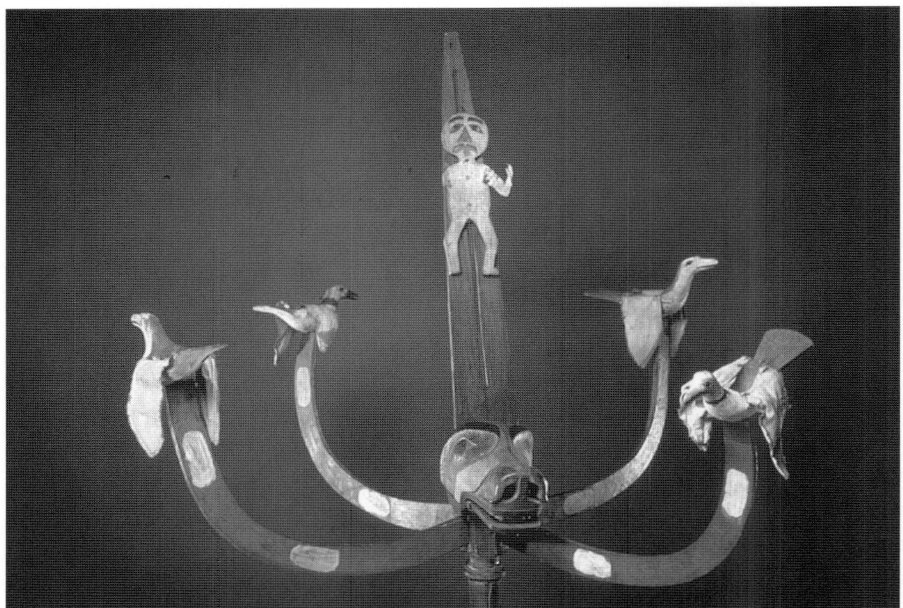

4.5 Sea Otter mask, 19th century. Hopetown. Wood, rope, cloth, paint. L: 170 cm. AMNH 16/8530 AJ, neg. 4588; courtesy Department of Library Services.

The entire tribe tried to capture him, but he eluded their grasp, changing himself into various creatures, represented as masks and other objects in the AMNH collection. First he appeared as a bullhead or sculpin, then as a whale with both its own tail and that of the sculpin, and also with an eagle that had descended and perched on its back. Next, Born-to-Be-Head-of-the-World became a sea otter with gulls flying around his head, illustrated by another mask that includes a clever mechanism which enables small, carved birds with flexible cloth wings to whirl around the sea otter's head when a cord is pulled (Figure 4.5). Ultimately, Born-to-Be-Head-of-the-World became a man again and instructed his tribe to bring gravel and fill in the watery gap between the shore of the village and Monster-Receptacle, creating a new site, a suitable place for the supernatural house of Ḵumugwe'. There Born-to-Be-Head-of-the-World held a Winter Dance for the Kwakwa̱ka̱'wakw.

This story, very briefly summarized here, is a part of the history of the Gwawa̱'enux̱w people, and its narration alone would have contextualized the exhibition of the mask set in *Chiefly Feasts* according to its historical function. Fortunately, even more information was brought to light, revealing both a historical relationship with another mask set as well as the contemporary significance of the Undersea Kingdom collection.

In May 1990, when the delegation of Kwakwaka'wakw advisors visited New York, each Undersea Kingdom mask was brought out so that they could discuss its function and appearance. Unexpectedly one of the guests, Gwawa'enuxw Chief Tom Willie, rose from his seat and began to recite his own version of this legend in Kwak̓wala. Chief Willie owns the exclusive privilege of telling his version of the Siwidi story today, which he chose to demonstrate dramatically in a museum setting, just as Agnes Cranmer had publicly demonstrated her dance privilege so far from home. The story commanded the rapt attention of Kwakwaka'wakw guests and non-native museum personnel alike, who witnessed Tom Willie's public oration. His prerogatives were validated, informally, in New York, in a larger sphere than is routinely possible at a potlatch, although no payments were made on this occasion. Employees of the AMNH, however, were given something of value for their services as witnesses, if not potlatch goods. They were able to perform a scholarly coup, contextualizing these masks from the museum's collection within a long-standing Kwakwaka'wakw ceremonial tradition. As a result of the elders' visit, we now know that the Siwidi masks at the American Museum of Natural History represent just one generation in a continuing tradition, demonstrated in this case through oratory rather than through the physical appearance of the masks themselves.

Chief Willie also maintains the exclusive prerogative to have these masks recarved and danced, which he has demonstrated at several potlatches during the last few years. The Campbell River Museum on Vancouver Island, British Columbia, has negotiated a special partnership with him and has commissioned a new set of Undersea Kingdom masks by contemporary Kwakwaka'wakw carvers. This project has been in progress since 1987. The masks are usually exhibited at the museum but may be removed for use at potlatch performances staged by Chief Willie.[22] Although the new generation of Undersea Kingdom or Siwidi masks at Campbell River has been carved to represent the same aquatic creatures appropriate to the ancient legend, they are independent from the AMNH set as works of art. They bear little or no visual resemblance to the nineteenth-century set in New York, which prompted Chief Willie's oration, although they may quote sea creature masks produced during the intervening generations of the last 100 years. Most of the masks, like the Sea Eagle, for instance, part of an entire costume by Calvin Hunt, have no counterpart in the nineteenth-century collection at the American Museum of Natural History. Similarly, there is no K̓umugwe', or undersea chief, like the one carved by Tony Hunt Jr. for the Campbell River set, no Dzonoquis, like the new one by Mervyn Child, and no Sea Monster similar to the one carved by Stan Hunt among those collected by George Hunt for Franz Boas.[23] On the other hand, the AMNH collection includes pieces like the killerwhale feast dishes and a Speaker's mask, not seen in the Campbell River collection.

A different grouping of objects, with some parallels, make up each of these two Undersea Kingdom ensembles. Although George Hunt may not have collected every mask used for the Undersea Kingdom dance during his generation, there is no reason to believe that the AMNH masks would be replicated for contemporary use, in the artistic handling of their appearance, even if he had. Contemporary carvers are asked to carve particular creatures known to the current owner of the dance privilege. Artists do take some liberties in their work. They may express their own vision or refer to any number of other masks that represent appropriate aquatic animals. Although they may not start from scratch, inventing unheard of beings or unprecedented formats as western artists do, they are not required to reproduce the characteristics of specific historical examples. New-generation masks need not resemble their predecessors, even when they represent the same creature, from the same legend. Their reliability in social context depends not upon the vision of their creators, but rather comes from the legitimacy of their use.

The new Sea Otter mask, carved and painted by Joe Peters Jr., for instance, corresponds with a creature represented among the old masks; however, it is visually distinct from the version in New York (Figure 4.6). Although the features of a sea otter are similarly conventionalized in both masks, the new one lacks the special extensions that support the small birds with cloth wings and the mechanism that causes them to whirl dramatically. Similarly, the Raven-of-the-Sea mask by Tony Hunt, from the Campbell River set, is painted with a slick black beak, has small wings carved above its brow, and is ornamented with copper on its teeth, eyes, and eyebrows (Figure 4.7). There are two Raven-of-the-Sea masks in the AMNH set, but they are colored very differently and bear no resemblance to Tony Hunt's vision of this creature. The relationship that endures between these masks and the two entire sets, for that matter, is their function—to display the dance privilege and the continuous relationship between the generations in Kwakwa̱ka'wakw culture—which is embodied in the exclusive right to tell the Siwidi story. This is not signaled in particular by the idiosyncratic vision of their makers. Although visually impressive masks that elicit "oohs" and "aahs" from the witnesses at a potlatch are valued, the continuing significance of the Siwidi set is not strictly linked with form or the visual affinity between dance masks of different generations.

Requirements for the physical appearance of these elaborate theatrical dance props on the Northwest Coast, whether mask sets, costumes or screens, puppets, or backdrops of various types, are not absolutely fixed through time. Perhaps they may vary because they are, in a sense, incidental to the central works on view at a potlatch. Although considered treasures, they function as props for the danced displays of privilege, which are primary in this setting. The opportunity to retell the histories and validate claims to their ownership is most important here and

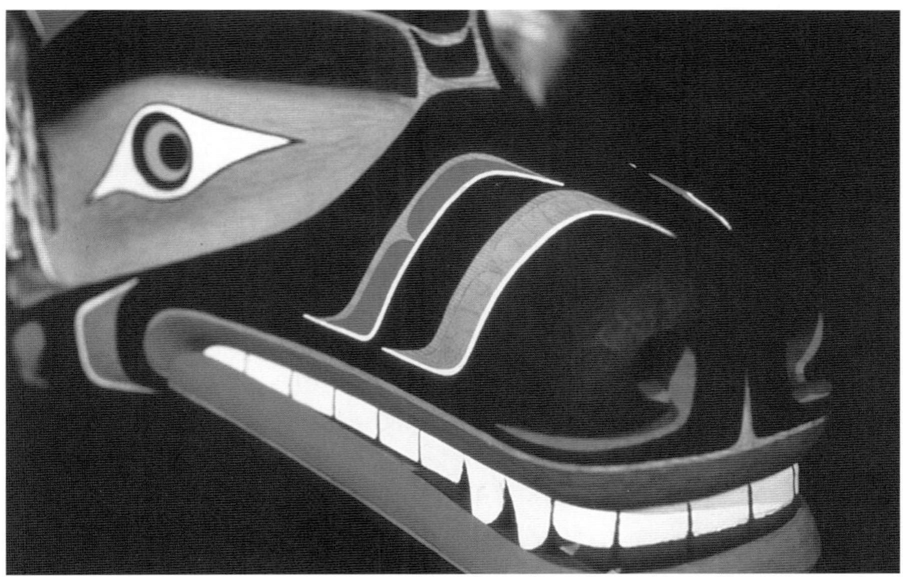

4.6 *Sea Otter mask by Joe Peters, Jr., 1988. Wood, paint. H: 24 cm. L: 41 cm. W: 27.5 cm. Photo: courtesy family of Joe Peters, Jr., and the Museum at Campbell River, B.C.; 988.29*

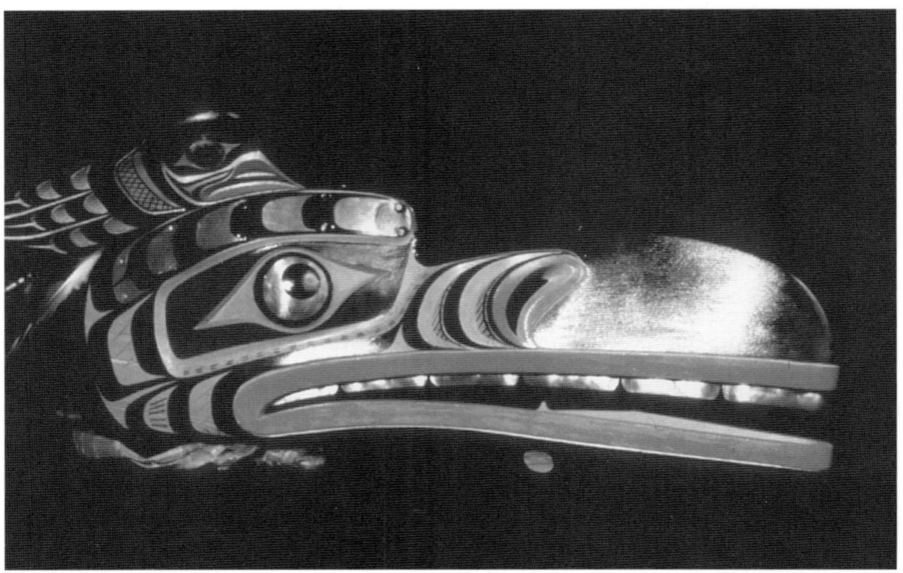

4.7 *Raven-of-the-Sea mask by Tony Hunt, 1989. Red cedar, acrylic paint, eagle feathers, copper. H: 36.5 cm. L: 91 cm. W: 27.5 cm. Courtesy Tony Hunt and the Museum at Campbell River, B.C.; 989.50.*

recurs at each and every potlatch. Objects and performances may vary over time, but they are as meaningful for each new generation as they were for the one before it, even as they signal new affiliations and up-to-the-minute concerns.

Masks and screens deteriorate over time and must be replaced periodically. Speeches may differ in format from one occasion to the next. Yet potlatches remain occasions to display enduring song and dance privileges and to renew individual and family claims to position. Without this continuing reproduction of form and ceremony, the legitimacy of these claims might be questioned within the community. The community or "big" houses where these events take place are therefore not considered museums or art galleries meant for the exhibition of carvings as the tours de force of artist-personalities. They are arenas for a continuing process of historical retrieval and selective refinement for appropriate contemporary use.

A Mirror to the Past: Authenticity and Value in the Marketplace

Unlike the Undersea Kingdom set, artworks carved strictly for non-native patrons like the *nułami'sta yelxts!ayo* screens at the American Museum of Natural History and many of the pieces carved for sale in art galleries, are identified almost entirely by their degree of visual or formal affinity with historical works. The many versions of the Clayoquot fish rattle or the Bella Coola Sun mask, for instance, have been unabashedly inspired by the appearance of older models. Although such specific visual references to the past are not strictly called for when a mask or other work is destined for ceremonial use, some visual likeness from one generation of traditional carvings to the next may occur incidentally. Continuity in style may sometimes be found in the historical record, accounted for by the influence of a master carver upon his apprentices. The persistence of some compositional devices may result from the habitual combination of forms required for the display of complex crest images.[24] The use of calipers and tracing paper is rarely called for, however, when artworks are created strictly for potlatch use. Nuu-chah-nulth artist Art Thompson has commented on this phenomenon: "There is less replication for native traditional use because these people [the Nuu-chah-nulth] respect who I am. We're living in 1993. Yes, we love historical things, but leave the past in the past. What we draw from the past makes us better, it advances the arts, advances the culture" (June 10, 1993: interview).

Museum curators, art gallery directors, and non-native collectors, less concerned with advance—uncharted territory in Indian art—do require similitude in the replicas that they commission. As early as 1952, Mungo Martin was hired by the British Columbia Provincial Museum (now the Royal British Columbia

Museum) to replicate old totem poles in Victoria's Thunderbird Park.[25] Martin originated the practice of duplication that continues to this day among the artists who have worked in the museum's carving shed to create the "Potlatch Collection," copying many old pieces from various Northwest Coast traditions. Some artists who also produce striking original pieces, such as Richard Hunt, Calvin Hunt, and Art Thompson, have become quite skilled at the replication process and are often commissioned to produce close copies. As historical documents, these painstakingly carved works are clearly of value. They are also easy to identify as examples of "authentic" native art while experimental works may be more difficult to categorize.

Ongoing change in the lives of contemporary First Nations people makes it difficult to articulate accurate and neat definitions of their identity. Yet native artworks that clearly refer to the past, conceptualized by some connoisseurs as less hybrid, bear concrete evidence of "authenticity." Their pedigrees may be traced to the imagined purity of the precontact period, helping to certify them as native, a category useful in non-native transactions. Certified native art by gifted artists may not command the high prices or the critical attention of a Picasso, or a Kostabi for that matter, but it may be associated, when considered authentic, with a particular valuable status. Furthermore, as James Clifford has reminded us, the "good collector," or connoisseur of value and artistic merit, "will be expected to label them [his personal treasures], to know their dynasty . . . to tell 'interesting' things about them, to distinguish copies from originals" (1988: 219). Ironically, native Northwest Coast artworks that refer directly to the past may become more like the originals valued by museums, scholars, and collectors. They may seem more like "the real thing" when their particular attributes can be named, traced to historical precedent, and their values appraised. Therefore formal indications of historical accuracy have been encouraged by non-native art professionals. Northwest Coast artworks currently made for the commercial marketplace are very often near-replicas or the popularly termed "take-offs" on nineteenth-century works.

Practices related to the manufacture of these objects for the art market were also developed in relation to a system of indigenous use with conventions for design and ceremonial function already in place. This phenomenon, the production of new artworks based upon existing models, may be better understood for this particular situation on the Northwest Coast when contrasted with the origin of commercial arts among other nonwestern groups. Certain Inuit artworks from the Canadian Arctic, for instance, appear to be similarly motivated by historicism. Most Inuit art made for sale over the last fifty years, however, was probably reinvented almost in complete response to the encouragement of outsiders at mid-twentieth century and not significantly based upon local precedent. When the Hudson's Bay Company set up trading posts for white fox early in the twenti-eth century, only a minor amount of souvenir or indigenous art-making existed in the area. Some small toys and charms, perhaps loosely related to the carved and incised works of the Dorset and Thule traditions, were known. Non-Inuit intervened, however, in response to the extreme poverty engendered by the breakdown of nomadic life in the area and the accompanying loss of hunting technologies. As a proposed solution, these outsiders encouraged craft produc-tion. Early government efforts had been relatively ineffective, but in 1948, Cana-dian artist James Houston visited eastern Hudson's Bay and taught soapstone carving to the native people. At his behest, the Canadian Handicrafts Guild in Montreal became involved in publicizing these works. With some support from the government and a system of credit established by the Hudson's Bay Com-pany, a market for Inuit arts and crafts was established. Again, with government support in the 1950s, Houston introduced block, stencil, and stone engraving as printmaking techniques, at first on Baffin Island, which resulted in successful ex-hibitions both in Montreal and Ottawa. Houston was followed by other white teachers. Today printmaking is an important form of artistic expression for the Inuit, and printmakers' cooperatives have become a significant social force in Inuit life.[26]

The prints and soapstone carvings produced under these conditions relied until recently on stylized interpretations of traditional mythological themes and depictions of native people and indigenous animals that no longer strictly relate to the circumstances of contemporary Inuit life. This process of historification, in which hunting scenes and images of igloos were given prominence, was created to a large extent to address the interests of buyers outside the community. It is also possible that Inuit artists may have been expressing their own nostalgia for the past by these artistic means. In any case, these circumstances contrast with the continuing production of native Northwest Coast art and its relationship to historical subject matter. Also revitalized since the 1950s, the growth of Northwest Coast art traditions has taken place under very different circumstances. The mar-keting of Northwest Coast works was developed along with ongoing ceremonial requirements and an evolution of formal concerns invented by and considered acceptable to native practitioners themselves, even as it was encouraged by non-native buyers.

As a consequence of this phenomenon, replicas or creative translations, and even more experimental works in recognizable Northwest Coast style that have been developed for the marketplace are valued for their certifiable relationship with continuing native cultural practice. The survival of native art traditions adds even greater value to the collections of institutions and individuals, as evidenced by the interest that museum curators and even some art gallery directors take in the ceremonial life of contemporary people and, not incidently, their relative willingness to loan these pieces out for potlatch use. The status of these works, at least as designated by the non-native world, would be less certain if they exceeded the limits of traditionalism entirely. Individual masks and other works of Northwest Coast art that may be identified with particular historical models as well as with traditional practice continue to proliferate and command very high prices in the art market.

For these reasons, contemporary works of Northwest Coast native art in the galleries and museums are almost always associated with their predecessors and in this manner are maintained as units in what may be understood as a loose series. For instance, a curator may be aware that their collection includes a K̲umugwe' mask or a Raven mask, and that many more such masks in other collections may also be identified by such names and their uses in traditional culture. Such masks may even be considered as a type of multiple, known by association with others of their lineage. Interestingly, Igor Kopytoff has suggested (1986: 64–91) that a certain lack of "singularity," as seen in one-of-a-kind objects, actually defines the status of true commodities. Although these masks and other works are certainly not completely lacking in individuality (they will have characteristics particular to their artistic manufacture or use), they are recognized and even appraised for their relative value by their contextualization against other similar members of their class. This recognition factor may be said to define their commodity status to outsiders and also to assign them demonstrable value.

A contemporary rattle, for instance, may be placed and validated when its buyers know that it is based upon the form of a museum piece, verifying its descent within the tradition. Although its unique life story may be known—the details of its cultural biography include the relative skill of the artist and the prestige of this particular historical model—it will not likely be associated with the modernist's drive to exceed commodity status and above all else to create a work that stands alone, supposedly unique. Therefore it must remain outside the category of most valuable and most critically acclaimed works of western art.

Position and Marginality

Proponents of both modern and postmodern critical history have extolled the singular work of artists whose vision is thought to be so personal that it cites no predecessors and acknowledges no collaborators. Rosalind Krauss has contested the integrity of such a strict autobiographical approach, associated only with the personality of the artist, and points to the analysis of these works as "an art history turned militantly away from all that is transpersonal in history—style, social

and economic context, archive, structure. . . ." (1985: 25; 23–40; 151–170; and passim). Complete self-reference and originality may in fact be an impossible fiction
constructed by art professionals, collectors, and institutions seeking clarity and
an endless stream of new products.

Contemporary native artists working in a traditional manner, however,
continually cite matters of "transpersonal" concern related to history and group
affiliation. Furthermore, art historians and anthropologists habitually highlight
the social context of their works. These pieces are understood to be shaped by
stylistic conventions, distinct references to the past, and indicators of relative social standing. They are therefore not presented as newly invented or the art of the
"cutting edge," even by the most appreciative admirers. Recognized in this manner, Indian artists may flourish close to home or among specialized collectors. On
a more global level, however, they are compelled to accept a position of some dis-
empowerment. The informed choice to maintain native identity by working in
the style of one's ancestors, a position evaluated by many outsiders as that of a traditional craftsperson, not a fine artist, consigns the overwhelming majority of
contemporary native Northwest Coast artists to marginality. Because most of
these artists do not place the greatest emphasis in their own work on individual
identity and progress, they are regarded as working outside of a broader discourse
that is defined by "advance."

A very few native Northwest Coast artists, however, have transcended a clear
distinction between the two art traditions, maintaining references to Indian identity in the imagery of their work but experimenting with the application of these
forms. Lawrence Paul Yuxweluptun of the Cowichan Salish tribe, for instance,
refers to his native heritage in his paintings but addresses a broader range of formal concerns, often to highlight controversial political issues. His painting *The
Environmentalist,* for example, extracts elements of formline design, such as the
split U's and ovoids that Bill Holm named, from their usual context and has them
depend loosely, like the melting clocks of a Salvador Dali painting, from trees and
mountains in a surrealistic landscape (Plate 14). A male figure in the painting,
drawn naturalistically from the neck down but with a gaping hole in its chest,
supports the stylized form of a Northwest Coast mask as its head. These images
suggest contemporary issues of ecological concern and illustrate Indian disem-
powerment and the clash of native and non-native conventions—used here to
make up the composition.

Yuxweluptun, who has also experimented with virtual reality as a medium
for his work, was educated at the Emily Carr College of Art and Design in Vancouver. His work has been included in the *Juried Third Biennial Native American
Fine Arts Invitational* at the Heard Museum in Phoenix, Arizona, and was prominently featured as well in the prestigious exhibition of 1992 *Land, Spirit, Power,*

held at the National Gallery of Canada in Ottawa. In 1995 he had a solo exhibition at the Morris and Helen Belkin Art Gallery at the University of British Columbia. Although he paints on a reserve and dances in traditional ceremonies, he recognizes the unique position that his work occupies in referring to issues that are deeply affected by native life, but functioning outside of traditional means of expression.

> My work is very different from traditional art work. How do you paint a land claim? You can't carve a totem pole that has a beer bottle on it. . . . Painting is a form of political activism, a way to exercise my inherent right, my right to authority, my freedom. . . . I can speak out in my paintings even without the recognition of self-government. . . . Always, I create art to communicate with others, to let other cultures see things for themselves. (Nemiroff, Houle, and Townsend-Gault 1992: 220–27; also Gerber and Katz-Lahaigue 1989: 110–19)

Lawrence Paul Yuxweluptun clearly addresses himself to a broader audience, including non-natives with authority in both artistic and political spheres. His dialogue with outsiders results in a unique if jarring blend of elements that functions favorably within the criteria established by western art curators for individual vision and progress.

Some other Northwest Coast artists have focused on the refinement of formal vocabularies that make their works compelling to non-natives as well, although they may not undertake Yuxweluptun's extraordinary adaptations of content. They accomplish this through style and composition, and although they continue to refer to crest art images, their facility with abstraction in particular permits greater communication with non-native audiences. Doug Cranmer, for instance, who has produced a great many traditional Kwakwa̲ka'wakw carvings on commission, has also made visual experiments with elements derived from the formline tradition. His paintings *Killerwhale* and *Canoe*, first introduced to a broader public as far back as the *Legacy* exhibition of 1970 at the Royal British Columbia Museum, were lauded by curator Peter Macnair as abstract designs based on an extreme competency within the tradition. These images, according to Macnair, resulted from personal experience and "intense introspection." Cranmer had arranged the stylized shapes of dorsal fins and canoe prows so that they were reassembled as visual puzzles. When viewed as strictly abstract paintings, they are intricately constructed designs that move across wooden panels in an elegant manner that allows them to stand on their own, without the necessity of any reference to their subject matter (Macnair et al., 1984: 101; figs. 98–99).

Recently Cranmer has begun to apply his interest in abstract design to three-dimensional media. His latest works include log carvings composed of these detached, stylized elements and allowed to animate the surface of the wood; they are only loosely reminiscent of totem poles. Cranmer contends that there are no models for these experiments, but that his ideas come to him "out of a coffee pot," or from his private musings with caffeine in hand (June 20, 1993: interview). This artist, completely conversant with the conventions of Northwest Coast native art, has followed a personal muse in some of his work that moves it outside of existing definitions for the traditional.

Halkomelem Salish artist Susan Point has also experimented with elements derived from old Coast Salish designs, which she manipulates in her own distinct manner to fit within shaped formats. Some of these paintings, prints, and sculptures exceed any simplistic definition dependent solely on the artist's ethnic background. Ironically, the format she has most frequently worked with is the circle, derived from the traditional form of spindle whorls. In an early painting *Salmon Run* (1989), however, elements are set in a square frame (Figure 4.8). This work was inspired by a modular design on an old Salish mortuary box in the collection of the University of British Columbia Museum of Anthropology.[27] Point's sense of flat design is both astute and complex, and her translation of these historical elements, such as the rectangular profile faces of fish, are oriented in various directions in the compartments of an irregular grid. This lively composition, constructed from the many ramifications of the single fish form, suggests the conventions of western abstraction as much as it does Salish art.

Point has received some major commissions for works of public art, including cast metal grates for the streets of Seattle, Washington, more recently an installation of a huge spindle whorl-like carving at the Vancouver airport and a housepost or interior pole titled *Female Welcome Figure* that is placed with works by other Coast Salish artists. Operating in contexts that demand certain cross-cultural means of expression, Point understands that the mission of her work is to be effective in increasing public awareness of Coast Salish art (Gerber and Katz-Lahaigue 1989: 87). Point's facility with abstraction may provide a medium through which this dialogue may be conducted.

Tlingit artist Jim Schoppert's work should be mentioned here as well, not only because it is extraordinary, but because it, too, often benefits from the language of abstraction in order to communicate with a more diverse group of viewers. Although Schoppert had considerable experience carving masks and other items of regalia in both Northwest Coast and Eskimo style, many examples of his work, such as *Blueberries* (1986), for instance, were meant to make a broader statement. This work is composed as a combination of wood panels carved in relief with truncated sections of formline shapes and other geometric elements (Figure 4.9). These displaced forms that seem like fragments or the close-up de-

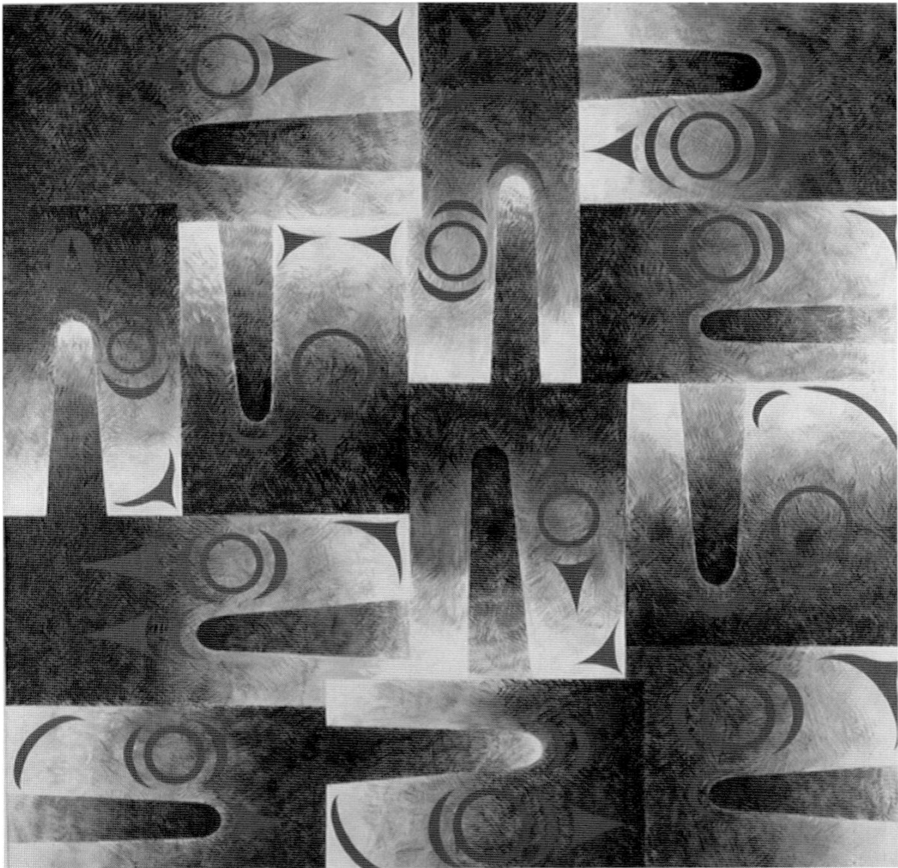

4.8 Salmon Run *by Susan Point, 1989. Acrylic on canvas. H: 100 cm. W: 100 cm. Courtesy Susan Point and Völkerkundemuseum Universität Zürich.*

tails of a larger, more traditional piece such as a bentwood box or facade paint-ing have been strategically placed, tinted with colored washes, and marked with painted strokes to play with the height and depth implied by the carving. Schop-pert's abstract pieces may be compared with Cranmer's and Point's projects, but he may be more explicit in the use he made of nonrepresentational strategies to break down clear boundaries that qualify certain works as strictly native, perhaps minimizing what is "transpersonal." For instance, he liked to illustrate his state-ments about the customary necessity of representation in traditional art by quot-ing Bill Reid's complaint that unless his jewelry had eyes and teeth, no one wanted it (Schoppert 1997: 32). However Schoppert said he wanted to take Northwest Coast art "into [a] more modern context. . . . One, I removed the cultural rele-

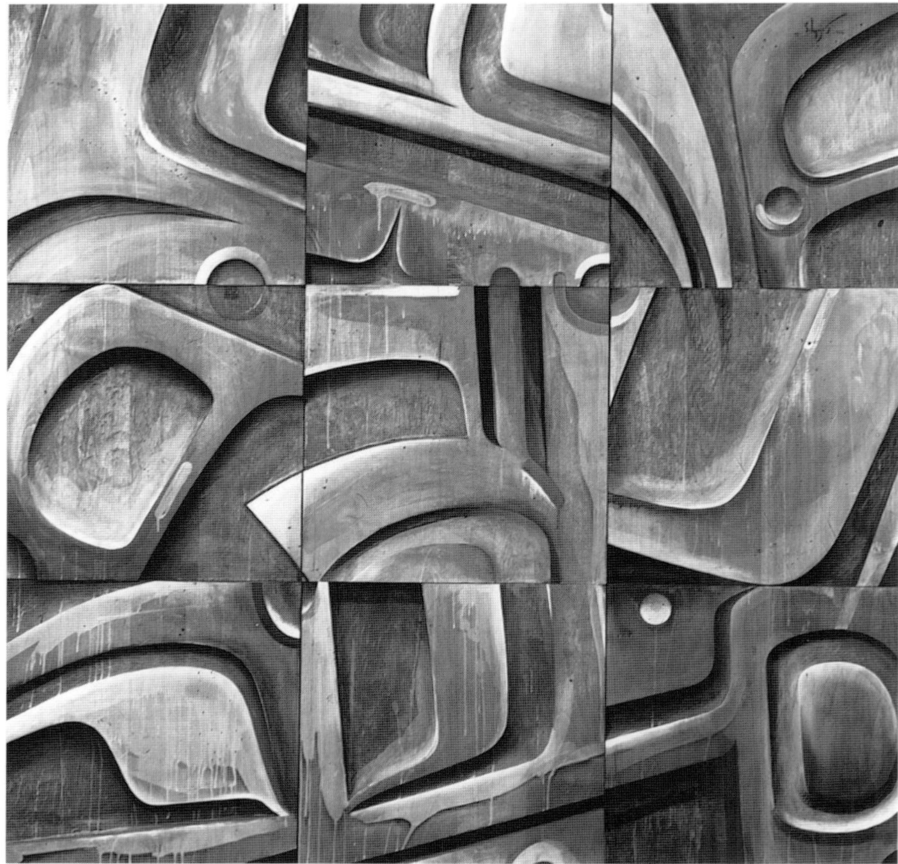

4.9 Blueberries *by Jim Schoppert, 1986. Carved poplar panel. H: 72 in. W: 72 in. Photo: courtesy the estate of Jim Schoppert and the Anchorage Museum of History and Art.*

vancy of it. Two, I got rid of the traditional use of black and red colors. Third, I got rid of the focused specific image. Then I started adding to it. I fragmented the work. I began abstracting some of it."[28]

Experimental works such as these may one day come to exceed current definitions for the category of Indian art and may cause some breakdown of canonical requirements for authenticity. These productions, very unusual on the Northwest Coast, are better known in other regions of the United States and Canada through the experimental works of artists of native descent, such as Jimmy Durham and Kay Walkingstick. Formal definitions of traditional native art and the delineation of design rules that direct its forms might ultimately be dropped from art-historical discourse as incidental to more contemporary concerns for individual expression and advance. Discussions of slight variation and experimentation within the confines of native art traditions, already justified in the literature by Holm (1965), Macnair (1984), and others, might then no longer serve us well enough.

At this point, however, these works are still exceptional on the Northwest Coast, and all of them still maintain some references to native identity.[29] The vast majority of these artists continue to choose the traditional approach, producing works for sale to outsiders that do not differ in any distinguishable manner from those used at potlatches. At present, the market and many influential patrons of native art support this choice, but financial success may not be the only factor at work in the continuing proliferation of historically based works of art. The conservative stance of traditional Northwest Coast artists cannot be understood when viewed as a completely passive one, implying their complete reliance upon the rewards of the marketplace or indicating a lack of political awareness. Instead, the position of Northwest Coast native artists working in this manner may be more active, related in part to issues of "identity politics," just as they are for other nonwestern artists. Cornel West has discussed the works of African-American artists in a way that might be analogous. He has suggested that the option exercised by artists of color to "revel in parochialism" rather than pursue the "legitimizing power of the mainstream" denies the complete authority of outsiders, formerly understood as indispensable. As a parallel, the exclusive production of artworks that refer to native life may qualify the choices of some Northwest Coast artists as tacit participation in what West has called "the new cultural politics of difference." Contemporary nonwestern artists may take positions anywhere along a continuum, ranging from compliance with mainstream sensibilities to a completely insular perspective, based solely upon ethnic identity, and thus advertising that difference (West 1990: 19–36). These choices may be understood as considered ones, resulting from the informed participation of contemporary native artists in the culture of their ancestors.

The legitimizing power of the mainstream may be particularly hard to come by for native artists so that their persistent assertion of ethnic identity, a choice that contributes to their plight and maintains their position on the margin of art historical discourse, may indicate a statement of some resistance. According to bell hooks, this may be an elected "space of refusal." It may be "a message from that space on the margin that is a site of creativity and power, that inclusive space where we recover ourselves. . . ." (hooks 1990: 341–43). Tony Hunt's Raven-of-the-Sea mask from the contemporary Undersea Kingdom set, for example, may be composed of graphic elements that are as sleek and refined as a ship's hull or machine part, but they are combined in a manner sanctioned by his ancestors and put to use by the descendants of Siwidi. They are configured to advertise the

Kwakw<u>a</u>ka'wakw hero's hard-earned prerogatives. Tom Hunt as well may have taken great liberties in his carved execution of the *nułami'sta yelxts!ayo* screen, but he accomplished this with the split **U**'s and ovoids of the northern Northwest Coast graphic tradition and by doing so helped to pass on his grandmother's song and dance privilege in a public forum.

Some statement of refusal may be embedded in the work of contemporary Northwest Coast artists, particularly those conversant with western art forms, when they maintain references to native life and identity. It is implicit in their integration of indispensable traditional concerns with their own contemporary sensibilities, a combination that drives the appearance of many new works. Ironically, this historicism is currently strengthened on two fronts. These works meet the requirements of both Indian artists and their patrons, each asserting their decision-making capacities within the forums that are open to them. Therefore, these works do not move art history along its imagined course. The contribution of these artists as members of a community less dazzled by invention for its own sake may help redefine that course as one approach among many. Their decisions may help reposition a supposed center of cultural power, dispersing it to various locations.

CHAPTER FIVE

The Style in Which They Were Imagined

In fact, all communities larger than primordial villages of face-to-face contact (and perhaps even these) are imagined. Communities are to be distinguished, not by their falsity/genuineness, but by the style in which they are imagined.
—Benedict Anderson, *Imagined Communities* 1983: 6

FACSIMILES AND COPIES IN NATIVE ART are imagined as well, but their significance need not be reduced to a matter of artful deception if their reworked forms are considered to be enlightening on the subject of the communities they represent. The cultural biographies of the old and not-so-old buildings, transplanted totem poles, updated dance presentations, carefully crafted speeches, masks, and other works of art discussed here so far indicate that these are not simulacra, as qualified by lack of reference or mere pretense. They result instead from various creative processes developed by influential artists and other authorities. As a result, native Northwest Coast replicas may be said to function as do many other works of art, by selectively referencing history. Although indicators of historical accuracy are almost always devised and announced by participants in projects that describe Indian art and culture, in the end the designation of authority, the prerogative to make decisions (not the inheritance of privilege), has emerged as central. Where these items that refer to the native past will be displayed, toward whom the construction of their meaning will be directed, and who will participate in their execution appears to matter even more than the accurate representation of formal details known through precedent. Rather than mourning this development—the privileging of formal regulation over exact historical duplication—the study of many new projects reveals that this contest for authority is precisely what defines this art as vital and still signifi-cant for its community.

Recently the admissability of native art in public settings has been submitted for popular debate in increasingly broad forums to a larger community. Litera-ture, museum display, theatrical works, commercial messages, and in particular films that include the representation of ethnic minorities in the United States and Canada are currently evaluated in the media, before the eyes of the general pub-lic, in direct reference to their propriety. This is measured in two ways: through the construction of appropriate portrayals as sanctioned by native advisors, and by the presence of certain essential indicators of historical accuracy that are strate-gically inserted into projects through relatively new processes of collaboration.

A case in point that was discussed to a remarkable degree in the press and among the parents of young children in the summer of 1995 is the movie *Pocahontas*, released by Walt Disney Pictures in June of that year. It presents the "updated" story of an Indian princess, daughter of Chief Powhatan, who lived in the vicinity of what became Jamestown, Virginia, at the beginning of the seven-teenth century. Eric Goldberg, the director of the film, set the tone for the public by placing the diligent recovery of historical material at center stage:

> When you bring visual details to a film, you're also bringing a sense of the culture. . . . You can't disengage the two. With 'Pocahontas,' it would have been very easy to Hollywoodize the story and use a lot of tepees and totem poles. But it didn't happen to be what the Powhatan Indians were like, and we tried to reflect that. (*New York Times*, June 11, 1995: section 2: 1f)

It was clearly put about that the Disney studio had done its homework un-der the direction of proper authorities. It sought validation of the film through the bruiting of selected indicators of historical accuracy; the film's creative team visited Jamestown, various museums, and consulted with some "American Indian organizations, historians, academics and even descendants of Pocahontas" (ibid.). Their efforts, and the comments of native activist and actor Russell Means (Oglala Lakota) as a spokesperson (who also provided the voice for Chief Powhatan in the movie), were highlighted in the news media, backing this claim of legitimacy for the project, after all "just" a children's cartoon.

Along with the absence of tepees and totem poles, the selection of another native person, Irene Bedard (Inupiaq) to create the voice of Pocahontas, and also Chief Powhatan's shift, in the script, to the use of the title "Daughter" to address the young woman instead of her proper name, were cited as indications of rigor-ous research and the desire to portray native history appropriately (ibid.). But not surprisingly, some elements of the story played out in glorious song and image had to depart from the history or truth that is only recoverable on a hypothetical basis, in any case. One such disparity is demonstrated in the Oglala Lakota identity of Means and the Inupiaq or Native Alaskan background of Bedard, presented in this project as equivalent, as "American Indian," and therefore suitable for the reconstruction of the Powhatan tribe's history. Of greater significance to some native people who critiqued the film is the fact that Pocahontas is portrayed as being older than she would have been at the time that the events in the picture were supposed to have taken place. Represented as in her twenties, instead of as a twelve-year-old, she is also shown as amazingly athletic, spiritually inclined, and feminist in her approach, in spite of the Barbie doll-like figure and provocative clothing that the studio designed for her. The age change is accounted for as being more appropriate to the portrayal of her love affair with Captain John Smith—central to the *Pocahontas* film plot—according to contemporary sensibilities (ibid.). Yet much of the historical accuracy that is compromised in the movie may actually be traced to parts of the story that were not told on screen. The historical Pocahontas left her native home and traveled to England, where she married a tobacco farmer and then died quite soon—certainly a disappointing end for this young woman whom Disney and various other apocryphal accounts identify as a peacemaker and visionary in the service of her people.

In spite of these discrepancies, Russell Means has commented positively on this version of history the film presents. He was apparently quite affected by the cheerful greed and completely self-centered views celebrated in song by the English adventurers in Smith's party just as they hit landfall:

> When I first read the script, I was impressed with the beginning of the film. In fact, I was overwhelmed by it. It tells the truth about the motives for Europeans initially coming to the so-called New World. I find it astounding that Americans and the Disney Studios are willing to tell the truth. (Edgerton 1996: 260)

Another consultant, Shirley (Little Dove) Custalow-McGowan, a Powhatan who works as a native teacher and historian, was not so pleased. Despite the relatively positive image suggested for the Powhatan people in the film—they were, not surprisingly, portrayed as highly attuned to nature and largely ethical conservationists—this was not the story that she wanted told. "My heart sorrowed within me. . . . Ten-year-old Pocahontas has become twenty-year-old Pocahontas. The movie was no longer historically accurate" (Kilpatrick 1995: 37). Simon Schama, a non-native, has teased out several interesting themes from the film that do not derive from the native past, but may be traced instead to Euro-American legendary history, and again, the continuing message of superior ecological concern that often characterizes non-native depictions of Indian loftiness: "No one, though, is in much danger of confusing 'Pocahontas' with a history lesson," he wrote (1995: A21), but this is arguable. Many children and their parents may actually rely on this film as the correct model.

A variety of authorities were actually responsible for this contested story line and profile of the Pocahontas character, including the invention of features that will probably be read by contemporary viewers as heroic and redeeming. It is unlikely that all of these "updated" details as well as those strategies that affected the marketing of the film were invented solely on the basis of the much-touted native point of view. The public announcement of historically accurate details and the appropriate lineage of some members of the consultation team are just a few features among many that determined the type of influential public statement that the film was able to make. According to this new emphasis on propriety, however, historical inaccuracies and non-native interventions are considered deceptive and are therefore glossed over to gain public approval.

Although difficult to recognize at first glance, the origin and nature of modifications of the past in the film may actually be the most telling indicators of social clout, and may offer the best picture of contemporary native and non-native interaction available to date—in fact, of art history in the making. This information was not offered to Disney audiences. In this regard, Annie E. Coombes has offered a trenchant critique of the popularity of recent transcultural forms that are now celebrated by museum curators as a new acceptance of cultural diversity. Coombes (1994: 89–114) suggests that appreciative viewers of hybrid productions at these more traditional venues miss out on how key differences may have been constituted as well as on issues of differential access to cultural authority. The same may be said of the construction of new popular culture representations that appear to descend to us, at least in part, from the recent history of museum practice. For instance, museum representations, although still largely contextualized by non-native administration, were the first to be affected by native advice, with the result that museum visitors as well as observant film studios and theme parks executives have now been educated on the necessity of this practice.

Many readers will be familiar with the exhibitions that first included the significant participation of native advisors and presented the issue of native consultation itself to the public. These were: *A Time of Gathering: Native Heritage in Washington State*, at the Burke Museum in 1991; *Chiefly Feasts*, which opened in New York the same year; and the First Peoples Hall, recently inaugurated at the CMC in Canada. Now, in the late 1990s, comprehensive plans are being forged at the National Museum of the American Indian under the supervision of complex native consultation teams. The museum is scheduled to open to the public on the mall in Washington, D.C. in 2002, and updates on the progress of the museum and also its elaborate storage facility in Suitland, Maryland, appear in *The New York Times* with some regularity.

Even individual native artists who direct themselves to the commercial marketplace play certain roles as "advisors" in the presentation of their cultures of origin to larger audiences. While advancing their own goals, they, and all of these parties, lend as a by-product what amounts to their "seals of approval" to the complex art forms that result from collaboration. They make and authorize works that encode a sometimes bumpy and inequitable process of interaction. Although they habitually devise some indicators of historical accuracy for their projects, in the end, the right to designate permissable variation from past form may be their highest credential. This is why Disney is astute in indicating the native identities of some, if not all, of their consultants. As history is edited to meet new requirements, the identity of these editors is as important as the nature of the revisions themselves. Greater analyses of the conditions of the consultation process itself may then be essential to the explication of difference and the relative access to power that Coombes has so far found lacking.

Obviously, as in the projects used as examples in this study, some individuals play a greater role in the arbitration of new form and meaning than do others. Some Indian representatives may be appointed to the role of consultant because they come forward on their own, but others are designated by outsiders like Disney or the American Museum of Natural History as key players. These individuals may be better informed about native history, or have the inherited right to speak about a particular work of art (a position which may be contested by others), or they may be the only individuals available who have an interest in participating in such interactions. Their appointment as consultants, according to these variable qualifications, is now de rigeur for projects that cite native life all over North America.

The Northwest Coast case, however, is unique. In this part of the world, self-representation by simple participation is further compounded by long-standing cultural practices for exclusive jurisdiction. This zealous desire to own the past is reiterated in British Columbia and Southeast Alaska by the crest art system, an indigenous condition that still operates among native traditionalists, but is now complicated by other strategies to claim authority at non-native venues. In this region, verbal and visual discourse about ownership is carried out locally through the relatively unambiguous formal devices that document precedent: the bears, ravens, and sea creatures that figure in exclusive traditional histories. The necessity to assert authority in non-native settings, however, may not parallel crest affiliation. The studies cited here indicate just how crest ownership may be tenaciously guarded or, on the contrary, allowed to deteriorate, as new opportunities for representation in public places become available. These processes began soon after contact.

For example, it is clear that the form of the Chief Shakes Community House was developed over time with differing degrees of Tlingit participation. When Chief Shakes IV relocated the Nanya.ayí clan to the Wrangell site, no doubt he and other high-ranking family members determined which artistic elements were to be transported from the old house. Shakes V also maintained his role as chiefly arbiter of form. George Shakes did the same, but his times were quite different and demanded some deference to the standards of new, non-native authority figures. Missionary influence in particular affected the appearance of the house during his lifetime, accounting for the presence of the religious posters tacked up right next to the extremely prestigious Shark posts, and probably of various other furnishings considered appropriate to a proper and civilized way of life.

During the tenure of the Civilian Conservation Corps in Southeast Alaska, the house was revamped from the ground up on the basis of historical citation, but as translated by certain Tlingit workers under the supervision of non-native authorities. It is most important to note that in this period, the authority to invent form appropriate to the house passed out of Nanya.ayí hands. For the first time in the history of the house, the advisors were Tlingit, but not of the clan of those direct inheritors of the Shakes line who had been led up the mountain by the Brown Bear. Charley Jones, named Chief Shakes VII for ceremonial purposes during that period, claimed the right to that title with the support of the various businesses and committees involved in the project. His claim, however, is not universally accepted. Tom Ukas was also influential because of his artistic ability and knowledge of Tlingit history, but he was not a descendant of Shakes. For the 1984 project, the replication of the old houseposts, again a collaborative effort, was undertaken. Native organizations worked with non-native museum personnel, supervising a diverse carving team headed by a non-native artist.

Who was influential in Hull, Quebec? The construction of the Grand Hall village at the Canadian Museum of Civilization was also clearly a group effort. Yet the authority to reimagine the forms included in the hall was broadly distributed, not only between native and non-native parties but also in reference to the particular artists and other consultants selected for participation. Native project supervisors for each of the six house-building teams were chosen for the most part by Bill McLennan of the University of British Columbia on the basis of their artistic knowledge, their prominence in their home communities, and their availability for this kind of employment. It should be stated here that many people who maintain historical knowledge and receive artistic training in native communities come from families who have long played a prominent role in the ceremonial, political, and artistic life of the group. For the most part, however, the CMC project supervisors were unrelated to the families or other social divisions with the right to represent the crests that may be observed in the hall. As we have seen, these family connections are indispensable on home territory. The notable exceptions to this rule were Ron Hamilton in the design process for the Nuu-chah-nulth house facade and Doug Cranmer, who was largely responsible for the appearance of the Kwakwaka'wakw housefront painting and is a descendant of Chief Wakas, the legitimate owner of the prototype. Cranmer insists, however, that his family affiliations had nothing to do with his participation (June 20, 1993: interview). It should be reiterated that Andrea LaForet of the CMC did consult with various descendants of the house groups represented in the hall. But the recovery of explicit visual information that may have affected the crest imagery on the houses did not result from this process, probably because of the loss of significant local knowledge about these art forms.

At the American Museum of Natural History, the dance reenactment made to celebrate the opening of the *Chiefly Feasts* exhibition was influenced most by George Hunt's descendants, who live in Alert Bay and Fort Rupert on Vancouver Island today. Their affiliations with a number of different families and Kwakwaka'wakw tribes with different dance privileges—Kwagu'ł, 'Namgis, Gwawa'enuxw, and Lekwiltok for instance—is worth noting again, as it indicates the necessity to cross the boundaries of traditional divisions in order to participate in many new and influential public projects.

Individual artists working on smaller-scale projects usually operate with even greater autonomy in regard to traditional regulation. Many of their works that refer to historical models are produced, at least in principle, under the aegis of museum staffs and other outsiders, usually without direct reference to crest ownership. For example, Calvin Hunt's painted screen with puppets and the similar take-off produced by his nephew, Tom Hunt, were both made for non-native patrons on the basis of their Kwakwaka'wakw identities and not because of their specific family or band affiliations. Later, on the Northwest Coast, these artworks were redefined to some extent when they were associated with specific family privileges.

Certainly the group of prominent Northwest Coast artists who replicated the Undersea Kingdom set of masks for the Campbell River Museum and Gwawa'enuxw Chief Tom Willie were affiliated with a range of different bands and families. Other artists discussed in Chapter Four, whose works incorporate references to western art and who function increasingly on their own, may be influenced by the comments and examples set by others, but any references that they may make to family histories are largely indiscernible to the audiences most familiar with their work. Like other artists around the world, they may be motivated to develop imagery on the basis of artistic precedent or financial gain, the desire for acclaim, or their own private muses.

These examples and others suggest that the production of replicated works of art seen in public places, made by contemporary native Northwest Coast artists, are rarely reinvented under the sole authorization of legitimate crest owners. Although works commissioned primarily for potlatch use are still made for bona fide owners of traditional privilege, and several contemporary native artists observe traditional courtesies in public on their own recognizance, productions that address a broader audience are often adjusted beyond the visual requirements of native communities. Recent shifts in patronage, from traditional authority to public commission and contemporary market forces, now parallel the circumstances affecting non-native artists who were released from institutional and religious authorization centuries ago. This phenomenon unwittingly encourages some infractions against history. Contemporary native participation may insure the presence of some aspects of historical accuracy in museums, films, and in gallery art, but they are frequently founded upon the power bases of the present. This shifts the emphasis from the reproduction of the "past" alone, but the general public may not be aware of this. This phenomenon seems rather ironic in light of the continuing interest in historical accuracy at popular venues and its frequent assertion in the public record.

How then have these newly appointed coauthors from the Northwest Coast imagined the art form as it goes forward, even as they refer incessantly to some aspects of the past, and how does that form differ from those installments of native art history that have come before it? I submit that these new authorities, collaborating with each other and participating in the undertakings of non-natives, have contributed to a certain course of generalization that now affects the representation of native cultures beyond the discrete divisions that the art of the past was directed to maintain. Outsiders, with the exception of some connoisseurs, have encouraged various artistic expressions of larger group identity for the Northwest Coast, particularly in grand-scale projects that will educate the public about the past.

Museum visitors have long been educated about the existence of gross cultural units like "the Northwest Coast," "the Tlingit," or "the Kwakwaka'wakw," unqualified in terms of their smaller subdivisions. Strict adherence to the identifiers that originate with the crest system in these environments would not even be perceived by the overwhelming majority of white viewers. Native Northwest Coast people themselves now routinely consult, carve, paint, and dance in these settings, and they often maintain finer traditional distinctions subtley expressed behind the scenes, as it were. Some additional signs of difference, discreetly worked out among insiders, as seen in the cooperative approach of native artists to problems with protocol in the Grand Hall project and at the *Chiefly Feasts* dances, for instance, may forecast a future of public presentations that will be characterized by the construction of what amounts to parallel realities. Relatively generalized expressions at public venues, along with certain permissible instances of historical inaccuracy, may even serve an additional purpose: to confirm the outsider status of non-native audiences.

For white viewers, the function of source materials such as photographs, archaeological evidence, and stylistic continuity with precontact or early post-contact works is understood as being documentary and therefore is most effective. A prerogative system based upon appropriate affiliation known through the recitation of legendary history and not on so-called scientific evidence may be too esoteric, requiring too much specialized knowledge. Thus the historical record may actually be compromised, permitting, for example, a combination of totem poles that violates the distinct boundaries for such placements according to traditional protocols. On native land, outside of museums, however, these poles continue to display a number of images that refer to the unique history and affiliations of individuals, families, and clans. They were, and are, actually meant to announce and establish the claims of those units. Consultants may also authorize a theme of unity in dance display, but privately subvert it by making small cash payments that validate traditional distinctions among players. These points are advertised only to "those in the know."

Even the salmon-attracting rattle described in Chapter Four, a small piece, was originally carved as a part of a complex of privileges belonging to a particular Clayoquot Nuu-chah-nulth chief. It has already inspired many take-offs recently seen on the art market, including examples made by a Kwakwaka'wakw artist and an Ojibway. The famous Nuxalk Sun Mask from the collection of the American Museum of Natural History has also been reimagined by both a Nuu-chah-nulth artist and one of Nuxalk descent. This phenomenon has even permitted Haida artist Robert Davidson to imaginatively "create crests" for some of his non-native clients. A request for a totem pole by a land developer in Toronto was fulfilled with a carving that incorporated an image of the legendary Raven bringing a house to the Haida people. Davidson has also included eagles in carvings made for several of his American non-native patrons in reference to their "national bird." The characteristic Haida totem pole image of the Three Watchmen, usually seen at the top of old poles, was placed at the bottom of a set of three separate new totem poles also destined for a Toronto location. These figures were altered again by positioning them back-to-back, a poetic modification created to refer to the complex and repetitive relationships between past, present, and future. "The story will evolve," commented Davidson, with "intuition and humor" (Mar. 26, 1993: interview).

Interestingly, the story of the various versions of the *nulami'sta yelxst!ayo* screen, and their public presentation as the prerogative of different individuals, illustrates an important exception to this generalizing tendency. Several different Kwakwa̱ka'wakw people laid claim to the screen image, but even this great license to appropriate from one group to another, now observed in so many commercial works from the Northwest Coast, may be reversed and astutely applied to cite difference. Again, the Kwakwa̱ka'wakw are still tenacious in maintaining opportunities, even under the most unusual circumstances, to display their exclusive prerogatives.

Artworks such as these become quite influential, both in the ongoing careers and promotion of certain native artists and for the education and pleasure of various outsiders. Therefore Benedict Anderson's work (1991) is again helpful here because of his many suggestions that the policies of nineteenth-century colonial states contributed to the imagining of national identities, and that some of these eventually exceeded their original defining roles. These affected the consciousness of populations and were made to serve ends that could not have been foreseen. Similarly art, now an expression of existing conditions, may come to affect life in the future on the Northwest Coast. Many opportunities for artistic expression in prestigious venues and the demonstration of authoritative knowledge in the non-native context have already been created by non-Indian sponsors to accompany this generalization of identities, as described above. In some cases, therefore, definitions of individual and family identity that conferred power in the past may eventually be obscured, or augmented, by greater affiliation with larger groups who have more influence. Considerable knowledge about membership in small subdivisions is already lost, although it may be recovered or even reconstructed. For now, relatively unified displays of ethnic identity are popular among outsider audiences, which frequently include those who patronize replicated works. More finely tuned divisions, however, still serve important purposes at home, on the reserves.

Artistic Differences

These practices suggest even greater differences in relation to the requirements set for non-Indian artists. Here in the meeting grounds of the West, where native history and lineage must at least appear to be accurate and seamless, some indication of community and historical reference will be displayed. The "copyist" strategies of white artists, who are thought to work completely on their own, however, high-light only disjunction and discontinuity of the generations. Rosalind Krauss in-advertently captured the essence of these artistic differences in her recent essay about Cindy Sherman's series *Film Stills,* photographed in the late 1970s and often thought to parrot movie images of women from the 1950s. The artist claims, "Some people have told me they remember the movie that one of my images is derived from, but in fact I had no film in mind at all." [1] Krauss (1993) identifies this lack of clear models or originals for the languid and lost young women in these black-and-white images with a kind of "intense, generalized memory" that informs the critical dialogues of Sherman's generation, but does not tell us any-thing more about Lana Turner's or Bette Davis's genre.

On the contrary, Northwest Coast works like Tom Hunt's *Tuxw'id Screen* (1990) have a much larger task. This piece must allude to the adventures of an ancient heroine, the conferring of her power on individuals of this generation, and its moving parts must also pique the interests of such contemporary wizards of undetermined cultural affiliation who people the corporate offices of, say, Microsoft. As Northwest Coast art moves into the public domain, it addresses contemporary outsiders, but it must continue to acknowledge history to main-tain its mystique—a drastic departure from the unspoken mandate applied to certain twentieth-century non-native "copyists" whose works assert iconoclasm. Warhol had no need to sell soup itself, only a multiplicity of soup-can images that challenged the hierarchy of subject matter which existed for fine art practice prior to the interventions of his generation.

Similar modern/postmodern practices may motivate native artists from other regions of the U.S. and Canada more directly than their Northwest Coast contemporaries. Important historical differences farther south and east—such as earlier sustained contact and greater economic devastation—made Indian au-tonomy even more difficult to maintain. At the same time, the discipline of the highly conventionalized formline system for flat art as well as standard require-ments for sculpture has been unique to the Northwest Coast. Although exclusive ownership may be associated with the painted designs known from tipi covers and war shirts on the Plains, most were created by nonspecialists in a freehand style on the basis of personal history or visionary experience. The design reper-toires of some Pueblo potters encoded important information about the home and identity of the artists, but Bunzel (1929) was just as impressed with the malleability of a system that permitted expressions from the artists' dreams. On the Northwest Coast, only the shaman created artworks completely on the basis of his personal experiences.

The range of artistic approaches on display at the National Gallery of Canada show *Land, Spirit, Power* of 1992 has already been described as being related to regional affiliation. James Luna, a Luiseño-Diestueño from California, for example, maintains an enormous amount of flexibility in negotiating the full spectrum of requirements set by both his native and non-native viewers. Luna discloses that he is well aware of the diversity of his audience, but claims, "I make my art for Indian people first, that is to say, I do not make it for the approval of the people, but so that they will get it" (quoted in Townsend-Gault 1992: 191). For Luna, it is possible to display four pairs of women's underpants on hangers—in yellow, black, white, and red—to proclaim that *The Sacred Colors Are Everywhere* (1992). He may transform the traditional with fewer limits than those required in discourse with the native community in the Northwest. His canny ability to "out" native perspectives for a more general audience, and probably amuse many traditional people at the same time, is more reminiscent of Cindy Sherman's knack for speaking to contemporary women and men by appropriating signs that originate in her mother's generation.

Rick Rivet, a Métis artist from Aklavik in the Northwest Territories (not the Northwest Coast) works in acrylic on canvas in a painterly style that he defines as "an expressionist/primitivist approach" (quoted in McMaster and Martin 1992: 170). His work is extremely provocative as a reversal of Northwest Coast citation of native historical imagery. Rivet has used some well-known historical photographs of non-native protagonists posed at certain defining moments of colonial history as models for his paintings. Images of General Custer, or an armored conquistador with the face of a boar in *Legacy*, are no match for the devastation described in his painting *Wounded Knee #2* (1991), which is clearly a new version of George Trager's famous photograph, *The Dead at the Battle of Wounded Knee, S.D.* Rivet includes the image of the conquistador at the scene, a Nazi officer and other military figures plucked from history, and a Ku Klux Klan member. They preside over the grisly deposit of corpses into a trench, a mass burial that elicits associated nightmare memories of the Holocaust. This artist takes what he needs from the non-native past to create this dark vision.

On the Northwest Coast, such liberties are taken only by the exceptional Lawrence Paul Yuxweluptun. Generally Northwest Coast artists are different, motivated to refer to their own histories or those of their immediate neighbors. They may be willing to transgress band affiliations or family distinctions within their own region for the sake of art or for a greater public voice, but at present that is the limit of the mix. Artists from other regions continue to cross more distant borders, national and international. One may find a Tony Hunt piece or Nathan Jackson's work in Germany or New York, but their art speaks to Vancouver Island or Southeast Alaska and to those who admire Northwest Coast cultures.

Implications for Repatriation

This difference, the Northwest Coast perspective that enables the recycling of form, may come to function beyond strictly artistic or market applications. The reuse of historical models may have some implications for repatriation issues that will only be of use in this region. The return of cultural property has been of greater concern to museum curators and others since the passage of the Native American Grave Protection and Repatriation Act in 1990. Some native groups in Canada and the United States have already been called upon to consider replication as one solution to the intricate problems related to these new requests for the return of selected works of art to native hands.

The descendants of Oglala Lakota survivors of the Wounded Knee massacre of 1890 were recently made aware of such an option in Barre, Massachusetts. A small one-room museum located in the town's library was informed that its collection of beaded shirts, leggings, wooden pipes, and locks of human hair were actually taken from the bodies of Wounded Knee victims. The Wounded Knee Survivors Association and the Oglala Lakota tribe are now seeking the return of those artifacts. A lawyer for the survivors' association has suggested that the library association's fears that objects of historical value will be buried and lost forever may be alleviated by a replication project. His plan calls for Lakota artists to recreate some of them—those not considered sacred—for display at the library. Some native people, however, have taken issue with the right of the library even to exhibit facsimiles of what they consider "stolen" property, yet others are pleased with the library's museum for having preserved these important objects (*New York Times* Feb. 19, 1993: A12).

This approach is unlikely to succeed in the southwestern United States. It appears that some Zuni masks and perhaps other ceremonial objects were probably created as replicas specifically for collectors like Stewart Culin of The Brooklyn Museum and Matilda Coxe Stevenson of the Smithsonian Institution (then the U.S. National Museum) in the late nineteenth and early twentieth centuries. Although these artworks may never have been used in traditional contexts, the Zuni are adamant about their right to regain control over their disposition. They have justified their position by citing a case from the 1950s, when they discovered that a group of Boy Scouts from La Junta, California had reproduced certain Zuni masks for their own "mock" Indian dances. A series of communications between the Boy Scouts and the Zuni, along with a complaint that some religious leaders brought to the Commissioner of Indian Affairs, convinced the Scouts to give up their masks (Merrill, Ladd, and Ferguson 1993: 523–67; Fane June 20, 1995: interview). Zuni leaders still claim that the correct combination of specific mask features functions as a type of formula. The proper configuration of eyes, snouts, and other identifying characteristics "calls the deity" and imbues the mask with a sacred character, regardless of the materials or cultural origin of its maker.[2]

As may be expected, on the Northwest Coast similar proposals for replication may not be rejected across the board. In 1958, chiefs of the Kitwancool in British Columbia negotiated with Wilson Duff and Michael Kew of the British Columbia Provincial Museum and the British Columbia Totem Pole Preservation Committee to allow the removal of several old totem poles for preservation. Their agreement included a requirement that exact replicas of these poles would be provided for Kitwancool (Royal British Columbia Museum 1959).

Several years ago, the Moachat Nuu-chah-nulth band was consulted by Aldona Jonaitis, then of the American Museum of Natural History, and Richard Inglis, then of the Royal British Columbia Museum, on the appropriate handling and research of a complex of artifacts known as The Whale Shrine. The combination of architectural elements, carved figures, and human skulls is a part of the AMNH collection and was being considered at that point for reinstallation in an exhibition gallery. Unlike the Oglala Lakota or Zuni examples, a replicated version of the piece was suggested for use in the native location, near the town of Gold River on the west coast of Vancouver Island, rather than for the halls of the museum. This project was considered with enthusiasm by some Moachat as a symbol of cultural pride as well as a financial asset if popularized as a tourist attraction. Other members of the community were more concerned that their ability to control the powerful magic of the shrine, even in replicated form, was lost along with the songs and other ceremonial practices that would have been known in the past by a specialist. In any case, unrelated factors have delayed this project indefinitely.[3]

As a related example, George MacDonald of the Canadian Museum of Civilization reports that he has sent an extensive photographic record of the museum's collection to members of a Tsimshian tribal council at Port Simpson in the form of a laser disk. He expects that some of these pieces will be copied by native trainees in a proposed carving program there (Nov. 19, 1992: interview). Although MacDonald did not send the disk in relation to a specific repatriation project, this gesture may eventually return historical images to their community of origin. (Recall as well that the house plans from the Grand Hall at the CMC have already been reappropriated by a Tsimshian group.)

A variety of responses to such proposals will emerge. It is likely that the greatest success with repatriation by replica will be seen on the Northwest Coast. Here a long history of such transactions exists—traditional images, even ones that represent high privileges, have been sold, transferred, altered, and put on public display. As discussed in Chapter Four, many Northwest Coast objects in museum collections may already be "new generation" pieces, although curators and other custodians may not realize this.

It is also a matter of public knowledge that some contemporary Northwest Coast groups already incorporate close copies of important old pieces in their current ceremonial practices. A number of important *at.óow* or "owned or purchased things," items of regalia of the T'akdeintaan Tlingit for instance, were destroyed in a clan house fire in Hoonah in 1944. Several clan hats and other extremely valuable objects were lost, and very similar replacements have since been carved for them. Among these is the Mountain Tribe Dog Hat, a historically important image that relates to clan oratory. The new piece has been used for traditional display purposes, for instance at a memorial potlatch held for Willie Marks, a prominent member of the community, in October, 1981; Marks himself had carved this version of the hat. In contemporary T'akdeintaan ceremony, these replicated items of regalia are apparently regarded as authentic expressions of the ancient stories and clan history (Henrikson Dec. 7, 1992: letter to author; Davenhauer and Davenhauer 1990: 102; passim).

In the same manner, a wooden crest hat in the form of a frog, the property of the Kiks.ádi Tlingit clan, was sold at auction to the Alaska State Museum in 1975. The Kiks.ádi maintain the right to borrow the hat from the museum for traditional ceremonies, but a replica was also produced as part of the sales agreement. Interestingly, the new version of the hat was carved by non-native artist John Livingston. It too is brought out with reverence at potlatches, sometimes placed directly next to the old one on a table that displays various important items of regalia (Henrikson Dec. 7, 1992: letter to author). This matter of replacement by replica is quite complex, however, and it should be noted that new pieces are not simply interchangeable with old ones. Very old regalia is considered even more prestigious by the Tlingit, as these items may continue to gain in value both as spiritual objects and as property that has been "paid for" repeatedly, after having made multiple potlatch appearances.

I too have seen newly made take-offs deriving from old Kwakwaka'wakw masks from the collection of the American Museum of Natural History, which were used both at a potlatch and at a feast in Alert Bay in 1993. The older prototypes became well known after the publication of the *Chiefly Feasts* exhibition catalog in 1991 and may have inspired a new Xwixwi mask, a transformation mask that resembles the hero Siwidi from the Undersea Kingdom story, and an Echo mask with various interchangeable snouts and beaks. The new masks were admired in the big house and accepted without comment, at least in a public forum.

This acceptance of recreated items of regalia for traditional ceremonial purposes should not be regarded as uniform practice on the Northwest Coast. Evidence also indicates that certain very special old objects are considered to have historical importance that may not be transferred by simple formal transcription. Again the Tlingit consider some old artworks as having historical importance based upon "physical evidence" intrinsic to their individual histories. For example, a crest hat in the form of a Brown Bear's head was the property of the Kiks.ádi clan, and its construction is documented by Swanton (1908: 419, fig. 105). The original owner was said to have fought the bear after it had attacked and killed several people. The offending animal was then destroyed with an ax blow to its head, and its skin was used to make the hat. These wounds were left on the pelt at the top of the hat as evidence of the encounter, and of the owner's heroic deed. Other similar cases are known. The importance of the skin and teeth of the supposed "original" Nanya.ayí Brown Bear that saved the clan from a great flood has already been described in Chapters One and Four (see Plate 3). The Coho clan in Sitka also owns such an object, a robe torn by a bullet during the Battle of Sitka in 1804. Similarly, the Kiks.ádi clan's Raven Hat was worn at one time by their ancestor Katlean and is said to incorporate the very hair of the slaves who were killed to commission the manufacture of the hat.[4]

The Tlingit are not the only group that may accord specific one-of-a-kind objects a special status on the basis of their history. In the best known repatriation case on the Northwest Coast, Kwakwaka'wakw representatives achieved the return of most of the potlatch artifacts taken from them in 1922, seized under duress from some of the twenty-two individuals arrested for participation in the grand-scale potlatch on Village Island, which was held in defiance of non-native law at the end of 1921. This process of repatriation took a great deal of time and the devotion of many members of the Kwakwaka'wakw community. Negotiations began in the early 1970s. Two native-run museums were funded and built to prepare for the return of these objects, the Kwagiulth Museum in Cape Mudge and the U'mista Cultural Centre in Alert Bay, completed in 1979 and 1980 respectively. The "Potlatch Collection" held by the Canadian Museum of Civilization was the first portion returned, but not until 1987 did the Royal Ontario Museum return the second one, and only after heated and lengthy negotiations. More recently The Museum of the American Indian / George Heye Foundation (now The National Museum of the American Indian) also returned some of the objects that it held (Webster 1988: 43–44; Clifford 1991: 212–54). These specific properties could never have been replaced by formal reference or facsimile.

Therefore the question of repatriation by replica on the Northwest Coast remains open. Although some cases suggest that updated versions of older works may "stand in" for their predecessors in ceremony, and certainly in non-native displays, we must return here to the question of authorization. Some circumstances, worked out by specific individuals, may someday permit commissioned substitutions. Yet the resulting forms will not tell us all that we need to know about the significance of these replicas, no matter how accurately they mirror the older pieces. The composition of those groups that govern their production and arbitrate the style and site of their display will be just as significant. Repatriation negotiations, like the processes associated with other forms of art reproduction on the Northwest Coast, are complex ones relating to assertions of ownership of the native past and to a lesser extent to issues of historical accuracy.

The Northwest Coast, Native North America, and Others

The most accurate Northwest Coast replicas as well as the newest variations on the old themes, those that acknowledge history only obliquely, are still outstanding and different when considered against the vehement avant-gardism of the modern west. As yet Northwest Coast artists have little incentive to emulate the conceptual models posed by non-native traditions. The resulting works of art are therefore usually understood by outsiders to be of some educational value rather than of artistic interest, or perhaps merely nostalgic, particularly when sponsored by white authorities. To a greater extent than the paintings and performance pieces made by native artists from other regions in North America, such works have been thought to highlight an admirable past that can only be shadowed by a repetitive and disempowered present.

Some greater insight has been achieved through the study of individual style and the recognition of change in native Northwest Coast art, but these investigations grow from our own familiar pursuits. Studies by non-native scholars have, until recently, been preoccupied with the identification of formal attributes observed apart from their selective use and the contemporary shifts in authority that affect their public image.

Although the art of the Northwest Coast is clearly motivated by unique concerns, it is possible that a growing corpus of indigenous art forms that originate in other parts of the world may also cite local histories in a variety of ways that affect their reception by outsiders. Other "art revivals" have expanded the international market for ethnic arts. Some of these new or recreated traditions are also produced with accompanying discourses that position them in relation to the arts made by the genetic forebears of the artists.

As Fred Myers has suggested in relation to acrylic paintings by the contemporary Pintupi, an Australian Aboriginal people, these discourses may be wildly variable depending whether they originate from local producing communities or, instead, from their new international audiences. Again we have the sense of parallel realities. In the Aboriginal case, the painted designs are said to originate with "the Dreamings," which are owned by certain groups through inheritance and associated with specific locales. As Myers explains, however, outsiders tend to recognize a number of qualities that they are predisposed to appreciate in this art form which do not quite correlate with Pintupi ideas of the work. The antiquity of Aboriginal art and its basis in certain spiritual practices are considered to be admirable, as are the political assertions that relate to Aboriginal identity and claims to land as they are understood by non-Aboriginals. These ideas about Pintupi life and history have become associated with the acrylic paintings and enhance their interest in the eyes of some white viewers. At the same time, these images are appreciated in relation to modernist ideas of fine art, particularly as powerful abstract compositions casually associated with paintings by non-native artists which are familiar to New York gallery visitors and art critics (Myers 1992: 319–55).

The history and context of nonwestern art forms, as announced by related texts, marketing strategies, and popular media (recall the *Pocahontas* debate) will usually attempt to define their relationship to or departure from historical antecedents. The Inuit soapstone carvings discussed earlier (pp. 129–30) were first marketed in the late 1940s, and their positive reception was orchestrated in relation to the supposed legitimacy of their connection with the late archaeological and early postcontact arts of the Arctic region. James Houston argued for this continuity with the past. But Nelson Graburn and Edmund Carpenter contended that the overwhelming majority of Inuit claimed never to have carved soapstone before they were encouraged to do so for the art market, although some relatively unadorned soapstone seal-oil lamps and cooking pots were known.[5]

Postcontact arts from Africa created specifically for the art market were negatively evaluated as soon as they departed from the assumed legitimacy of the African past. These sentiments may have been suggested to students of African art for the first time by William Fagg in his early designation of African traditions as "classical" and not "romantic," despite his own groundbreaking studies that identified the individual styles of particular master artists in Africa. He clearly states his views on the subject and the high value he attaches to artistic productions made in support of history and community, rather than as the uncertain expressions of feeling and originality. Fagg's legacy may have been established by his statement that "Western art is still wallowing, even though ever more uncertainly, in the lotus-eating autoeroticism engendered by the romantic movement" (1969: 42–57). Contemporary artists in Africa, he argued, might be "true artists," but "they are not truly African artists" (ibid.: 45). Contemporary African artists are received with much greater interest today, though this idea of insurmountable disjunction between the practices of the past and the present may not be entirely forgotten. For example, The National Museum of African Art in Washington, D.C., has conceived two discrete curatorial positions in reference to the custodianship and scholarship that it will contribute to the field—one for classical African art and one for modern African art.[6] This distinction reflects the extraordinary status still attributed to past practice.

It should be understood that public images constructed for these diverse nonwestern art traditions have so far been largely informed by the comments of outsiders. The new popularity of consultation processes in the creation and display of Native American and Native Canadian art may now just begin to reveal the perspectives of insiders. Similar developments are almost certainly in store for indigenous people from other parts of the world, but they will make something completely different of it.

On the Northwest Coast, artistic references to the past are still clear and recognizable. They have previously been known by the extraordinary conventions developed for this purpose over thousands of years. Now we may look to these representations and wonder exactly who it was that imagined them. Superficially their visualizations appear to be uniform and anonymous. One Brown Bear with its mouth stretched wide and its internal organs as uncannily visible as its broad grin may appear to differ little from another. We may find its features described on an old totem pole, on a piece of stationary in a gift shop, in a serigraph print, or with its dismembered parts distributed in a different manner than ever before by holograph or in pixels. Now, however, it is possible to follow from the outset some of the latest cross-cultural transactions that parallel the making of such images. These negotiations may even be documented while in process and so reveal the completely individual regard for the past that each close copy substantiates.

Notes

Introduction

1. The term 'Northwest Coast,' as it is used here, refers to a "culture area" that has been defined according to certain shared practices, such as traditional subsistence technology, ceremonial practice, and the use of conventionalized forms elaborated in art and architecture. The area corresponds to slightly variable geographical boundaries that define the North Pacific coast of North America. On the north, the area is delineated by the Copper River delta on the Gulf of Alaska. The panhandle and the islands off its shores from as far as Yakutat Bay are the northern reaches of traditional Tlingit territory. The Queen Charlotte Islands, or Haida Gwaii, British Columbia, is the home of the Haida people, a distinct group. A portion of the Haida population also live across Dixon Entrance on the southern part of Prince of Wales Island in southeastern Alaska. The Tsimshian speaking peoples—including the Southern Tsimshian, Coast Tsimshian, Nis'ga and Gitksan—live in northwestern British Columbia, traditionally along the Nass and Skeena Rivers. The Haisla, Bella Bella (now called Heiltsuk people), the Bella Coola (now Nuxalk), and Oowekeeno live farther south. The group known as Kwakiutl now call themselves Kwakwa̱ka'wakw or Kwagiulth and live on the north and eastern portions of Vancouver Island as well as in the coastal villages along the waterways, islands, and mainland opposite. The west coast of Vancouver Island is the traditional home of the Nuu-chah-nulth people (formerly known as Nootka) and the southern part of the island is Coast Salish territory, as is a large portion of the mainland of British Columbia opposite. The coast of Washington in the United States is the traditional home of the Makah, Quileute, and other groups that share cultural traits with those who live in this region.

2. James Clifford's new work (1997) describes some of the long history of interaction among native and non-native groups as the reciprocal activities of travelers. He proposes that our knowledge of other cultures has been informed, at least in part, by the experiences of "insider-outsiders, good translators and explicators, they've been around. The people studied by anthropologists have seldom been homebodies" (p. 19). Now travelers of both native and non-native descent have more information about others available to them than ever before.

3. Interestingly, Lawrence Paul Yuxweluptun's (Cowichan-Okanagan) experimental works were included in this exhibition as well. At present, he is the only Northwest Coast native artist who paints in a somewhat Surrealist style and has made some forays into the medium of "virtual reality." His work is discussed in greater detail in Chapter Four.

4. *Reserve*, a Canadian term, is used throughout this volume. American readers are more familiar with the term *reservation*.

5. Certain terms familiar to anthropologists are used in this section. For other readers, a few brief definitions may be useful: *Clans* are social divisions, usually thought to descend from a common ancestor, that function in some ways as groups. *Lineages* usually refer to traceable lines of descent from an ancestor. *Moieties* are the two primary subdivisions, or halves, of a larger tribal group that maintain certain reciprocal responsibilities.

6. Holm 1983: 28–29, 88–93; Macnair et al. 1984: 75–77. The cannibal bird masks discussed in both of these volumes are also illustrated on these pages.

7. For an explanation of the stylistic conventions associated with the northern Northwest Coast graphic tradition see Holm (1965). For more information on the relationship of formal rules to Haida argillite production during chronologically delineated periods see Macnair and Hoover (1984).

8. I have discussed this issue with Gerald McMaster, Curator of Contemporary Indian Art at the Canadian Museum of Civilization, and he corroborates my observation that no contemporary Northwest Coast artists have yet strayed completely from traditional art (telephone interview, July 17, 1995).

9. Krauss (1993) has challenged this formal and socially decontextualized break with the past that is claimed for the avant garde.

10. See Clifford 1986: 98–121. A supposed "golden age," a romantic and static past commonly thought to define native cultures, is discussed on these pages.

11. Anson Rabinach has effectively argued that Benjamin's historical approach does not simply equate authority with the legitimate claim to great historical depth and tradition: "Benjamin's anti-canon of discontinuity is too strong, his sense of rupture too great, to permit the paternal triad of Law, constraint and identity to become a binding force" (1979: 60–64).

Chapter One

Expedience and Classicism at the Chief Shakes Community House

1. For a discussion of the exclusion of tourist arts from public discourse, see Ruth Phillips (1998, 1992). Jonaitis (1993) explores the subject of the supposed loss of tradition in the evaluation of Haida argillite carvings by scholars and museum anthropologists.

2. These early descriptions of Tlingit-style houses are summarized in Emmons/de Laguna 1991: 64–65 in Frederica de Laguna's additions to the text. She refers to Malaspina 1849 and Suria, ed. Wagner, 1936.

3. It is interesting to note here that the house posts from the Chief Shakes house were sketched by Emmons, illustrating their importance as carved crest images. See Emmons/de Laguna 1991: 205.

4. For additional discussion of the concept of crest privilege on the Northwest Coast, Introduction, above, pp. 5–6.

5. Steve Brown suggests this date (1991: personal interview). The fragment of the screen is from the Burke Museum, cat. no. 1–1463. I was able to examine this object in February, 1993.

6. The story of the Nanya.ayí Brown Bear is recorded in Swanton 1909: 231.

7. Tradition has it that each time the skin on this mask wore out, it was refurbished with new fur. Also see Chapter Four, below, on the contemporary revival of this mask image in Northwest Coast native art.

8. No date is known for the beginning of Shakes IV's reign, but it continued until he died, in 1840, after the clan had migrated to the present site in Wrangell. The history of the Nanya.ayí as well as the genealogical ties among the various generations of the Shakes line is succinctly explained in Keithahn 1981: 1–7.

9. It should be noted here that the Hudson's Bay Company made an agreement with the Russian-American Company to lease all of its territory on the mainland south of Cape Spencer for a period of ten years with an option to renew, beginning on June 1, 1840. The Russian redoubt was then renamed Fort Stikine by the British, who were also awarded sole rights to purchase fur from the natives living there, including the Stikines (see Arndt 1983). I believe Tolmie is describing Shakes IV in the quote from his text because these negotiations for non-native settlement of the Stikine took place before 1840, the year that the HBC was established at the fort and coincidentally, the year of Shakes IV's death.

10. Keithahn reports that there were at least twenty-seven community houses at the old site when first encountered by a trader called Captain Haines early in the nineteenth century (1981: 5−6).

11. The Gonakadet legend is recorded by Swanton 1909: 165−73. Steve Brown has associated the double-headed killer whale image on the totem pole with two earlier models. One is a carved crest hat from the AMNH collection (cat. no. E2092, collected ca. 1882 by George T. Emmons). The other is a tobacco pipe now in the collection of the Burke Museum (cat. no. 2.5E561). See Brown 1994: 77. The pipe is also described in Holm 1987: 202 and is illustrated as Plate 83.

12. The Muybridge photograph of the Gonakadet pole is in the National Anthropological Archives, Smithsonian Institution, Washington D.C., neg. no. 56054.

13. Photograph by Partridge, ca. 1886. Peabody Museum, Harvard University (Holm 1987: 195).

14. For Muir's drawing, see *Sierra Club Bulletin* 10: 1 (Jan. 1916): Plate CXLII, John Muir Memorial Number. For the photograph see neg. no. 73.3.13.15, photographer unknown, Archives of the Tongass Historical Museum.

15. Photograph probably by George Davidson, May 1878, USNM cat. no. 4780.

16. Sturtevant defined the "Museum Period" as the years between the 1840s and 1890 (1969: 622). George Stocking, however, dates the beginning of the period to coincide with the opening of the Peabody Museum of Archaeology and Ethnology in 1866 (1985: 7). Douglas Cole traced the activities of museums that vied for the collection of Northwest Coast native artifacts during this period and claims that the "scramble" was over by 1906 (1985: 212). Martha Black (1992) has already associated this period with the development of photography.

17. See for instance Harlan E. Smith, 1909, AMNH neg. no. 46122.

18. Harlan E. Smith, 1909, AMNH neg. nos. 46123 and 46124.

19. Archives, American Museum of Natural History. See Emmons/de Laguna 1991: 205 for an example.

20. Brown 1987: 160. Brown tracks the earliest works of this artist to as far back as 1775 (ibid.: 164). Barbeau says the posts were installed at Wrangell at least from 1869 (1950: 610). They may be as much as 200 years old today.

21. Some other photographs of the Shakes house interior during that period, which may also be classified as such "contents displays," are RBCM photograph no. 1662, photographer unknown, ca. 1900, described in detail by Keithahn 1963: 95. From the University of Washington Libraries, Special Collections: photograph no. 2557, Arthur Pillsbury, 1898. From the Viola Garfield Collection photograph no. 3732, photographer unknown, ca. 1900−1916.

22. The photograph with large framed objects is from the University of Washington Libraries, Special Collections, neg. no. NA 3732, ca. 1900−1916. Other photographs of the period that coincides with George Shakes' tenure as chief (after 1878−1916) also include significant displays of prestige objects of both native and non-native manufacture. Also from the University of Washington Libraries, Special Collections, neg. no. NA 2548, is a scene photographed by Partridge in 1887. Here framed pictures, patterned cloth, and a clock are shown with various traditional Tlingit garments decorated with crest images. The cast-iron stove presides at the center of the space at this date, as it also does in a photograph from the collection of the Royal British Columbia Museum (neg. PN 1662, ca. 1900, photographer unknown), here amid a dazzling collection of Tlingit masks and other regalia.

23. This letter from Fort Wrangell, Alaska, dated August 5, 1879, was the personal property of George Shakes during his lifetime. This document and other "papers" of George Shakes are now in the Alaska State Historical Library and Archives in Juneau. Some of these empowered and authorized him to act as native policeman. In addition to the letter quoted in the text, see, for instance, November 2, 1881, from the Deputy Collector of the Customs House of Alaska authorizing an arrest in a smuggling case. A letter dated March 4, 1894, from the U.S. Marshal's Office of the District of Alaska authorized Shakes to break up illegal distilleries. A letter dated January 29, 1898, from W. A. Kelly, Superintendent of Schools in Sitka, reminded Shakes of his responsibility as "chief of police" to have the native children in Wrangell attend school. A letter from John Brady, Governor of Alaska, dated November 22, 1898, terminates George Shakes' position as Indian Policeman.

24. For the CCC Totem Parks, see Gower 1972; Keithahn 1963: 116–17; Katherine Kuh 1946; Garfield and Forrest 1961; Duff, Wallen and Clark 1969; Rakestraw n.d.; Jonaitis 1989. First initiated in the winter of 1933–34, the corps was known at first as the ECW (Emergency Conservation Work). Later, in 1937, the program was called by its popular name, the CCC (Civilian Conservation Corps). There were CCC

camps at Juneau, Ketchikan, Petersburg, Cordova, and Sitka. In 1937 a federal policy decision mandated that 50 percent of the enrollees in the CCC in Alaska must be Alaska natives (Indian and Eskimo), and that native CCC projects be listed for the years between 1937 and 1941. At this time, men in their thirties, forties, and above were hired for the program, which had originally been established for younger men. These new policies were developed in response to a protest against discriminatory CCC hiring practices made by the Alaska Native Brotherhood. In 1936 hearings were held before a Senate subcommittee on Indian Affairs in Ketchikan and Juneau (Paige 1985; Sorensen, Rakestraw, and Martin 1986: 5–7).

25. A report written for the Wrangell Cooperative Association by Pat Greene Ockert, "Wrangell Totem Poles and Chief Shakes Island Preservation and Restoration Project" (n.d.), explains: "Those holding title to the island during the 1930s decided to turn over their deeds to the U.S. Forest Service so that the island should be turned into a totem park. . . . The *title* to the island was turned over to the Bureau of Indian Affairs to manage. Local management of the island has been tossed back and forth between the BIA and various local organizations since 1940. *Title* to the island was transferred back to the Wrangell Cooperative Association (IRA Council). The transfer marked an end to over forty years of the local people fighting for the return of the island."

26. Linn Forrest had been a member of the group of architects that designed the Timberline Lodge on Mount Hood, Oregon. His first work in the Alaska National Forests was to redraft the design of the old Son-I-hat building, or "Whale House," at Old Kasaan (Archbold 1939: 16–18).

27. Thomas Ukas was author of "The Chief Shakes House," *The Alaska Sportsman* (Oct. 1968): 14–15. Brown gives the year of

Thomas Ukas' birth as 1890, and for the first time links his work with that of his father, the carver William Ukas (1994: 84).

28. Interview, Oct. 31, 1983, on the reconstruction of the Chief Shakes Community House with Linn Forrest Sr., project architect; transcript on file at the Wrangell Museum.

29. Copies by Ukas and Thomas are the Sea Lion Prince Pole, Kadashan Red Snapper Pole, Kadashan Crane Pole, Underwater Grizzly Pole, Three Frogs Pole, Bear-up-the-Mountain Pole, Sea Serpent Pole. The two originals carved by these men in 1940 are the Sun Totem and Eagle Totem.

30. Ritter and Voelckers 1983: interview with Linn Forrest; Ockert 1981.

31. Also from the 1983 Ritter and Voelkers interview, Forrest claims that he was inspired to design a facade painting or "front carved motif" by "early lithographs," especially one that he calls "The House of Many Faces," which he apparently studied in researching old Tlingit houses. Although he has referred to a historical model, his choice was probably inaccurate, since this is the Dogfish House, not the Brown Bear House. Forrest, incidentally, is not responsible for the later production of the interior screen that resembles the semi-abstract design motifs of a Chilkat robe.

32. Emmons describes similar construction technology for the Whale House at Klukwan: "Midway along each of the two sides and in the middle of the back wall was an intermediate upright, correspondingly grooved along both edges to take the other ends of the horizontal wall planks. Across the front, two heavy timbers or planks, one resting on the other, extended from corner post to corner post and built up the front wall to the height of the door sill. The upper member of this pair was grooved along its upper edge to hold the lower ends of the vertical planks that formed the house front" (1991: 61).

33. At the age of 76, Jones, also known as Kudanake and reported to be the seventh lineal descendant of Shakes I, was installed as Chief Shakes VII at a special ceremony at the Wrangell ANB building. Other individuals and families, however, have reported a stronger claim to the Shakes title than that of Charley Jones and his descendants. In 1970, for instance, Forrest DeWitt Sr. carved and raised a 45-foot totem pole in honor of his son Jonathan DeWitt in Ketchikan. The accompanying festivities were meant to validate his claim to the Shakes title. This claim has not been recognized at Wrangell, however, and the Tlingit community remains divided on this issue.

34. *The Alaskan* (a monthly publication of the Alaska CCC), June 20, 1940: 6. The official program of the Wrangell Potlatch is published in *The Wrangell Sentinel*, May 31, 1940: 1, and in a booklet circulated by Wrangell Potlatch Inc., with a cover letter by E. L. Keithahn, manager, dated May 10, 1940; on file at the Wrangell Museum. The 1983 interview with Linn Forrest specifies that the Indian communities were contacted in person and that Forrest acted as escort for a group from Ketchikan. Native groups from Kake, Klawok, and Hydaburg also attended the celebration.

35. *The Wrangell Sentinel*, May 31, 1940: 1, and the Wrangell Potlatch booklet on file at the Wrangell Museum.

36. Mrs. Marge Byrd of Wrangell and others teach and organize the activities of the *Shx'at K̲waan* dancers (August 26, 1992: interview).

37. The Kiks.ádi Totem, Raven Totem, Kit Totem, the One-Legged Fisherman Totem, and the Bear-up-the-Mountain and Gonakadet poles were recarved in 1984, along with the four Shark posts. Funding for this project was established in 1980 by the Office of History and Archaeology, matched with local funds and in-kind services by the Alaska State Museum, and was associated with a training program for young carvers.

38. Contract on file at The Wrangell Museum; courtesy of Patricia Greene Ockert, project director.

39. Brown (1987: 174n7) explains that the face below the tail of the new Shark-Octopus post, "The tail of the main Shark, and the head of the secondary Shark on the right were ceremonially chopped off and distributed to bereaved families of a canoe-load of potlatch guests who drowned on their way to Khasitláan." This was reported to him by Ms. Ethel Lund, formerly of Wrangell. Herem offers the late Herb Bradley's explanation for the missing parts, stating that one of the owners, an early Chief Shakes, hacked them off the house posts at a potlatch to pay in advance for any mishaps that might occur to his guests on their way home (1978: 50–51).

40. On August 26, 1992, I interviewed Nellie Torgramsen, who claims to be a descendant of Chief Shakes. She expressed the artistic perspective recorded here.

Chapter 2

The Map and the Territory in the Grand Hall at the Canadian Museum of Civilization

1. For information on Boas and museum display see Jacknis 1985: 75–111. For dioramas or "life groups" that depict Northwest Coast culture in particular, see Jonaitis 1988: 135, and Cole 1985: 135–39.

2. The woman working with cedar bark is a part of a "life group" designed by Boas for the Northwest Coast Hall at the American Museum of Natural History. The Grizzly Bear dancer appears in the film *From the Land of the War Canoes* (1914) by Edward Curtis.

3. For studies of criteria applied in the process of museum collection, see essays in Stocking 1985; Cole 1985; Lumley 1988; and Berlo 1992.

4. See essays in *Art/artifact* (1988), the catalog that accompanied the exhibition at The Center for African Art in New York, on the differences between the contextualization of "fine arts" and "ethnographic arts." See also R. Krauss (1985) on issues of style, social and economic context that have, until now, received less attention in Western art history.

Interestingly, my perusal (Dec. 15, 1994) of the small Northwest Coast native art collection at the Metropolitan Museum of Art in New York revealed some methodological differences between ethnological and art museum practices. The Northwest Coast pieces at the Met were acquired for the most part in the same manner as the western artworks in its collections—at auction and as gifts from private collectors. Therefore museum records reveal almost no collection data, not even reliable villages of origin, for these objects.

5. Baudrillard 1983: 2. I would like to mention here that my use of the map analogy coincides with Baudrillard's sense of abstraction and the reference to larger realities by signs. I will refer later to Benedict Anderson's chapter, "Census, Map, Museum" in *Imagined Communities* (1983) and influential classifications of larger territory.

6. See Boorstin (1961: 99) for the term "cultural mirage" as a phenomenon that he recognized as being common to "tourist oases everywhere."

7. "Grand Hall Exhibit: Pacific Coast Indian Village, Interpretive Plan," CMC, Grand Hall files, n.d.

8. See Sturtevant 1969: 622; Stocking 1985: 7; and Cole 1985: 212 on the Museum Period of Anthropology. Chapter One, n16, above, provides additional information.

9. Approximate dimensions are based upon "Grand Hall Exhibit: Pacific Coast Indian Village, Interpretive Plan," CMC, Grand Hall files, n.d.; and Grand Hall floor plan, ibid. It should be noted here as well that according to Andrea LaForet all of the houses in the hall were planned to be executed to the same standards. She claims that size differences, significant only in the depth of the houses, was coincidental. She also states that due to budgetary problems, the elaboration of the interior of Kwakwaka'wakw house was not followed immediately by the development of the interiors of the other houses (telephone interview, April 21, 1995).

10. Complete lists of the artists who participated in the Grand Hall project and the supervisor of each team have been published in LaForet 1992: 75.

11. For additional information on construction practices see LaForet 1992: 14–22.

12. It should be noted here that the Grand Hall functions already as a public space available for hire for receptions and parties. Douglas Cardinal, Ian Gregory, and George MacDonald 1992: personal interviews.

13. George MacDonald, Andrea LaForet 1992; Bill McLennan, Joe Becker, Glen Tallio, Jim Hart, and Terry Starr 1993: personal interviews. It is also interesting to note that no ceremonial dancing marked the opening of the exhibition *Chiefly Feasts: The Enduring Kwakiutl Potlatch* during the time that it appeared at the CMC (in the Fall of 1994). Chapter Three below describes the elaborate ceremonies that marked the opening of this show in New York. Despite careful provisions made for theatrical presentations in the Grand Hall, native participation in the form of customary dancing has so far only rarely been included at the CMC.

14. The dedication of the Hesquiaht Nuu-chah-nulth totem pole included a Sea Serpent dance, speeches by Hesquiaht elders and other important participants in the project. A video tape that records the event is on file at the Royal British Columbia Museum. Information about the location of the Hesquiaht ceremony was verified by Andrea LaForet (April 21, 1995: telephone interview).

15. Joe Becker, the project supervisor for the Coast Salish house, has indicated that he and other Coast Salish advisors were consulted about the development of a new exhibition for the interior of the house in the Grand Hall. The consensus among this group is for the reproduction of a nineteenth-century house interior (March 23, 1993: personal interview). The CMC, however, has hired anthropologist Margaret Stott to develop a plan for this exhibition. Stott does not plan to suggest a traditional interior (November 19, 1992: telephone interview).

16. It should be noted here as well that the following descriptions of the house interiors relate to their appearance in 1992. The interior of the Alert Bay house, photographed in the 1930s, belonged to Ed Whannock (Gloria Cranmer Webster June 23, 1993: personal interview). Whannock was also influential in the dances for outsiders designed in the 1950s and 60s, discussed in detail in Chapter Three, below.

17. Sources for the description of Coast Salish House types are Waterman and Greiner 1921; Drucker 1955: 54–63, 1965: 25–27; Barnett 1955; Vastokas 1966: 61–64; "The Coast Salish Shed Roof House" 1988: CMC, Grand Hall files; Nabokov and Easton 1989: 233–39.

18. Joe Becker recounts that he was advised to use this technique by his elders and had seen old examples at Musqueam. This was the first time that he had tried to work with cedar withes, but he "went ahead and just hoped that it would work out." March 23, 1993: personal interview.

19. The purpose of this platform is referred to in Waterman and Greiner 1921: 18–19; Barnett 1955: 38, 42; and in "Coast Salish" 1988: CMC, Grand Hall files (folder: Coast Salish House), (October 2: 23–24).

20. Barnett 1955: 38, 42–43; Waterman and Greiner 1921: Plate II shows a carved figure before a Northern Salish house, originally from Hill-Tout 1907: *British North America, I: The Far West, the Home of the*

Salish and Dene. (The Native Races of the British Empire) London: Archibald Constable. Plate IX. This could be an interior figure moved to the front of the house for the benefit of the photographer. See also Waterman and Greiner 1921: 27–28 and LaForet (1992: 23–24).

21. Mary Jane Lenz, Associate Curator for NMAI, has informed me that Coast Salish interior houseposts that may serve as models for one or more carved figures to be installed in the future near the Coast Salish house at the CMC were borrowed from NMAI (January 30, 1995: personal interview).

22. The impact of museum practice on public display and the history of exhibition construction is discussed in essays in Ivan Karp and Steven D. Lavine (eds.) 1991; Janet C. Berlo (ed.) 1992; Robert Lumley (ed.) 1988; and George Stocking Jr. (ed.) 1985.

23. Nuu-chah-nulth or "Nootka" architecture is described in Drucker 1951: 67–77, 1965: 145–148; Vastokas 1966: 56–60; Gunther (1972: 27–28) summarizes the observations of Cook and his party.

24. It should be noted that in addition to traditional devices, cement columns and some lug bolts are used in the construction of the Grand Hall houses to meet both engineering and insurance requirements.

25. Drucker mentioned that the houses were usually built broadside to the beach, but more recent examples "were set end-on to the waterfront" (1951: 69).

26. This individual may be Tom Sayachapis who is indicated as the builder of the original house in the CMC's document "Interpretive Unit 1: The Meeting of Two Worlds" (n.d.: 2).

27. This museum representation based upon both oral, and due to Sapir's efforts, written tradition may be compared with Jonaitis' account of model totem pole carving for the American Museum of Natural History by Charles Edenshaw. The museum

pole was carved on the basis of oral tradition, not modeled upon any physical carving that Swanton was aware of. Jonaitis has called this "invented art" in Berlo (1992: 38).

28. A brief biography of Ron Hamilton is available in Macnair et al. (1984: 184).

29. According to exhibition designer Ian Gregory, the original house design called for four birds instead of the moon images (November 17, 1992: personal interview).

30. The N. B. Miller photograph at the Smithsonian is no. 56, 438. A. J. Brabazon's photograph is PA 37738 in the Public Archives of Canada.

31. LaForet 1992: 32–33, and "The Wakas Pole," CMC files (n.d.: 12–14); Doug Cranmer June 20, 1993: personal interview. See also photographic evidence (PAC 16938 and Newcombe BCPM E 143). It is also interesting to note here that a replica of the Wakas pole was created as well for Edward Curtis' film *In the Land of the War Canoes* (Holm and Quimby 1980: 44, figs. 13, 30).

32. It should be noted here that Cranmer's father was the nephew of Wakas, which accounts for his greater familiarity with the history of the house. Cranmer claims, however, that he was not commissioned for these projects on the basis of this affiliation (June 20, 1993: personal interview).

33. See LaForet 1992: 37 and telephone interview, April 21, 1995, for issue of European influence and the Nuxalk house. For a description of the Jacobsen tour see Cole 1985: 68–72.

34. RBCM no. PN4575, Photo: I. Fougner.

35. As discussed in LaForet March 1986: 9, "Changes in Houses in Bella Coola 1875 to 1925," Ms. CMC Grand Hall files. Photographic evidence derives from AMNH neg. no. 335773 and RBCM no. 4571.

36. More complete descriptions of these totem poles are published in LaForet 1992: 38–39.

37. Personal interviews: Glen Tallio,

Bill McLennan: 1993. The Kwakw<u>a</u>'wakw feast dish referred to here is a huge carving that represents the legendary figure, Dzunu<u>k</u>wa. This dish is moved from time to time and is not always in front of the Nuxalk house.

38. LaForet met with various band councils, elders' groups and the descendants of house owners when possible. Gloria Cranmer Webster and Doug Cranmer were consulted about the Wakas house; Mrs. Mabel Hall, Mrs. Lina Cole, and Lawrence Putlas were consulted on the Clellamin house; and Adam Sheewish discussed the Tsesha'ath house with her (November 17, 1992: personal interview).

39. For the Haida house see Vastokas 1966: 27–34; MacDonald 1983: 18–19, Blackman 1990, 7: 242–43, Nabokov and Eastman 1989: 270–71.

40. For a brief history of these poles see LaForet 1992: 40–45. Chief Wiah's house is described in MacDonald 1983: 142.

41. Jim Hart. Personal interview. March 26, 1993. On the day following our interview, Hart called me to reiterate that he and the crew "feel good" about the Haida house at the CMC.

42. For descriptions of Tsimshian architecture see Boas 1916: 46–48, 1896: 580–83; Drucker 1965: 119–21; Vastokas 1966: 38–42; Nabokov and Easton 1989: 280–81; Halpin and Seguin 1990: 7: 271–72.

43. McLennan has been working on "The Imagery Recovery Project" at the University of British Columbia, Museum of Anthropology with the assistance of the Canada Council and the Canadian Museum of Civilization.

44. Terry Starr. Personal interview. March 25, 1993. Starr also feels that the correct identity of the proper owner of the old screen has yet to be established.

45. 'First Nations' is a term most frequently used in Canada, but only occasionally in the United States, to refer to native groups.

46. For more complete descriptions of these totem poles see LaForet 1992: 48–50.

47. LaForet, *The Book of the Grand Hall* (1992) is a slim, soft-covered volume that is sold in the CMC book shop and is designed for a general audience.

48. Stephen Fjellman asserts this role for Walt Disney World (1992: 8–9) and identifies Antonio Gramsci's writings on cultural authority in "Notes on Italian History," in Quintin Hoare and Geoffrey Nowell Smith (eds.) 1971: 103–104. See also Gramsci's writings on the relationship between ideology, the formation of class divisions and education (ibid.: 26–43).

49. See also Bourdieu and Passeron (1977) for a more complete discussion of legitimacy and the basis of its force in symbolic systems. These issues of power relations in education have been constructed in response to Marxist theories of the mechanics of class relations. See also Louis Althusser (1971) on "ideological state apparatuses." In reference to the "reproduction of the culture of the dominant classes" and postmodernism, see Chris Jenks (1993).

Chapter 3

Making Dance History: Kwakw<u>a</u>'wakw Performance Art at the American Museum of Natural History

1. A shorter and less detailed version of this chapter was presented as a paper at the November 1993 Native American Art Studies Association Conference and was subsequently published in *American Indian Art Magazine* 20: 1 (Winter 1994): 54–61.

2. See, for example, articles by Blackman, Holm, Kenyon, Stearns, and Elmendorf in *Arctic Anthropology* 14: 1 (1977), edited by Margaret B. Blackman, and originally prepared as papers for a 1974 symposium of the American Anthropological

Association in Mexico City on the subject of continuity and change in Northwest Coast ceremonialism.

3. See Phillips (1993, 1998), for instance, for discussions of artifacts originally created as items for sale to tourists, frequently excluded from museum displays.

4. These accounts appeared in *The Pioneer Journal*, the local newspaper published by Ron Shukar, a non-native resident of Alert Bay, who also owned the small department store known as Ronnie's. Apparently Shukar was held in high regard by the native people of Alert Bay, as in 1959, the "cedar bark headdress" was conferred upon him in recognition of the co-operation he had given the 'Namgis people (*Pioneer Journal*, June 24, 1959: 2). The paper was later renamed *The North Island Gazette* and Shukar's son became the publisher. Bill Holm recalls that "Most everyone who read newspapers took *The Pioneer Journal* . . . whether Indian or white" (January 24, 1994: letter to author).

5. See Holm (1977: 7) for his comments on Boas's dance descriptions, repeatedly used for later analyses of Kwakwaka'wakw potlatching and ceremonialism. Holm claims that early accounts, particularly those made about the dances held in Fort Rupert in 1894, were sometimes faulty. Although corrections were made in later publications, they have seldom been noted.

6. Cole 1985: 202. For the tour of the Bella Coola dancers, see ibid.: 68–71. For some description of the Chicago World's Fair performances, also see ibid.: 129–31 and photo documentation, some of which is on file at AMNH. Dances performed in St. Louis in 1904 are recounted in both Ford 1941: 186–90 and Cole 1985: 202.

7. Mungo Martin's Victoria potlatch is described in Duff (1961) and was recorded on tape by Richard Waterman; on file at the RBCM.

8. These dance presentations were predated by a celebration in Alert Bay in honor of the coronation of George VI. Native participants included the 'Namgis as well as visitors from New Vancouver and Village Island. While there was no dancing, participants displayed full regalia in the form of masks, headdresses, robes, and button blankets. This event is documented in photographs now in the achieves of the RBCM.

9. Spradley 1969: 158–62; Cole and Chaikin 1990: 169. Sewid was a major protagonist in the introduction and adaptation of traditional dance for the entertainment of outsiders, as is elaborated in this chapter. In this light, it is interesting to note that he is said to have renounced the potlatch and that he even spoke against it in church before he "came back around to it" in the 1950s. Bill Holm recalls that Sewid danced and participated in a big potlatch on Turnour Island in January 1959 (January 24, 1994: letter to the author; Spradley 1969: 109–10).

10. Holm recalls Bill Scow's leading role in interpreting this and future ceremonies for non-Indian audiences, especially for the affairs attended by guests with political importance: "He was called upon because he was knowledgeable and articulate, even though he himself had left the potlatch system and never attended if he wasn't called upon for this duty." (January 24, 1994: letter to the author).

11. It is also important to note here that Dan Cranmer's 1921 potlatch on Village Island had resulted in the arrest of some participants and the confiscation of potlatch regalia by Canadian authorities.

12. Other dances included in this event were the display of a "Simpleton" masker, a Mosquito, and a Wolf (*Pioneer Journal*, May 30, 1951: 1–2; Cole and Chaikin 1990: 169).

13. The Heron was described as "having an exceptionally long beak which opened and closed with a snapping sound as the performer gave out with his distinctive call" (*Pioneer Journal*, May 22, 1952). This long

beak and snapping call are consistent with the characteristics of the Cannibal Birds. It might have been a Raven or Huxwhukw, both the servants of Baxwbakwalanux-wsiwe' (along with the Crooked-Beak-of-Heaven), who is the initiating spirit of the *hamat'sa*.

14. I would like to acknowledge both Gloria Cranmer Webster and her mother, Agnes Cranmer (now deceased), who first suggested to me that the productions of the Kwak̓wala Arts and Crafts Organization may have served as a form of precedent for the *Chiefly Feasts* ceremonies and other contemporary performances like it (1993: personal interviews).

15. Spradley 1969: 236–37. I note here with considerable sadness that in September 1997 the Alert Bay big house was destroyed in a fire. Reconstruction was promptly carried out, and a new building was inaugurated in May 1999.

16. Drew Oswell, a non-native resident of Alert Bay in the early 1960s, was a member of the local Board of Trade. He claims that he and a member of the Company of Young Canadians (a service organization similar to the Peace Corps in the United States) approached the purser of the cruise ship and offered him a commission on every printed program and ticket he sold. The net proceeds from such sales went to the Kwak̓wala Arts and Crafts Organization (Oswell, October 12, 1993: telephone interview). Members also sold crafts, baskets in particular, to the tourists.

17. A copy of the printed program is on file at the U'mista Cultural Centre in Alert Bay, British Columbia. These dances selected for the tourist performances were in many ways similar to those performed at potlatches, though they may be titled differently and were generally fewer in number and shorter in length (Agnes Cranmer, Ethel Alfred, Margaret Cook, 1993: personal communications; Bill Holm, Jan. 23, 1994: letter to the author). Bill Holm also indi-cates that the dances "were not accompanied by potlatch business and often had a 'skeleton' cast consisting mostly of older women, young people and one or two older, retired men for singers, etc. These took place mainly in the summer when most young and middle aged men were away fishing or otherwise occupied. Still there was always an effort to restrict the performances to dances that could properly be presented by those present" (ibid.).

18. These women, along with Gloria Cranmer Webster, Tony Hunt, William Hunt, Bill Cranmer, Adam Dick, Pam Baker, and various other *Chiefly Feasts* participants attended two planning meetings—one in Alert Bay and another in a New York hotel room just before the performances. There selections were made for the dance repertoire, and other details of protocol were settled (Gloria Cranmer Webster, June 22, 1993: personal interview; Tony Hunt, June 8, 1993: personal interview; Bill Cranmer, June 21, 1993: personal interview). According to Webster, such meetings, usually attended by the old people, take place before potlatches as well (1991: 232).

19. Bill Holm recalls that other women were involved in the activities of the Kwak̓wala Arts and Crafts Organization. These were Emma Beans, Lucy Brown, Helen Knox (then of Fort Rupert), and Emma Hunt (then living most of the time in Victoria). Regular participants also included Katie Scow, Agnes Alfred, Dorothy Hawkins, Vera Cranmer (now Newman) and others (Jan. 24, 1994: letter to the author).

20. In early 1992, for instance, the family of Chief Tom Willie (see Chapter 4, below) traveled to New York to perform at the American Museum of Natural History. There, in the Kaufman Auditorium, they staged a version of the Dance of the Undersea Kingdom, the exclusive dance prerogative of Chief Willie.

21. Translated from Kwakwala by Gloria Cranmer Webster in 1993.

22. William Hunt sang the Kwagu'ł mourning song, Bill Cranmer the 'Na̱mgis', and Tom Willie the Gwawa̱'enux̱w. Songs owned by four chiefs are usually sung at a potlatch (Bill Cranmer, June 21, 1993: personal interview).

23. Tony Hunt, June 8, 1993: personal interview). Hunt is referring to those people who were arrested following Dan Cranmer's famous potlatch in 1921 on Village Island.

24. This mask was removed from display in "The Potlatch Today" section of the exhibition for this purpose, making this performance especially meaningful for the museum staff, who are more accustomed to the "kid glove handling" of artifacts.

25. In the past, certain masked dancers helped to insure appropriate behavior and correct protocol at a potlatch. Boas recorded detailed accounts of the roles of both the Fool dancer or *nułamał* (1897: 544–620) and Grizzly Bear (ibid.: 467–69) in this regard. Bill Cranmer also reports that the function of the *emas* or ancestral mask that circles the house before the start of the *hamat'sa* ceremonies is to make sure that all is in order. Correct protocol in seating would be one of its concerns. In Cranmer's memory, no actual objections have been made by the masker. Mistakes in dance execution or even breaches of proper behavior in everyday life should be corrected either immediately or at a future potlatch with the distribution of payment. This is usually accomplished following the last dance of the *hamat'sa* series when all of the tamed *hamat'sa* in the house circle the floor in grand procession. Then the chief responsible for the past infraction dances, or his representative will, wearing the chief's headgear and singing the song that his tribe owns for such occasions. Then he distributes payment to "wipe his body clean" (Bill Cranmer, June 21, 1993: personal interview). I witnessed this procedure for correc-

tion at a memorial potlatch for Chief Albert Alfred in Alert Bay, June 1994.

26. This quote was taken from a videotape of the *Chiefly Feasts* ceremonies now on file at AMNH. It was translated for me by Tony Hunt during a 1993 interview.

27. Tony Hunt. *Tradition and Innovation in Northwest Coast Indian Art*, October 19, 1991. Audio tape on file AMNH. Other speakers at this event, which continued on October 20, 1991, included Peter Macnair, Aldona Jonaitis, Gloria Cranmer Webster, Art Thompson, Ira Jacknis, Bill Holm, Steve Brown, Wayne Suttles, Debbie Sparrow, Janet Catherine Berlo, Margaret Blackman, Robert Davidson, Robin Wright, and Richard Inglis.

28. Tony Hunt first suggested to me that the *Chiefly Feasts* ceremonies might be understood as "Aldona's [Jonaitis] play potlatch" (June 8, 1993: personal interview).

29. Young Kwakwa̱ka̱'wakw singers and dancers are now being trained to make their own dance history. Children learn to dance in cultural programs at the T'lisa lagi'lakw School in Alert Bay, and for a couple of years, young urban Kwakwa̱ka̱'wakw were taught to sing by both Adam Dick and Tony Hunt at Mungo Martin's house in Thunderbird Park, Victoria. Their education differs from that of their parents and grandparents, who were privately trained by members of their own families. Adam Dick recalls his own childhood experiences that qualify him to officiate as song leader at a great many potlatches today and to be a teacher in Victoria. He remembers that he was not allowed to play, like an ordinary child, but sat in instead upon the conferences of his elders that took place behind the village. He had to stay awake late at night "to listen to that grown-up business" (June 7, 1993: telephone interview).

Tony Hunt has commented that some knowledge has not been passed on in an ideal manner. He laments the "language problem" (many young people cannot

speak Kwak̓wala). He is optimistic, however, and accepts the challenges that teaching presents. "When we started in Mungo's
house, they didn't know one song. Now
they know thirty" (June 8, 1993: personal interview).

Chapter Four

False Cognates: Looking Backward at the Latest Thing in Contemporary Northwest Coast Art

1. The rattle (AMNH 16/1966), col-
lected in 1897 by Filip Jacobsen for the Jesup
North Pacific Expedition, is illustrated in
Jonaitis 1988: 168, Plate 72.

2. Richard Inglis, 1991: personal interview. Inglis, together with Aldona Jonaitis
had been researching correspondence and
manuscripts related to the collection of
certain Nuu-chah-nulth artifacts in the
AMNH collection.

3. For the recontextualization of the
Zande net, see Center for African Art 1988:
16–17 and illustrations on page 175 and book
cover.

4. Leona Latimer, Aug. 23, 1991: personal interview. It is important to note that
not all dealers in native art share this perspective. Gary Wyatt, formerly of the Inuit
Gallery and now of The Spirit Wrestler in
Vancouver, for instance, believes that collectors have more interest in acquiring outstanding one-of-a-kind works (March 24,
1993: personal interview). However, even
these pieces are done in recognizable and
formally "correct" Northwest Coast styles.

5. Many helpful suggestions on the
identification of historical models for these
masks came from personal interviews with
Peter Macnair, then of the Royal British
Columbia Museum in Victoria, and Randall Macnair (July 19, 1991); Isabelle Proctor
of Derek Simpkins Gallery of Tribal Arts in

Vancouver (July 23, 1991); and Gary Wyatt,
then of the Inuit Gallery, also in Vancouver
(Mar. 24, 1993).

6. Thompson requested a profile view
photograph from AMNH during my tenure
as Jonaitis' research assistant in 1991 so he
could accurately reproduce the proportions
of the Nuxalk mask.

7. For the old Bear mask (Plate 3 in this
volume), see Holm 1987: 193. This is one of
many examples in which imagery is appropriated from one native group by a member
of another. Most Northwest Coast artists
have dabbled with the styles and images of
other groups "for art's sake," but continue
to observe the exclusive right of individuals
and families to show privately held crest art
privileges in the context of a potlatch. See
the discussion of such "privileges" in the Introduction, above, pp. 5–6.

8. The simultaneity of modernist criteria for originality and postmodern interest
in the recontextualization of extant images
may be associated with the claim of some
scholars that the periodization of these concerns may be too strictly delineated. Charles
Jencks, for instance, has suggested the term
'Late-Modern' as a more descriptive alter-
native (1992: 13).

9. Marginalization, or the contextualization of native or various "ethnic" arts
within mainstream discourse, has been the
subject of recent consideration in art historical literature. See for instance Lippard
(1990); Phillips (1989); Clifford, Groys,
Owens, Storr, and Wallace (1989); Spivak
(1988) in Nelson and Grossberg; Rushing
and WalkingStick, eds., *Art Journal* 51: 3
(1992), an issue on "Recent Native American Art"; Fergusen, Gever, Minh-ha, West
(eds.) (1990); Duffek and Hill (1989);
Nemiroff, Houle, Townsend-Gault (1992);
McMaster and Martin (1992).

10. For William Fagg's contribution to
the identification of individual master artists in African art, see Fagg's *Nigerian Images* (1963): 119–21; Fagg and Plass, *African*

Sculpture: An Anthology (1964): 74, 88–93, 102–103, 111; Fagg, "The African Artist," in Biebuyck (1969): 42–57; and Fagg, *Yoruba Sculpture of West Africa* (1982): 35–49.

11. For a more complete example of a "cultural biography," see Chapter One above, on the many restoration projects affecting the form of the Chief Shakes Community House. I have adapted this term from Igor Kopytoff (1986).

12. This section elaborates data I reported in Ostrowitz and Jonaitis in Jonaitis 1991: 62–64. No analysis of the accompanying adjustments in social reality that follow upon the various new versions of the screen, as discussed here, is made in the catalogue caption. Neither is Tom Hunt's version of the screen discussed. The catalogue number for the old screen is AMNH 16/9484AL; the painted replica by Calvin Hunt is AMNH 16.1–2630AB.

13. These features, which identify the collaged nature of this artifact from various component pieces perhaps not originally intended to be configured as they were for the *Chiefly Feasts* exhibition, were discovered by Peter Macnair and communicated to me in 1990.

14. The genealogy of this inherited dance privilege is then problematic as it relates to this particular prop, because the people of New Vancouver are of the Da̱'naxda'x̱w tribe. Yet actual artworks as well as dance privileges were, and continue to be, transferred to distant locations on various occasions. As a woman's dance, the possibility of a marriage gift comes to mind.

15. It was my responsibility, as Jonaitis' research assistant, to gather information on this particular work and to write the essay and label information for it which was used in both the exhibition itself and in the accompanying catalog (See note 12 above).

16. This suggestion is also supported by Franz Boas's handwritten entry in an AMNH catalog ledger, stating that the screen should be called a *nō'nlemg·ila*, an entry that he made after George Hunt's designation, when the artifact arrived at the museum in 1904. This is the Kwaḵwala term used for puppets that respond to the supernatural commands of a *tuxw'id*. Illustrations of *nō'nlemg·ila* puppets may be seen in Boas 1897: 507–10. In addition, undated computer records in the AMNH catalog contain entries by Bill Holm, who also stated that the prop was probably used for a *tuxw'id* dance.

17. Interestingly, in 1991 Calvin Hunt also created an edition of serigraph prints, titled *Kwa-giulth Tokwit Screen '91*, that illustrate his version of the *nuɫami'sta yelxts!ayo*. This may be considered another version of the same image.

18. Emma Hunt and Tom Hunt, Sept. 1991: telephone interviews. Mrs. Hunt also told me that she sang but did not dance at the Legacy opening because she was not well enough at the time. The *tuxw'id* dance, she explained, has "quite a beat."

19. Also see the Introduction, above, pp. 8 ff., for comments on related works by Baudrillard, Benjamin, and Eco. Additional discussion on Baudrillard's definition of decontextualized art appears in Chapter Two, p. 48.

20. Consultants Peter Macnair, Gloria Cranmer Webster, Wayne Suttles, research assistant Stacy Marcus, and I contributed to this research. This process of discovery is also documented by Ostrowitz and Jonaitis in Jonaitis (1991: 251–82), where all of the related artifacts are also illustrated. No analysis of the formal relationship (or its lack) between the AMNH set and the Campbell River collection is made in the catalog essay.

21. Boas recorded two additional versions of the same story, both called *Sī'wit* (1935: 175-90). Masks and other objects noted are from the AMNH collection. The Killerwhale dishes are cat. nos. 16/8527 and 8528; the Bullhead 16/8942; the Whale 16/8390; and the Sea Otter 16/8530AJ.

22. Just before her death in 1993, Tom

Willie's wife, Elsie Williams, expressed her desire to commission the carving of an entirely new set of Undersea Kingdom masks, this time without the participation of the Campbell River Museum. Some of these masks may now be completed (Elsie Williams, June 22, 1993: personal interview).

23. Other creatures represented in the Campbell River set that are not included in the nineteenth-century ensemble in New York are Bill Henderson's Octopus mask, Bruce Stephen's carving of a Supernatural Codfish, and Tony Dawson's Sea Monster.

24. See the repetitive imagery that continues as the crest prerogatives of the various generations of the Shakes family, Chapter One. Also see Robin Wright's work (1983, 1985, 1992) on configurations typical of the Haida carver.

25. Macnair et al. 1984: 185. Mungo Martin was hired a year or two earlier by the Museum of Anthropology at the University of British Columbia to restore and replicate old totem poles as well.

26. For more information on the early intervention of outsiders in the production of Inuit arts and crafts in the Canadian Arctic, see Houston (1969, 1975); Swinton (1972, 1978); Graburn (1976); and Blodgett (1991).

27. Illustrated and discussed in Gerber and Katz-Lahaigue 1989: 94; and Karen Duffek, July 23, 1991: personal interview.

28. Henrikson 1997: 10. Henrikson takes this statement of Schoppert's from an earlier piece by Robert Breunig and Erin Younger, "The Second Biennial Native American Fine Arts Invitational," *American Indian Arts Magazine* 11: 2 (Spring 1986): 60–65.

29. I have consulted with Gerald McMaster, Curator of Contemporary Indian Art at the CMC, who corroborates my understanding that no contemporary Northwest Coast native artists are working without some reference to native tradition at this point (July 17, 1995: telephone interview).

Chapter Five

The Style in Which They Were Imagined

1. Krauss begins her essay "Film Stills" (1993) with this quote, originally recorded by Lisbet Nilson in "Q&A: Cindy Sherman," *American Photographer* (September 1983): 77.

2. I attended a meeting in the Fall of 1996 at The Brooklyn Museum of Art in which representatives from Zuni Pueblo responded to questions about masks made on commission for the museum collection under the supervision of the trader Andrew Vanderwagen during Culin's tenure as Curator of Ethnology.

3. Aldona Jonaitis, Richard Inglis, 1990, 1991: personal interviews; Jonaitis, Aug. 11, 1995: telephone interview. Jonaitis's book on the history of the representation of this complex work of art to the non-native public is in progress.

4. I would like to thank Steve Henrikson of the Alaska State Museum for suggesting these examples, the crest hats and the robe, which may be considered as having historical importance (December 7, 1992: letter to the author).

5. An overview of these events is available in Nelson Graburn's "Eskimo Art: The Eastern Canadian Arctic," in Graburn (ed.) (1976): 39–55.

6. Alisa LaGamma, Assistant Curator for the Department of the Arts of Africa, Oceania and the Americas at the Metropolitan Museum of Art, brought this information to my attention.

References

Abbreviations:
AMNH   American Museum of Natural History
CMC   Canadian Museum of Civilization, Hull, Quebec

The Alaskan. June 20, 1940: 1f. "Many Visitors at Potlatch."
Althusser, Louis. 1971. "Ideology and Ideological State Apparatuses." *Lenin and Philosophy and Other Essays.* Trans. Ben Brewster. New York: Monthly Review Press, 127–86.
Anderson, Benedict. 1983. "Census Map, Museum," in *Imagined Communities: Reflections on the Origin and Spread of Nationalism.* Reprint, London: Verso, 1991.
Archbold, C. M. 1939. "Restoration." *The Alaska Sportsman* 5(3): 16–19.
Arndt, Katherine L. 1984. "Russian Relations with the Stikine Tlingit, 1833–1867." Paper presented at the Sixth Annual Alaska History Symposium, Sitka. November 4.
Barbeau, Marius. 1958. *Pathfinders in the North Pacific.* N.p: The Caxton Printers Ltd.
———. 1990. *Totem Poles, According to Crests and Topics.* With a Foreword by George F. MacDonald. 2 vols. Hull, Quebec: Canadian Museum of Civilization. 2nd ed.
Barnett, Homer G. 1955. *The Coast Salish of British Columbia.* Eugene: University of Oregon.
Baudrillard, Jean. 1983. *Simulations.* Trans. Paul Foss, Paul Patton, and Phillip Beitchman. New York: Semiotext(e), Inc.
———. *Simulacra and Simulation.* 1994. Trans. Sheila Faria Glaser. Ann Arbor: The University of Michigan Press.
Belting, Hans. 1987. *The End of the History of Art?* Trans. Christopher S. Wood. Chicago: The University of Chicago Press.
Benjamin, Walter. 1968. "The Work of Art in the Age of Mechanical Reproduction." *Illuminations.* Hannah Arendt, ed. New York: Schocken Books, 217–51.
———. 1979. "Doctrine of the Similar." Trans. Knut Tarnowski. *New German Critique* 17: 65–69.
Berger, Peter L., and Thomas Luckmann, eds. 1976. *The Social Construction of Reality: A Treatise in the Sociology of Knowledge.* New York: Anchor Press.

Berlo, Janet Catherine, ed. 1992. *The Early Years of Native American Art History: The Politics of Scholarship and Collecting.* Seattle: University of Washington Press.

Black, Martha. 1992. "Displays and Captures: Some Historic Photographs from the Northwest Coast." *American Indian Art Magazine* 18(1): 68–75.

Blackman, Margaret B., ed. 1977. "Continuity and Change in Northwest Coast Ceremonialism." Papers from a Symposium Presented at the 1974 Meetings of the American Anthropological Association in Mexico City. *Arctic Anthropology* 14(1): 1–93.

———. 1982. "The Afterimage and Image After: Visual Documents and the Renaissance in Northwest Coast Art." *American Indian Art Magazine* 7(2): 30–39.

———. 1990. "Facing the Future, Envisioning the Past: Visual Literature and Contemporary Northwest Coast Masks." *Arctic Anthropology* 27(2): 27–40.

———. 1990. "Haida Traditional Culture." *Handbook of North American Indians: Northwest Coast*, vol. 7. Washington, D.C.: Smithsonian Institution, 240–60.

Blodgett, Jean. 1991. *In Cape Dorset We Do It This Way: Three Decades of Inuit Printmaking.* Kleinburg, Ontario: McMichael Canadian Art Collection.

Boas, Franz. 1896. "Sixth Report on the Indians of British Columbia." *66th Report of the British Association for the Advancement of Science for 1896.* London: 569–91.

———. 1897. "The Social Organization and the Secret Societies of the Kwakiutl Indians." *Report of the United States National Museum for 1895.* Washington, D.C.: 311–738.

———. 1919. "Tsimshian Mythology." Based on Texts Recorded by Henry W. Tate. *31st Annual Report of the Bureau of American Ethnology for the Years 1909–1910.* Washington, D.C.: 29–1037.

———. 1921. "Ethnology of the Kwakiutl (Based on Data Collected by George Hunt)." 2 pts. *35th Annual Report of the Bureau of American Ethnology for the Years 1913–1914.* Washington, D.C.

———. 1927. *Primitive Art.* Cambridge, Mass: Harvard University Press. Reprint, New York: Dover Publications, 1955.

———. 1935 *Kwakiutl Tales.* New York: Columbia University Press.

Boas, Franz, and George Hunt. 1902–1905. "Kwakiutl Texts." *American Museum of Natural History Memoirs 5.* Publications of the Jesup North Pacific Expeditions.

———. 1906. "Kwakiutl Texts, Second Series." *American Museum of Natural History Memoirs 14.* Publications of the Jesup North Pacific Expeditions.

Boorstin, Daniel. 1961. *The Image: A Guide to Pseudo-events in America.* New York: Harper & Row.

Bourdieu, Pierre. 1977. *Outline of a Theory of Practice.* Cambridge: Cambridge University Press.

Bourdieu, Pierre, and Jean-Claude Passeron. 1977. *Reproduction in Education, Society and Culture.* London: Sage Publications.

Brady, John G. November 22, 1898. Letter to George Shakes. Alaska State Library and Archives, Juneau.

Brown, Steve. 1987. "From Taquan to Klukwan: Tracing the Work of an Early Tlingit Master Artist," in *Faces, Voices & Dreams: A Celebration of the Centennial of the Sheldon Jackson Museum.* Peter L. Corey, ed. Sitka: Division of Alaska State Museums and the Friends of the Alaska State Museum, 157–75.

———. 1994. "In the Shadow of the Wrangell Master: Photo Documentation of the Work of Two Nineteenth-century Tlingit Artists." *American Indian Art Magazine* 19(4): 74–85, 104.

Bruner, Edward M. 1994. "Abraham Lincoln as Authentic Reproduction: A Critique of Postmodernism." *American Anthropologist* 2: 397–415.

Bunzel, Ruth. 1929. *The Pueblo Potter: A Study of Creative Imagination in Primitive Art.* Reprint, New York: Dover Publications, 1972.

Canadian Museum of Civilization. n.d. "Interpretive Unit 1: The Meeting of Two Worlds." Grand Hall Files.

———. n.d. *Grand Hall Exhibit: Pacific Coast Indian Village, Interpretive Plan.* Grand Hall files.

———. Oct. 2, 1988. "Coast Salish." Ms. Grand Hall Files, folder: Coast Salish House.

———. 1988. "The Coast Salish Shed Roof House." Ms. Grand Hall files.

———. 1989. *Totem Ceremony.* Performance, Hesquiaht Nuu-chah-nulth. Videocassette. Royal British Columbia Museum files.

Carlson, Roy L., ed. 1983. "Prehistory of the Northwest Coast," in *Indian Traditions of the Northwest Coast.* Burnaby, B.C.: Archaeology Press, Simon Fraser University.

The Center for African Art. 1988. *Art/artifact: African Art in Anthropology Collections.* Introduction by Susan Vogel. New York: The Center for African Art.

Chiefly Feasts: The Enduring Kwakiutl Potlatch. 1991. Opening celebration, videocassette. Judith Ostrowitz and Geralyn Abinader, eds. New York: American Museum of Natural History.

Clifford, James. 1986. "On Ethnographic Analogy," in *Writing Culture: The Poetics and Politics of Ethnography.* J. Clifford and George E. Marcus. eds. Berkeley: University of California Press: 98–121.

———. 1988. *The Predicament of Culture: Twentieth-Century Ethnography, Literature, and Art.* Cambridge: Harvard University Press.

———. 1991. "Four Northwest Coast Museums." In *Exhibiting Cultures: The*

Poetics and Politics of Museum Display. Ivan Karp and Steven D. Lavine, eds. Washington, D.C.: Smithsonian Institution Press: 212–54.

———. 1997. *Routes: Travel and Translation in the Late Twentieth Century.* Cambridge and London: Harvard University Press.

Clifford, James, Boris Groys, Craig Owens, Martha Rosler, Robert Storr, and Michelle Wallace. 1989. "The Global Issue: A Symposium." *Art in America* 77(7): 86–89, 151–53.

Codere, Helen. 1956. "The Amiable Side of Kwakiutl Life: The Potlatch and the Play Potlatch." *American Anthropologist* 58(2): 334–51.

———. 1990. "Kwakiutl Traditional Culture." *Handbook of North American Indians: Northwest Coast.* Vol. 7. Washington, D.C.: Smithsonian Institution, 359–77.

Cole, Douglas. 1985. *Captured Heritage: The Scramble for Northwest Coast Artifacts.* Seattle: University of Washington Press.

Cole, Douglas, and Ira Chaikin. 1990. *An Iron Hand Upon the People: The Law against the Potlatch on the Northwest Coast.* Vancouver: Douglas & McIntyre.

Coombes, Annie E. 1994. "The Recalcitrant Object: Culture Contact and the Question of Hybridity." *Colonial Discourse/Postcolonial Theory.* New York: St. Martin's Press.

Corser, H. P. n.d. [1931]. *Totem Lore of the Alaska Indians.* 3rd ed. Ketchikan: Ryus Drug Co.

Curtis, Edward S. 1915. *The North American Indian.* Vol. 10, *The Kwakiutl.* Frederick W. Hodge, ed. Norwood, Mass.: Plimpton Press.

Dauenhauer, Nora Marks, and Richard Dauenhauer. 1987. *Haa Shuká, Our Ancestors: Tlingit Oral Narratives.* Classics of Tlingit Oral Literature 1. Seattle: University of Washington Press and Sealaska Heritage Foundation.

———. 1990. *Haa Tuwunáagu Yís, For Healing Our Spirit: Tlingit Oratory.* Classics of Tlingit Oral Literature 2. Seattle: University of Washington Press and Sealaska Heritage Foundation.

De Roos, Robert. 1994. "The Magic Worlds of Walt Disney." *Disney Discourse: Producing the Magic Kingdom.* Ed. Eric Smooden. New York: Routledge.

Drucker, Philip. 1951. "The Northern and Central Nootkan Tribes." *Bureau of American Ethnology Bulletin 144.* Washington: Smithsonian Institution.

———. 1955. *Indians of the Northwest Coast.* New York: McGraw-Hill for the American Museum of Natural History.

———. 1965. *Cultures of the North Pacific Coast.* San Francisco: Chandler Publishing Company.

Duff, Wilson, ed. 1959. *Histories, Territories, and Laws of the Kitwancool.* Victoria, B.C.: Royal British Columbia Museum (reprinted 1989).

———. 1961. "A Killer Whale Copper: A Chief's Memorial to His Son." *Report for the Year 1960*. Victoria, B.C.: British Columbia Provincial Museum of Natural History and Anthropology, Department of Education: B32–36.

Duff, Wilson, Jane Wallen, and Joe Clark. 1969. "Totem Pole Survey of Southeast Alaska: Report of Field Survey and Follow-Up Activities, June–October 1969." Ms. Juneau: The Alaska State Museum, n.p.

Duffek, Karen. *Bill Reid: Beyond the Essential Form*. Vancouver: University of British Columbia Press, 1986.

Duffek, Karen, and Tom Hill. 1989. *Beyond History*. Vancouver, B.C.: Vancouver Art Gallery.

Eco, Umberto. 1986. *Travels in Hyperreality*, trans. William Weaver. San Diego: Harcourt Brace Jovanovich.

Edgerton, Gary. 1996. "Redesigning Pocahontas." *Journal of Popular Film and Television*. 24(2): 259–67.

Emmons, George Thornton. 1916. "The Whale House of the Chilkat." *Anthropological Papers of the American Museum of Natural History*. Vol. 19, pt. 1. New York: American Museum of Natural History.

———. 1991. *The Tlingit Indians*. Edited with additions by Frederica de Laguna. Seattle: University of Washington Press.

Fagg, William. 1963. *Nigerian Images*. London: National Commissions for Museums & Monuments in association with Lund Humphries.

———. 1969. "The African Artist." In *Tradition and Creativity in Tribal Art*, Daniel Biebuyck, ed. Berkeley: University of California Press, 42–57.

———. 1982. *Yoruba Sculpture of West Africa*. New York: Alfred A. Knopf.

Fagg, William, and Margaret Plass. 1964. *African Sculpture: An Anthology*. London: Studio Vista Ltd.

Ferguson, Russell, Martha Gever, Trinh T. Minh-ha, and Cornel West. 1990. *Out There: Marginalization and Contemporary Cultures*. New York: The New Museum of Contemporary Art.

Fisher, Philip. 1991. *Making and Effacing Art: Modern American Art in a Culture of Museums*. New York: Oxford University Press, 1991.

Fjellman, Stephen M. 1992. *Vinyl Leaves: Walt Disney World and America*. Boulder: Westview Press.

Ford, Clellan S., ed. 1941. *Smoke From Their Fires: The Life of a Kwakiutl Chief*. New Haven: Yale University Press. Reprint, Hamden, Ct.: Archon Books, 1968.

Forrest, Linn. August 1, 1971. Interview with anonymous interviewer. Juneau: Alaska State Museum.

———. June 16, 1976. Interview. Juneau: Tongass Historical Museum.

Garfield, Viola E., and Linn A. Forrest. 1961. *The Wolf and the Raven*. Seattle: University of Washington Press.

Geertz, Clifford. 1986. "Making Experience, Authoring Selves." *The Anthropology of Experience.* Victor W. Turner and Edward M. Bruner, eds. Urbana: University of Illinois Press, 373–80.

Gerber, Peter R., and Vanina Katz-Lahaigue. 1989. *Susan A. Point, Joe David, Lawrence Paul: Native Artists from the Northwest Coast.* Zurich: Ethnological Museum of the University of Zurich.

Gower, Calvin W. 1972. "The CCC Indian Division: Aid for Depressed Americans, 1933–1942." *Minnesota History* 43: 3–13.

Graburn, Nelson, ed. 1976. *Ethnic and Tourist Arts: Cultural Expressions from the Fourth World.* Berkeley: University of California Press.

———. 1984. "The Evolution of Tourist Arts." *Annals of Tourism Research* 11(3): 393–420.

Gunther, Erna. 1972. *Indian Life on the Northwest Coast of North America: As Seen by the Early Explorers and Fur Traders during the Last Decades of the Eighteenth Century.* Chicago: University of Chicago Press, 1972.

Halpin, Marjorie M., and Margaret Seguin. 1990. "Tsimshian Peoples: Southern Tsimshian, Coast Tsimshian, Nishga, and Gitksan." *Handbook of North American Indians: Northwest Coast.* Vol. 7. Washington, D.C.: Smithsonian Institution, 267–84.

Harvey, David. 1990. *The Condition of Postmodernity: An Enquiry into the Origins of Cultural Change.* Cambridge, Mass.: Blackwell.

Hawthorn, Audrey. 1967. *Kwakiutl Art.* 2nd ed. Seattle: University of Washington Press.

Henrikson, Steve. 1997. "'Art is a One-eared Mad Man.' The Art of Jim Schoppert." *Instrument of Change: Jim Schoppert 1947–1992 Retrospective Exhibition.* Anchorage: Anchorage Museum of History and Art, 4–15.

Herem, Barry. 1978. "Oldest in Alaska? Chief Shakes Houseposts." *Alaska Magazine* January: 49–51.

———. 1990. "A Historic Tlingit Artist: The Trail of His Work and Its Modern Re-Creation." *American Indian Art Magazine* 15(3): 48–55.

Hoare, Quintin, and Geoffrey Nowell Smith, eds. 1971. *Selections from the Prison Notebooks of Antonio Gramsci.* London: Lawrence and Wishart, 1971.

Hobsbawm, Eric, and Terrance Ranger, eds. 1983. *The Invention of Tradition.* Cambridge: Cambridge University Press.

Holm, Bill. 1965. *Northwest Coast Indian Art: An Analysis of Form.* Thomas Burke Memorial Washington State Museum Monograph 1. Seattle: University of Washington Press.

———. 1977. "Traditional and Contemporary Southern Kwakiutl Winter Dance." *Arctic Anthropology* 15(1): 5–24.

———. 1983. *Smoky-Top: The Art and Times of Willie Seaweed.* Thomas Burke

Memorial Washington State Museum Monograph 3. Seattle: University of Washington Press, 1983.

———. 1987. *Spirit and Ancestor: A Century of Northwest Coast Indian Art at the Burke Museum.* Thomas Burke Memorial Washington State Museum Monograph 4. Seattle: University of Washington Press.

Holm, Bill, and George Irving Quimby. 1980. *Edward S. Curtis in the Land of the War Canoes: A Pioneer Cinematographer in the Pacific Northwest.* Seattle: University of Washington Press.

hooks, bell. 1990. "Marginality as Site of Resistance." *Out There: Marginalization and Contemporary Cultures.* Russell Fergusen, Martha Gever, Trinh T. Minh-ha, Cornell West, eds. New York: The New Museum of Contemporary Art: 341–43.

Houston, James. 1969. "Ten Years of Eskimo Printmaking." *Artist's Proof:* 90–97.

———. 1975. *Arts of the Eskimo: Prints.* Ed. Ernst Roche. Barre, Mass.: Barre Publishers.

Hunt, Tony. 1991. "The Hunt Family—An Artistic Tradition." *Tradition and Innovation in Northwest Coast Indian Art, A Symposium.* Audiocassette. New York: American Museum of Natural History, October 19.

Jacknis, Ira S. 1985. "Franz Boas and Exhibits: On the Limitations of the Museum Method of Anthropology," in *Objects and Others: Essays on Museums and Material Culture.* George W. Stocking, Jr., ed. History of Anthropology 3. Madison: University of Wisconsin Press.

Jameson, Frederic. 1991. *Postmodernism, or, The Cultural Logic of Late Capitalism.* Durham: Duke University Press.

Jencks, Charles. 1992. "The Post-Modern Agenda," in *The Post-Modern Reader.* Charles Jencks, ed. London: Academy Editions, 10–39.

Jenks, Chris. 1993. *Cultural Reproduction.* London: Routledge.

Jonaitis, Aldona. 1988. *From the Land of the Totem Poles: The Northwest Coast Indian Art Collection at the American Museum of Natural History.* New York: The American Museum of Natural History.

———. 1989. "Totem Poles and the Indian New Deal," *The Canadian Journal of Native Studies* 9(2): 237–52.

———. 1992. "Franz Boas, John Swanton, and the New Haida Sculpture at the American Museum of Natural History," in Janet Catherine Berlo, ed., *The Early Years of Native American Art History: The Politics of Scholarship and Collecting.* Seattle: University of Washington Press, 22–61.

———. 1993. "Traders of Tradition: The History of Haida Art." *Robert Davidson: Eagle of the Dawn.* Ian M. Thom, ed. Vancouver, B.C.: Vancouver Art Gallery, 3–23.

Jonaitis, Aldona, ed. 1991. *Chiefly Feasts: The Enduring Kwakiutl Potlatch.* New York: American Museum of Natural History.

Kaplan, James. 1994. "The Art of the Steal." *New York* 27(4): 28–34.

Karp, Ivan, and Steven D. Lavine. 1991. *Exhibiting Cultures: The Poetics and Politics of Museum Display.* Washington, D.C.: Smithsonian Institution Press.

Keithahn, Edward L. 1940. *The Authentic History of Shakes Island and Clan. The Wrangell Sentinel.* Reprint, Wrangell Historical Society, 1981.

———. 1963. *Monuments in Cedar.* Seattle: Superior Publishing Company.

Kelly, William A. January 29, 1898. Letter to George Shakes. Juneau: Alaska State Library and Archives.

Kennedy, Dorothy I. D., and Randall T. Bouchard. 1990. "Northern Coast Salish." *Handbook of North American Indians: Northwest Coast.* Vol. 7. Washington, D.C.: Smithsonian Institution, 441–52.

Kew, Michael. October 29, 1987. Letter to Andrea LaForet. Canadian Museum of Civilization, Grand Hall files.

Kilpatrick, Jacquelyn. 1995. "Disney's 'Politically Correct' *Pocahontas.*" *Cineaste* 21(4): 36–37.

Kimmelman, Michael. July 25, 1997. "Sought or Imposed, Limits Can Take Flight: At the Met with Chuck Close." *The New York Times:* C1, C23.

Kopytoff, Igor. 1986. "The Cultural Biography of Things: Commoditization as Process," in *The Social Life of Things: Commodities in Cultural Perspective.* Arjun Appadurai, ed. New York: Cambridge University Press, 64–91.

Kostabi, Mark. 1988. *Sadness Because the Video Store was Closed & Other Stories.* New York: Abbeville Press.

Krauss, Rosalind E. 1985. *The Originality of the Avant-Garde and Other Modernist Myths.* Cambridge: The MIT Press.

———. 1993. "Film Stills." In *Cindy Sherman, 1975–1993.* New York: Rizzoli, 17–61.

Kubler, George. 1962. *The Shape of Time: Remarks on the History of Things.* New Haven: Yale University Press.

Kuh, Katherine. 1946. "Preservation of Indian Art in Southeast Alaska, Part I." Juneau: Alaska State Library and Archives, unpublished typescript, n.p.

Kwa Kwa La Arts and Crafts. n.d. *Kila-Kias-La: 'Many Welcomes' to Alert Bay.* Alert Bay, B.C.: U'mista Cultural Centre Archives. Dance program, tickets, and brochure in booklet form.

LaForet, Andrea. 1986. "Changes in Houses in Bella Coola 1875 to 1925." CMC Grand Hall Files. Unpublished manuscript.

———. 1986. "Report on Fieldwork in British Columbia, May 22–June 13, 1986." CMC Grand Hall files. Unpublished manuscript.

———. 1991. "Time and the Grand Hall." CMC Grand Hall Files. Unpublished manuscript.

————. 1992. *The Book of the Grand Hall.* Hull, Quebec: Canadian Museum of Civilization.

————. n.d. "Nuxalk House." CMC Grand Hall Files. Unpublished manuscript.

————. n.d. "The Wakas House." CMC Grand Hall files. Unpublished manuscript.

————. n.d. "The Wakas Pole." CMC Grand Hall files. Unpublished manuscript.

Lippard, Lucy R. 1990. *Mixed Blessings: New Art in a Multicultural America.* New York: Pantheon Books.

Lowenthal, David. 1985. *The Past is a Foreign Country.* New York: Cambridge University Press.

Lumley, Robert, ed. 1988. *The Museum Time Machine: Putting Cultures on Display.* London: Routledge.

MacCannell, Dean. 1976. *The Tourist: A New Theory of the Leisure Class.* New York: Schocken Books.

————. 1973. "Staged Authenticity: Arrangements of Social Space in Tourist Settings." *American Journal of Sociology* 79(3): 589–603.

————. 1984. "Reconstructed Ethnicity: Tourism and Cultural Identity in Third World Communities." *Annals of Tourism Research* 11(3): 375–92.

MacDonald, George F. 1983. *Haida Monumental Art: Villages of the Queen Charlotte Islands.* Vancouver, B.C.: University of British Columbia Press.

————. 1990. "Foreword." In Barbeau 1990, *Totem Poles: According to Crests and Topics* [vol. 1, 1950], v–x. Hull, Quebec: Canadian Museum of Civilization.

MacDonald, George F., and Stephen Alsford. 1989. *Museum for the Global Village.* Hull, Quebec: Canadian Museum of Civilization.

————. 1990. *The Canadian Museum of Civilization.* Hull, Quebec: Canadian Museum of Civilization.

McIlwraith, Thomas F. 1948. *The Bella Coola Indians.* 2 vols. Toronto: University of Toronto Press.

McMaster, Gerald, and Lee-Ann Martin, eds. 1992. *Indigena: Contemporary Native Perspectives.* Hull, Quebec: Canadian Museum of Civilization.

Macnair, Peter L. and Alan Hoover. 1984. *The Magic Leaves: A History of Haida Argillite Carving.* Victoria: British Columbia Provincial Museum, Special Publication 7.

Macnair, Peter L., Alan L. Hoover, and Keven Neary. 1984. *The Legacy: Tradition and Innovation in Northwest Coast Indian Art.* Vancouver: Douglas & McIntyre.

Malaspina, Alejandro. 1849. "Viajo de . . . ." *Collección de Documentos Oneditos para la Historia de Espana.* Miguel Salva and Pedro Sainz de Baranda, eds. Vol. 15. Madrid: Imprenta de la Viuda de Calero.

Malcolm, Janet. 1994. "Profile: Forty-One False Starts." *The New Yorker.* July 11: 50–68.

Malin, Edward. 1986. *Totem Poles of the Pacific Northwest Coast.* Portland: Timber Press.

Mariani, P., and J. Crary. 1990. "In the Shadow of the West: Edward Said," in *Discourses: Conversations in Postmodern Art and Culture.* R. Fergusen, W. Olander, M. Tucker, K. Fiss, eds. New York: New Museum of Contemporary Art, 93–104.

Merrill, William J., Edmund J. Ladd, and T. J. Fergusen. 1993. "The Return of the Ahayuda: Lessons for Repatriation from Zuni Pueblo and the Smithsonian Institution." *Current Anthropology* 34(5): 523–67.

Muir, John. 1915. *Travels in Alaska.* Boston: Houghton Mifflin Co. Reprint, San Francisco: Sierra Club Books, 1988.

———. 1916. "Alaska Notebook." *Sierra Club Bulletin* 10(1): 31–37.

Meyers, Fred. 1992. "Representing Culture: The Production of Discourse(s) for Aboriginal Acrylic Paintings," in *Rereading Cultural Anthropology.* George E. Marcus, ed. Durham and London: Duke University Press, 319–55.

Nabokov, Peter, and Robert Easton. 1989. *Native American Architecture.* New York: Oxford University Press.

Nemiroff, Diana, Robert Houle, and Charlotte Towsend-Gault. 1992. *Land, Spirit, Power: First Nations at the National Gallery of Canada.* Ottawa: National Gallery of Canada.

The New York Times, June 11, 1955. "Moving Beyond Tepees and Totem Poles," sec. 2: 1+.

———. Feb. 19, 1993. "Museum Set to Lose Indian Treasures," A12.

Oakford, J. S., Deputy Collector. November 2, 1881. Letter to Shakes, Chief of the Stickeens. Juneau: Alaska State Library and Archives.

Ockert, Pat Greene. 1981. *Chief Shakes Island.* Pamphlet. Wrangell, Alaska: Wrangell Museum Archives.

———. n.d. "Wrangell Totem Poles and Shakes Island Preservation and Restoration Project." Wrangell, Alaska: Wrangell Cooperative Association.

Oguibe, Olu. 1993. "In the 'Heart of Darkness'." *Third Text* 23: 3–8.

Olbrechts, Frans M. 1946. *Plastiek van Kongo.* Antwerp: Standard.

Ostrowitz, Judith. 1994. "Privileging the Past: A Case Study in Contemporary Kwakwaka'wakw Performance Art." *American Indian Art Magazine* 20(1): 54–61.

Ostrowitz, Judith, and Aldona Jonaitis. 1991. "Postscript: The Treasures of Siwidi," in *Chiefly Feasts: The Enduring Kwakiutl Potlatch.* Aldona Jonaitis, ed. New York: American Museum of Natural History, 251–81.

Paalen, Wolfgang. 1943. "Totem Art." *Dyn: The Journal of the Durham University Anthropological Society* 4–5: 7–39.

Paige, John C. 1985. *The Civilian Conservation Corps and the National Park Service, 1933–1942: An Administrative History.* United States Department of the Interior, National Park Service.

Phillips, Ruth B. 1989. "What is 'Huron Art'? Native American Art and the New Art History." *The Canadian Journal of Native Studies* 9(2): 161–86.

———. 1993. "Why Not Tourist Art? Significant Silences in Native American Museum Representations," in *After Colonialism: Imperial Histories and Post-colonial Displacements.* Gyan Prakesh, ed. New York: Princeton University Press, 98–125.

———. 1998. *Trading Identities: The Souvenir in Native North American Art from the Northeast, 1700–1900.* Seattle: University of Washington Press.

The Pioneer Journal. May 23, 1951. "Special Celebrations Number."

———. May 30, 1951: 2. "Indian Dances Thrill Capacity Crowds in Highlights of Celebrations."

———. May 22, 1952: n.p. "Indian dances. . . ."

———. April 30, 1958: 1. "About 25 Indian Girls. . . ." (photo caption)

———. May 28, 1958: n.p. "Chief William Scow addressed the crowd. . . ." (photo caption)

———. June 11, 1958: 1. "Nothing Modern Allowed at Indian Celebrations."

———. July 16, 1958: n.p. "Princes Margaret meets Local Representative."

———. June 24, 1959: 1f. "Princess Leads Indian Celebrations Parade."

———. Dec. 31, 1959: 4. "Left centre is the modern R.C.M.P. patrol launch. . . ." (photo caption)

Plato. 1971. *The Republic of Plato.* Translation and notes by Francis MacDonald Cornford. London: Oxford University Press.

Rabinbach, Anson. 1979. "Critique and Commentary/Alchemy and Chemistry: Some Remarks on Walter Benjamin and this Issue." *New German Critique* 17: 3–14.

———. 1979. "Introduction to Walter Benjamin's "Doctrine of the Similar." *New German Critique* 17: 60–64.

Rakestraw, Lawrence. n.d. "A History of the Forest Service Role in Totem Pole Restoration and Preservation and An Index of Sources for United States Forest Service Work in Reference to Totem Poles, 1906–1971." United States Forest Service, Alaska Region. Unpublished manuscript, n.p.

Ritter, Richard, and Paul Voelckers. October 31, 1983. Interview with Linn Forrest. Wrangell, Alaska: Wrangell Museum Archives.

Rushing, W. Jackson, and Kay WalkingStick. 1992. "Recent Native American Art." Special issue of *Art Journal* 51(3): 1992.

Sapir, Edward. 1913. Canadian Museum of Civilization. Edward Sapir Collection, Tom 15. Unpublished manuscript.

Schama, Simon. 1995. "The Princess of Eco-Kitsch." *The New York Times,* June 14: A21.

Schapiro, Meyer. 1937. "Nature of Abstract Art." *Modern Art.* Reprint 1982. New York: Braziller, 185–211.

Schoppert, Jim. 1997. "Give It Eyes and Teeth and I'll Buy It: The Native Artist in the 80's." *Instrument of Change: James Schoppert 1947–1992 Retrospective Exhibition.* Anchorage: Anchorage Museum of History and Art, 29–33.

Seguin, Margaret, ed. 1985. *Interpretive Contexts for Traditional and Current Coast Tsimshian Feasts.* Ottawa: National Museum of Man, Ethnology Service Papers 98.

Shotridge, Louis. 1913. "Chilkat Houses." *University of Pennsylvania Museum Journal* 4: 81–99.

Sorensen, Conner, Lawrence Rakestraw, and Robert R. Martin, Sr. 1986. *Alaskan Native Participation in the Civilian Conservation Corps: A Finding Guide to Sources.* Alaska Historical Commission: Studies in History 206, n.p.

Spivak, Gayatri Chakravorty. 1988. "Can the Subaltern Speak?" *Marxism and the Interpretation of Culture.* Ed. Cary Nelson and Lawrence Grossberg. Urbana: University of Illinois Press, 271–313.

Spradley, James. 1969. *Guests Never Leave Hungry: The Autobiography of James Sewid, A Kwakiutl Indian.* New Haven: Yale University Press.

Stocking, George W., ed. 1985. *Objects and Others: Essays on Museums and Material Culture.* History of Anthropology 3. Madison: University of Wisconsin Press.

Sturtevant, William. 1969. "Does Anthropology Need Museums?" *Proceedings of the Biology Society,* vol. 82. Washington D.C.: 619–50.

Suria, Tomás de. 1791. "Journal of Tomás de Suria of His Voyage with Malaspina to the Northwest Coast of North America in 1791." Henry R. Wagner, ed. *Pacific Historical Review* 5: 3 (1936): 234–76.

Suttles, Wayne. 1990. "Introduction." *Handbook of North American Indians: Northwest Coast.* Vol. 7. Washington, D.C.: Smithsonian Institution, 1–15.

———. 1991. "The Shed-Roof House," in *A Time of Gathering.* Robin K. Wright, ed. Seattle: Burke Museum, 212–22.

Swanton, John R. 1908. "Social Conditions, Beliefs, and Linguistic Relationships of the Tlingit Indians." *26th Annual Report of the Bureau of American Ethnology for the Years 1904–1905.* Washington D.C.: 391–485.

———. 1909. "Tlingit Myths and Texts." *Bureau of American Ethnology Bulletin 39.* Washington, D.C.

Swinton, George. 1971. *Sculpture/Inuit: Masterworks of the Canadian Arctic.* Toronto: University of Toronto Press.

———. 1972. *Sculpture of the Eskimo.* New York Graphic Society.

———. 1978. "Eskimo Art: Beyond the Mythologized Past." *Artnews* 77(1): 78–82.

Taussig, Michael. 1993. *Mimesis and Alterity: A Particular History of the Senses.* New York: Routledge.

Thomas, William G. March 4, 1894. Letter to George Shakes. Juneau: Alaska State Library and Archives.

Townsend-Gault, Charlotte. 1992. "James Luna," in Nemiroff et al., eds., *Land, Spirit, Power: First Nations at the National Gallery of Canada.* Ottawa: National Gallery of Canada, 190–95.

Turner, Victor W. and Edward M. Bruner, eds. 1986. *The Anthropology of Experience.* Urbana: University of Illinois Press.

Ukas, Tom. 1968. "The Chief Shakes House." *Alaska Sportsman* 34(10): 14.

Van den Berghe, Pierre L., and Charles F. Keyes. 1984. "Introduction: Tourism and Re-created Ethnicity." *Annals of Tourism Research* 11(3): 343–52.

Vastokas, Joan M. 1966. *Architecture of the Northwest Coast Indians of America.* Ann Arbor: University Microfilms.

Waterman, T. T., and Ruth Greiner. 1921. *Indian Houses of Puget Sound.* Indian Notes and Monographs. Miscellaneous Series 9. New York: Museum of the American Indian, Heye Foundation.

Webster, Gloria Cranmer. 1988. "The 'R' Word." *Muse* 4(3): 43–44.

———. 1991. "The Contemporary Potlatch," in Aldona Jonaitis, ed. *Chiefly Feasts: The Enduring Kwakiutl Potlatch.* New York: American Museum of Natural History, 227–50.

West, Cornel. 1990. "The New Cultural Politics of Difference." *Out There: Marginalization and Contemporary Cultures.* Russell Fergusen, Martha Gever, Trinh T. Minh-ha, and Cornel West, eds. New York: The New Museum of Contemporary Art, 19–36.

Wrangell Potlatch. 1940. Wrangell, Alaska: Wrangell Museum Archives. Wrangell Potlatch, Inc., brochure.

The Wrangell Sentinel. March 29, 1940: 1. "Big Potlatch Planned in Wrangell June 3–4 for Island Dedication."

———. May 31, 1940: 1. "Mayor Fisk Extends Official Welcome to Potlatch Visitors."

———. June 7, 1940: 1. "Dedication Is Feature of Potlatch Event."

———. April 7, 1972: n.p. "Shakes House Dedication Seen in May."

———. Nov. 14, 1973: 1f. "Shakes Dedication Is Colorful."

———. Nov. 11, 1979: n.p. "Preservation Plans Begin for Houseposts and Totems."

———. April 23, 1980: 13. "Shakes Houseposts Project Granted Federal Assistance."

———. Jan. 1982: 18f (Southeastern Log). "Wrangell Totems Removed for
Work."

Wright, Robin K. 1982. "Haida Argillite: Carved for Sale." *American Indian Art
Magazine* 8(1): 48–55.

———. 1983. "Anonymous Attributions: A Tribute to a Mid-19th Century
Haida Argillite Carver, the Master of the Long Fingers." *Box of Daylight:
Northwest Coast Indian Art.* Bill Holm, ed. Seattle: Seattle Art Museum,
1983. 139–42.

———. 1985. "Nineteenth Century Haida Argillite Pipe Carvers: Stylistic Attribution." Ph.D. Dissertation, School of Art, University of Washington,
Seattle.

———. 1992. "Kadashan's Staff: The Work of a Mid-Nineteenth Century Haida
Argillite Carver in Another Medium." *American Indian Art Magazine* 17(4):
48–55.

———. 1998. "Two Haida Artists from Yan: Will John Gwaytihl and Simeon
Stilthda Please Step Apart?" *American Indian Art Magazine* 23(3): 42–57,
106–107.

Young, S. Hall. 1927. *Hall Young of Alaska: "The Mushing Parson."* New York:
Fleming S. Revell Company.

Young, S. Hall, A. L. Lindsley, M. Kendall, and Sheldon Jackson. August 5, 1879.
Letter of reference for George Shakes. Juneau: Alaska State Library and
Archives.

Interviews and Correspondence with Author

All interviews are quoted from the author's field notes and tape recordings.

Alfred, Ethel. June 23, 1993. Personal interview.

Austin-McKillop, Mardonna. Sept. 1991. Telephone interview.

Becker, Joe. Mar. 23, 1993. Personal interview.

Brown, Steve. Aug. 12, 1991. Personal interview.

Byrd, Marge. Aug. 26, 1992. Personal interview.

Cardinal, Douglas. Nov. 17, 1992. Personal interview.

Churchill, Edward P. Aug. 27, 1992. Personal interview.

Corey, Peter. Aug. 19, 1992. Personal interview.

Cranmer, Agnes. Mar. 1990; June 23, 1993. Personal interviews.

Cranmer, Bill. June 21, 1993. Personal interview.

Cranmer, Doug. June 20, 1993. Personal interview.

Davidson, Robert. Mar. 26, 1993. Personal interview.

DeWitt, Jonathan. 1993. Telephone interview.

Dick, Adam. June 7, 1993. Telephone interview.

Dick, Beau. Mar. 26, 1993. Personal interview.

Duffek, Karen. July 23, 1991. Personal interview.

Fane, Diana. June 20, 1995. Telephone interview.

Gregory, Ian. Nov. 17, 1992. Personal interview.

Hart, Jim. Mar. 26, 1993. Personal interview.

Henrikson, Steve. Dec. 7, 1992. Letter to author.

Holm, Bill. Jan. 24, 1994. Letter to author.

Hunt, Emma. Sept. 1991. Telephone interview.

Hunt, Richard. June 9, 1993. Personal interview.

Hunt, Tom. Sept. 1991. Telephone interview.

Hunt, Tony. June 8, 1993. Personal interview.

Inglis, Richard. 1990, 1991. Personal interviews.

Jackson, Nathan. Aug. 29, 1992. Telephone interview.

———. Aug. 31, 1992. Personal interview.

Jonaitis, Aldona. 1990; 1991; May 4, 1995. Personal interviews.

LaForet, Andrew. Nov. 17, 1992. Personal interview.

———. April 21, 1995. Telephone interviews.

Latimer, Leona. Aug. 23, 1991. Personal interview.

Lenz, Mary Jane. Jan. 30, 1995. Personal interview.

Levinson, Judith. 1992. Telephone interview.

MacDonald, George R. Nov. 19, 1992. Personal interview.

McLennan, Bill. Aug. 22, 1991; Mar. 22, 1993. Personal interviews.

McMaster, Gerald. Aug. 1, 1995. Telephone interview.

Macnair, Peter L. May 1990; July 19, 1991. Personal interviews.

Macnair, Randall. July 19, 1991. Personal interview.

Ockert, Pat Greene. Aug. 25, 1992. Personal interview.

Oswell, Drew. Oct. 12, 1993. Telephone interview.

Proctor, Isabel. July 23, 1991. Personal interview.

Starr, Terry. Mar. 25, 1993. Personal interview.

Stokes, Dick. Aug. 27 and 28, 1992. Personal interviews.

Stott, Margaret A. Nov. 19, 1992. Telephone interview.

Suttles, Wayne. May 25, 1995. Letter to author.

Tallio, Glen. Mar. 23, 1993. Personal interview.

Thompson, Art. June 10, 1993. Personal interview.

Torgramsen, Nellie. Aug. 26, 1992. Personal interview.

Webster, Gloria Cranmer. June 22 and 23, 1993. Personal interviews.

Williams, Elsie. June 23, 1993. Personal interview.

Wilson, Lyle. Aug. 22, 1991; Mar. 22, 1993. Personal interviews.

Wyatt, Gary. Mar. 24, 1993. Personal interview.

Index

Italic numbers refer to pages with illustrations.